A Miscellany

John Muir
A Miscellany

Introduction and selection
by Laurie Battle

Rucksack Editions

Galileo Publishers, Cambridge

Published by Galileo Publishers
16 Woodlands Road, Great Shelford,
Cambridge, UK, CB22 5LW

www.galileopublishing.co.uk

Galileo Publishers is an imprint of
Galileo Multimedia Ltd.

Selection and editorial material © Laurie Battle, 2017

The moral right of the editor of the selection has been
asserted.

ISBN 978-1-903385-58-6

Text design by James Shurmer

Cover design by NamdesignUK

Cover illustration by Katie Thompson

Rucksack Editions are based on an original concept by
Erlend Clouston

Printed in Lithuania

Also in the same series:

Edward Thomas: A Miscellany edited by Anna Stenning

William and Dorothy Wordsworth: A Miscellany edited by
Gavin Herbertson

Contents

California *continued*

Alaska

Author, Environmental Advocate

Introduction by Laurie Battle

The tendency nowadays to wander in wildernesses is delightful to see. Thousands of tired, nerve-shaken, over-civilized people are beginning to find out that going to the mountains is going home; that wildness is a necessity; and that mountain parks and reservations are useful not only as fountains of timber and irrigating rivers, but as fountains of life.[1]

The words could have been written yesterday, in any part of the world where people feel trapped by the excesses of modern life. John Muir's stature as a visionary leader was already on the rise by 1898, when the above passage first appeared in print. Muir was president of the Sierra Club, which he had cofounded in San Francisco six years earlier. Harvard University and the University of Wisconsin had recently awarded him honorary degrees. Influential editors were encouraging him to share his ideas with a wider audience. Muir's reverence for nature and uncompromising integrity would ultimately play a vital role in awakening the American public to the need to rein in rampant industrial development before it was too late.

…how many hearts with warm red blood in them are beating under cover of the woods, and how many teeth and eyes are shining! A multitude of animal people, intimately related to us, but of whose lives we know almost nothing, are as busy about their own affairs as we are about ours…[2]

A rough sketch of John Muir's life might resemble the

stories of countless other Scottish immigrants who came to America in the nineteenth century. What set him apart were his innate scientific talent, a loving heart that found beauty in everything he encountered, and the eleven years he spent living intimately with wild nature before settling into conventional family life.

John Muir was born in Dunbar, Scotland on April 21, 1838, the third child and first son of Daniel Muir and Ann Gilrye Muir. His father was a religious fundamentalist who mercilessly practiced "spare the rod and spoil the child." In 1849, when John was eleven years old, Daniel Muir uprooted his family and moved them across the Atlantic Ocean to the newly formed state of Wisconsin. His three sons were set to work clearing the untamed wilderness and building a farm. In the little time he could spare, John Muir taught himself mathematics, literature and philosophy, and tinkered with mechanical designs and inventions. At twenty-one, he left home and traveled to the capital city of Madison to show his work at the State Fair. His unique exhibit drew the attention of people who would become lifelong friends and mentors.

A freak accident changed the course of his life forever. After a handful of years spent studying at the University of Wisconsin and on botanizing treks in the Midwest and Canada, Muir went to work in an Indiana factory. His mechanical gifts again drew praise, and he might have joined the fast track to a prosperous career in industry. Then, one day in early March, 1867, a sharp file flew from his hand and pierced his right eye. For weeks he lay blinded in a dark room, not knowing if his eyesight would return. When a doctor offered hope that both eyes would fully recover, Muir realized he desired nothing more than to be out in nature. Six months after the accident, he packed up his botanizing tools, wrote "John Muir, Earth-planet, Universe" in his travel journal, and set out to walk a thousand miles to the Gulf of Mexico. He had vague ideas of ending up in South America, but, after falling ill in Florida, decided to go to California instead. He reached San Francisco in late March of 1868, immediately set out for Yosemite Valley and the High Sierra, and found his permanent home.

Night gathered, in most impressive repose; my blazing fire illumined the grand brown columns of my compassing cedars and a few withered briers and goldenrods that leaned forward between them, as if eager to drink the light. Stars glinted here and there through the rich plumes of my ceiling, and in front I could see a portion of the mighty cañon walls, dark against the sky, making me feel as if at the bottom of a sea. Few sounds reached me, excepting a few broken scraps of song from distant cascades. My weariness and the near soothing hush of the river made me drowsy. The breath of my cedar pillow was delicious, and I quickly drifted deep into the land of sleep.[3]

John Muir arrived in California at a pivotal time in American history. The nation's economy had entered a period of rapid growth following the Civil War. The new state's landscape, transformed by the 1849 Gold Rush, still held wilderness areas largely untouched by commercial development. Affluent Easterners would soon begin traveling west via the new transcontinental railroad to see firsthand what all the excitement was about.

In surveying Muir's writings for this anthology, his vibrant voice and personality immediately leaped off the pages. It seemed best to step aside and let him tell the stories he might wish to share if he could be here today.

He'd likely pick up where he left off in at least three distinct fields: as scientist, political activist, and advocate for the philosophy now known as deep ecology.

There are no accidents in Nature. Every motion of the constantly shifting bodies in the world is timed to the occasion for some definite, fore-ordered end. The flowers blossom in obedience to the same law that marks the course of constellations, and the song of a bird is the echo of a universal symphony. Nature is one, and to me the greatest delight of observation and study is to discover new unities in this all-embracing and eternal harmony.[4]

Muir saw the mystery of creation in nature and shared the wonder he found. He understood the power of democratic action to temper the destruction caused by large commercial interests chasing short-term profits. Today, he is honored as the father of America's national park system. Time has proven him right on the morality and the science of why human communities must learn to live sustainably within natural cycles.

Any fool can destroy trees. They cannot run away; and if they could, they would still be destroyed—chased and hunted down as long as fun or a dollar could be got out of their bark hides, branching horns, or magnificent bole backbones. Few that fell trees plant them; nor would planting avail much towards getting back anything like the noble primeval forests. During a man's life only saplings can be grown, in the place of the old trees—tens of centuries old—that have been destroyed. It took more than three thousand years to make some of the trees in these Western woods—trees that are still standing in perfect strength and beauty, waving and singing in the mighty forests of the Sierra. Through all the wonderful, eventful centuries since Christ's time—and long before that—God has cared for these trees, saved them from drought, disease, avalanches, and a thousand straining, leveling tempests and floods; but he cannot save them from fools—only Uncle Sam can do that.[5]

John Muir was happiest heading off into the wild with a loaf of bread, a bag of tea, a journal and sketchbook, and a head full of dreams. He was the quintessential mountain man, a modern-day Merlin who showed how much one determined, hard-working individual with a song in their heart can accomplish. His life is an inspiring reminder of the eternal vigilance needed to protect this Earth-planet we call home.

NOTES AND REFERENCES

1   John Muir, "The Wild Parks and Forest Reservations of the West," *The Atlantic Monthly, January 1, 1898.*

2   Ibid.

3   John Muir, "Hetch Hetchy Valley," *Boston Weekly Transcript,* March 25, 1873.

4   French Strother, "Three Days with John Muir," *The World's Work,* March, 1909.

5   John Muir, "The American Forests," *Our National Parks,* Ch. 10.

John Muir, Earth-planet, Universe

The Calypso Borealis

John Muir's first published piece of writing was excerpted from a letter to a friend and appeared under the byline of Prof. J.D. Butler, who had taught him classics at the University of Wisconsin. It describes a rare flower Muir discovered while traveling in Canada to study native plants.

~~~~~~~~~~

. . . I did find Calypso—but only once, far in the depths of the very wildest of Canadian dark woods, near those high, cold, moss-covered swamps where most of the peninsular streams of Canada West take their rise.

For several days in June I had been forcing my way through woods that seemed to become more and more dense, and among bogs more and more difficult to cross, when, one warm afternoon, after descending a hillside covered with huge half-dead hemlocks, I crossed an ice-cold stream, and espied two specimens of Calypso. There, upon an open plat of yellow moss, near an immense rotten log, were these little plants, so pure.

They were alone. Not a vine was near, nor a blade of grass, nor a bush. Nor were there any birds or insects, for great blocks of ice lay screened from the summer's sun by deep beds of moss, and chilled the water. They were indeed alone, for the dull ignoble hemlocks were not companions, nor was the nearer arbor-vitae, with its root-like pendulous branches decaying confusedly on the wet, cold ground.

I never before saw a plant so full of life, so perfectly spiritual, it seemed pure enough for the throne of its Creator. I felt as if I were in the presence of superior beings who loved me and beckoned me to come. I sat down beside them and wept for joy. Could angels in their better land show us a more beautiful plant? How good is our Heavenly Father in granting us such friends as are these plant-creatures, filling us wherever we go with pleasure so deep, so pure, so endless.

I cannot understand the nature of the curse, "Thorns and thistles shall it bring forth to thee." Is our world indeed the worse for this "thistly curse?" Are not all plants beautiful? or in some way useful? Would not the world suffer by the banishment of a single weed? The curse must be within ourselves.

Give me this keen relish for simple pleasures, and he that will may monopolize the lust of the flesh, the lust of the eye, the pride of life—yea, all pomps and marvels of the world.

(From "The Calypso Borealis: Botanical Enthusiasm", Prof. J.D. Butler, *The Boston Recorder*, December 21, 1866)

A Windswept Route

Following his recovery from a factory accident that nearly blinded him, Muir set out, at age 29, on a thousand-mile walk from Indiana to the Gulf of Mexico. Inscribing "John Muir, Earth-planet, Universe" with a flourish on his journal's inside cover, he aimed to reach South America and the Amazon River. A bout of malaria suffered along the way forced a change in plans, however, and Muir decided to visit California's healing climate before heading further south. He departed by boat from Cuba in early 1868.

The substance of the winds is too thin for human eyes, their written language is too difficult for human minds, and their spoken language mostly too faint for the ears. A mechanism is said to have been invented whereby the human organs of speech are made to write their own utterances. But without any extra mechanical contrivance, every speaker also writes as he speaks. All things in the creation of God register their own acts. The poet was mistaken when he said, "From the wing no scar the sky sustains." His eyes were simply too dim to see the scar. In sailing past Cuba I could see a fringe of foam along the coast, but could hear no sound of waves, simply because my ears could not hear wave-dashing at that distance. Yet every bit of spray was sounding in my ears.

The subject brings to mind a few recollections of the winds I heard in my late journey. In my walk from Indiana to the Gulf, earth and sky, plants and people, and all things changeable were constantly changing. Even in Kentucky nature and art have many a characteristic shibboleth. The people differ in language and in customs. Their architecture is generically different from that of their immediate neighbors on the north, not only in planters' mansions, but in barns and granaries and the cabins of the poor. But thousands of familiar flower faces looked from every hill and valley. I noted no difference in the sky, and the winds spoke the same things. I did not feel myself in a strange land.

In Tennessee my eyes rested upon the first mountain scenery I ever beheld. I was rising higher than ever before; strange trees were beginning to appear; alpine flowers and shrubs were meeting me at every step. But these Cumberland Mountains were timbered with oak, and were not unlike Wisconsin hills piled upon each other, and the strange plants were like those that were not strange. The sky was changed only a little, and the winds not by a single detectible note. Therefore, neither was Tennessee a strange land.

But soon came changes thick and fast. After passing the mountainous corner of North Carolina and a little way into Georgia, I beheld from one of the last ridge-summits of the Alleghanies that vast, smooth, sandy slope that reaches from the mountains to the sea. It is wooded with dark, branchy pines which were all strangers to me. Here the grasses, which are an earth-covering at the North, grow wide apart in tall clumps and tufts like saplings. My known flower companions were leaving me now, not one by one as in Kentucky and Tennessee, but in whole tribes and genera, and companies of shining strangers came trooping upon me in countless ranks. The sky, too, was changed, and I could detect strange sounds in the winds. Now I began to feel myself "a stranger in a strange land."

But in Florida came the greatest change of all, for here grows the palmetto, and here blow the winds so strangely toned by them. These palms and these winds severed the last strands of the cord that united me with home. Now I was a stranger, indeed. I was delighted, astonished, confounded, and gazed in wonderment blank and over-whelming as if I had fallen upon another star. But in all of this long, complex series of changes, one of the greatest, and the last of all, was the change I found in the tone and language of the winds. They no longer came with the old home music gathered from open prairies and waving fields of oak, but they passed over many a strange string. The leaves of magnolia, smooth like polished steel, the immense inverted forests of tillandsia banks, and the princely crowns of palms — upon these the winds made strange music, and at the coming-on of night had overwhelming power to present the distance from friends and home, and the completeness of my isolation from all things familiar.

Elsewhere I have already noted that when I was a day's journey from the Gulf, a wind blew upon me from the sea — the first sea breeze that had touched me in twenty years. I was plodding alone with my satchel and plants, leaning wearily forward, a little sore from approaching fever, when suddenly I felt the salt air, and before I had time to think, a whole flood of long-dormant associations rolled in upon me. The Firth of Forth, the Bass Rock, Dunbar Castle, and the winds and rocks and hills came upon the wings of that wind, and stood in as clear and sudden light as a landscape flashed upon the view by a blaze of lightning in a dark night.

I like to cling to a small chip of a ship like ours when the sea is rough, and long, comet-tailed streamers are blowing from the curled top of every wave. A big vessel responds awkwardly with mixed gestures to several waves at once, lumbering along like a loose floating island. But our little schooner, buoyant as a gull, glides up one side and down the other of each wave hill in delightful rhythm. As we advanced the scenery increased in grandeur and beauty. The waves heaved higher and grew wider, with corresponding motion. It was delightful to ride over this unsullied country of ever-changing water, and when looking upward from the shallow vales, or abroad over the round expanse from the tops of the wave hills, I almost forgot at times that the glassy, treeless country was forbidden to walkers. How delightful it would be to ramble over it on foot, enjoying the transparent crystal ground, and the music of its rising and falling hillocks, unmarred by the ropes and spars of a ship; to study the plants of these waving plains and their stream-currents; to sleep in wild weather in a bed of phosphorescent wave-foam, or briny scented seaweeds; to see the fishes by night in pathways of phosphorescent light; to walk the glassy plain in calm, with birds and flocks of glittering flying fishes here and there, or by night with every star pictured in its bosom!

But even of the land only a small portion is free to man, and if he, among other journeys on forbidden paths, ventures among the ice lands and hot lands, or up in the air in balloon bubbles, or on the ocean in ships, or down into it a little way in smothering diving-bells — in all such small adventures man is admonished and often punished in ways which clearly show him that he is in places for which, to use an approved phrase, he was never designed. However, in view of the rapid advancement of our time, no one can tell how far our star may finally be subdued to man's will. At all events I enjoyed this drifting locomotion to some extent.

(From *A Thousand Mile Walk to the Gulf*, Ch. 8)

California

"Any Place That is Wild"

Arriving by the Panama steamer, I stopped one day in San Francisco and then inquired for the nearest way out of town. "But where do you want to go?" asked the man to whom I had applied for this important information. "To any place that is wild," I said. This reply startled him. He seemed to fear I might be crazy and therefore the sooner I was out of town the better, so he directed me to the Oakland ferry.

So on the first of April, 1868, I set out afoot for Yosemite. It was the bloom-time of the year over the lowlands and coast ranges, the landscapes of the Santa Clara Valley were fairly drenched with sunshine, all the air was quivering with the songs of the meadow-larks, and the hills were so covered with flowers that they seemed to be painted. Slow indeed was my progress through these glorious gardens, the first of the California flora I had seen. Cattle and cultivation were making few scars as yet, and I wandered enchanted in long wavering curves, knowing by my pocket map that Yosemite Valley lay to the east and that I should surely find it.

(From *The Yosemite*, Ch. 1)

Rambles of a Botanist

On the second day of April, 1868, I left San Francisco for Yosemite Valley, companioned by a young Englishman. Our orthodox route of "nearest and quickest " was by steam to Stockton, thence by stage to Coulterville or Mariposa, and the remainder of the way over the mountains on horseback. But we had plenty of time, and proposed drifting leisurely mountainward, via the valley of San José, Pacheco Pass, and the plain of San Joaquin, and thence to Yosemite by any road that we chanced to find; enjoying the flowers and light, "camping out" in our blankets wherever overtaken by night, and paying very little compliance to roads or times. Accordingly, we crossed "the Bay" by the Oakland ferry, and proceeded up the valley of San José. This is one of the most fertile of the many small valleys of the coast; its rich bottoms are filled with wheat-fields and orchards and vineyards, and alfalfa meadows. It was now spring-time, and the weather was the best that we ever enjoyed. Larks and streams sang everywhere; the sky was cloudless, and the whole valley was a lake of light. The atmosphere was spicy and exhilarating; my companion acknowledging over his national prejudices that it was the best he ever breathed, — more deliciously fragrant than the hawthorn hedges of England. This San José sky was not simply pure and bright, and mixed with plenty of well-tempered sunshine, but it possessed a positive flavor, — a *taste*, that thrilled from the lungs throughout every tissue of the body; every inspiration yielded a corresponding well-defined piece of pleasure, that awakened thousands of new palates everywhere. Both my companion and myself had lived and dozed on common air for nearly thirty years, and never before this discovered that our bodies contained such multitudes of palates, or that this mortal flesh, so little valued by philosophers and teachers, was possessed of so vast a capacity for happiness.

We emerged from this ether baptism new creatures, born again; and truly not until this time were we fairly conscious that we were born at all. Never more, thought

I, as we strode forward at faster speed, never more shall I sentimentalize about getting out of the mortal coil: this flesh is not a coil, it is a sponge steeped in immortality.

The foothills (that form the sides of our blessed font) are in near view all the way to Gilroy; those of the Monte Diablo range on our left, those of Santa Cruz on our right; they are smooth and flowing, and come down to the bottom levels in curves of most surpassing beauty; they still wear natural flowers, which do not occur singly or in handfuls, scattered about in the grass, but they grow close together, in smooth, cloud-shaped companies, acres and hill-sides in size, white, purple, and yellow, separate, yet blending to each other like the hills upon which they grow. Besides the white, purple, and yellow clouds, we occasionally saw a thicket of scarlet castilleias and silvery-leaved lupines, also splendid fields of wild oats (*Avena fatua*). The delightful Gilia (*G. tricolor*) was very abundant in sweeping hill-side sheets, and a Leptosiphon (*L. androsca*) and Claytonias were everywhere by the roadsides, and lilies and dodecatheons by the streams: no wonder the air was so good, waving and rubbing on such a firmament of flowers! I tried to decide which of the plant-clouds was most fragant: perhaps it was the white, composed mostly of a delicate Boragewort; but doubtless all had a hand in balming the sky. Among trees we observed the laurel (*Oreodaphne californica*), and magnificent groves and tree-shaped groups of oaks, some specimens over seven feet in diameter; the white oaks (*Quercus lobata*) and (*Q. douglasii*), the black oak (*Q. sonomensis*), live-oak (*Q. agrifolia*), together with several dwarfy species on the hills, whose names we do not know. The prevailing northwest wind has permanently swayed all unsheltered trees up the valley; groves upon the more exposed hillsides lean forward like patches of lodged wheat. The Santa Cruz Mountains have grand forests of redwood (*Sequoia sempervirens*), some specimens near fifty feet in circumference.

The Pacheco Pass was scarcely less enchanting than the valley. It resounded with crystal waters, and the loud shouts of thousands of California quails. In size these about equal the eastern quail; not quite so plump in form. The male has a tall, slender crest, wider at top than bottom, which he can hold straight up, or droop backward on his neck, or forward over his bill, at pleasure; and, instead of Bob White, he shouts "pe-check-a," bearing down with a stiff, obstinate emphasis on "check."

Through a considerable portion of the pass the road bends and mazes along the groves of a stream, or down in its pebbly bed, leading one now deep in the shadows of dogwoods and alders, then out in the light, through dry chaparral, over green carex meadows banked with violets and ferns, and dry, plantless flood-beds of gravel and sand.

We found ferns in abundance all through the pass. Some far down in dark cañons, as the polypodium and rock fern, or high on sunlit braes, as *Pellaea mucronata*. Also we observed the delicate gold-powdered *Gymnogramma triangularis*, and *Pellaea andromedaefolia*, and the maidenhair (*Adiantum chilense*), and the broad-shouldered bracken (*Pteris aquilina*), which is everywhere; and an aspidium and cystopteris, and two or three others that I was not acquainted with. Also in this rich garden pass we gathered many fine grasses and carices, and brilliant pentstemons, azure and scarlet, and mints and lilies, and scores of others, strangers to us, but beautiful and pure as ever enjoyed the sun or shade of a mountain home....

...After we were fairly over the summit of the pass, and had reached an open hill-brow, a scene of peerless grandeur burst suddenly upon us. At our feet, basking in sungold, lay the Great Central Plain of California, bounded by the mountains on which we stood, and by the lofty, snowcapped Sierra Nevada; all in grandest simplicity, clear and bright as a new outspread map.

In half a day we were down over all the foot-hills, past the San Luis Gonzaga Ranch, and wading out in the grand level ocean of flowers. This plain, watered by the San Joaquin and Sacramento rivers, formed one flower-bed, nearly four hundred miles in length by thirty in width. In order that some definite conception may be formed of the richness of this flower-field, I will give a harvest gathered by me from one square yard of plain, opposite Hill's Ferry, a few miles from the coast-range foot-hills, and taken at random, like a cupful of water from a lake. An approximation was made to the number of grass flowers by counting the panicles, to the flowers of the *Compositae* by counting the heads. The mosses were roughly estimated by counting the number growing on one square inch. All the flowers of the other natural orders were counted one by one.

Natural orders	*No. of flowers*		*No. of species*
Gramineae	29,830	Panicles 1000	3
Compositae	132,125	Heads 3,305	2
Leguminosae	2,620		2
Umbelliferae	620		1
Polemoniaceae	401		2
Scrophulariaceae	169		1
————?	85		1
Rubiaceae	40		1
Geraniaceae	22		1
Musci	1,000,000	Funaria and Dicranum	2

Number of natural orders, 9 to 10. Of species, 16
Total number of open flowers, 165,912. Mosses, 1,000,000

In the above estimate, only open living flowers were taken into account. Those which were still in bud, together with those that were past flower, would number nearly as many more. The heads of the *Compositae* are usually regarded as one flower. Even then we would have seven thousand two hundred and sixty-two flowers, together with a thousand silky, transparent panicles of grasses, and a floor an inch thick of hooded mosses. The grasses have scarce any leaves, and do not interfere with the light of the other flowers, or with their color, in any marked degree.

The yellow of the *Compositae* is pure, deep, bossy solar gold, as if the sun had filled their rays and flowerets with the undiluted substance of his very self. In depth, the purple stratum was about ten or twelve inches; the yellow, seven or eight, and the moss stratum, of greenish yellow, one. But the purple stratum is dilute and transparent, so that the lower yellow is hardly dimmed; and only when a horizontal view is taken, so as to look edgewise through the upper stratum, does its color predominate. Therefore, when one stands on a wide level area, the gold immediately about him seems all in all; but on gradually looking wider the gold dims, and purple predominates.

In this botanist's better land, I drifted separate many days, the largest days of my life, resting at times from the blessed plants, in showers of bugs and sun-born butterflies; or I watched the smooth-bounding antelopes, or startled hares, skimming light and swift as eagles' shadows; or, turning from all this fervid life, contemplated the Sierras, that mighty wall uprising from the brink of this lake of gold, miles in the higher blue, bearing aloft its domes and spires in spotless white, unshining and beamless, yet pure as pearl, clear and undimmed as the flowers at my feet. Never were mortal eyes more thronged with beauty. When I walked, more than a hundred flowers touched my feet, at every step closing above them, as if wading in water. Go where I would, east or west, north or south, I still plashed and rippled in flower-gems; and at night I lay between two skies of silver and gold, spanned by a milky-way, and nestling deep in a goldy-way of vegetable suns....

...Ere we were ready to recommence our march to Yosemite, May was about half done. The flowers and grasses, so late in the pomp and power of full bloom, were dead, and their parched leaves crisped and crackled beneath our feet, as if they had literally been "cast into the oven." They were not given weeks and months to grow old; but they aged and died ere they could fade, standing side by side, erect and undecayed, bearing seed-cells and urns beautiful as corollas.

After travelling two days among the delightful death of this sunny winter, we came to another summer in the Sierra foothills. Flowers were spread confidingly open, and streams and winds were cool. Above Coulterville, forty or fifty miles farther in the mountains, we came to spring. The leaves of the mountain-oaks were small and drooping, and still wore their first tintings of crimson and purple; and the wrinkles of their bud-folds were still distinct, as if newly opened; and, scattered over banks and sunny slopes, thousands of gentle plants were tasting life for the first time. A few miles farther, on the Pilot Peak ridge, we came to the edge of a winter. Few growing leaves were to be seen; the highest and youngest of the lilies and spring violets were far below; winter scales were still wrapt close on the buds of dwarf oaks and hazels. The great sugar-pines waved their long arms, as if about to speak; and we soon were in deep snow. After we had reached the highest part of the ridge, clouds began to gather, storm-winds swept the forest, and snow began to fall thick and blinding.

Fortunately, we reached a sort of shingle cabin at Crane Flat, where we sheltered until the next day. Thus, in less than a week from the hot autumn of San Joaquin, we were struggling in a bewildering storm of mountain winter. This was on or about May 20, at an elevation of six thousand one hundred and thirty feet. Here the forest is magnificent, composed in part of the sugar-pine (*Pinus lambertiana*), which is the king of all pines, most noble in manners and language. Many specimens are over two hundred feet in height, and eight to ten in diameter, fresh and sound as the sun which made them. The yellow pine (*Pinus ponderosa*) also grows here, and the cedar (*Libocedrus decurrens*); but the bulk of the forest is made up of the two silver firs (*Picea grandis* and *Picea amabilis*), the former always greatly predominating at this altitude. Descending from this winter towards the Merced, the snow gradually disappeared from the ground and sky, tender leaves unfolded less and less doubtfully, violets and lilies shone about us once more, and at length, arriving in the glorious Yosemite, we found it full of summer and spring. Thus, as colors blend in a rainbow, and as mountains curve to a plain, so meet and blend the plants and seasons of this delightsome land.

(From "Rambles of a Botanist Among the Plants and Climates of California," *Old and New*, June 1, 1872)

Summer Job

Muir's first taste of the Sierra Nevada whet his appetite for more, and he postponed the idea of traveling to South America. The year after his arrival in California he took a job accompanying a flock of sheep into the mountains, work that would allow him plenty of free time to pursue his interests in exploring and studying the natural world.

In the great Central Valley of California there are only two seasons,—spring and summer. The spring begins with the first rainstorm, which usually falls in November. In a few months the wonderful flowery vegetation is in full bloom, and by the end of May it is dead and dry and crisp, as if every plant had been roasted in an oven.

Then the lolling, panting flocks and herds are driven to the high, cool, green pastures of the Sierra. I was longing for the mountains about this time, but money was scarce and I couldn't see how a bread supply was to be kept up. While I was anxiously brooding on the bread problem, so troublesome to wanderers, and trying to believe that I might learn to live like the wild animals, gleaning nourishment here and there from seeds, berries, etc., sauntering and climbing in joyful independence of money or baggage, Mr. Delaney, a sheep-owner, for whom I had worked a few weeks, called on me, and offered to engage me to go with his shepherd and flock to the headwaters of the Merced and Tuolumne rivers, —the very region I had most in mind. I was in the mood to accept work of any kind that would take me into the mountains whose treasures I had tasted last summer in the Yosemite region. The flock, he explained, would be moved gradually higher through the successive forest belts as the snow melted, stopping for a few weeks at the best places we came to. These I thought would be good centres of observation from which I might be able to make many telling excursions within a radius of eight or ten miles of the camps to learn something of the plants, animals, and rocks; for he assured me that I should be left perfectly free to follow my studies. I judged, however, that I was in no way the right man for the place, and freely explained my shortcomings, confessing that I was wholly unacquainted with the topography of the upper mountains, the streams that would have to be crossed, and the wild sheep-eating animals, etc.; in short that, what with bears, coyotes, rivers, cañons, and thorny, bewildering chaparral, I feared that half or more of his flock would be lost. Fortunately these shortcomings seemed insignificant to Mr. Delaney. The main thing, he said, was to have a man about the camp whom he could trust to see that the shepherd did his duty, and he assured me that the difficulties that seemed so formidable at a distance would vanish as we went on; encouraging me further by saying that the shepherd would do all the herding, that I could study plants and rocks and scenery as much as I liked, and that he would himself accompany us to the first main camp and make occasional visits to our higher ones to replenish our store of provisions and see how we prospered. Therefore I concluded to go, though still fearing, when I saw the silly sheep bouncing one by one through the narrow gate of the home corral to be counted, that of the two thousand and fifty many would never return.

I was fortunate in getting a fine St. Bernard dog for a companion. His master, a hunter with whom I was slightly acquainted, came to me as soon as he heard that I was going to spend the summer in the Sierra and begged me to take his favorite dog, Carlo, with me, for he feared that if he were compelled to stay all summer on the plains the fierce heat might be the death of him. "I think I can trust you to be kind to him," he said, "and I am sure he will be good to you. He knows all about the mountain animals, will guard the camp, assist in managing the sheep, and in every way be found able and faithful." Carlo knew we were talking about him, watched our faces, and listened so attentively that I fancied he understood us. Calling him by name, I asked him if he was willing to go with me. He looked me in the face with eyes expressing wonderful intelligence, then turned to his master, and after permission was given by a wave of the hand toward me and a farewell patting caress, he quietly followed me as if he perfectly understood all that had been said and had known me always.

June 3, 1869. —This morning provisions, camp-kettles, blankets, plant-press, etc., were packed on two horses, the flock headed for the tawny foothills, and away we sauntered in a cloud of dust: Mr. Delaney, bony and tall, with sharply hacked profile like Don Quixote, leading the pack-horses, Billy, the proud shepherd, a Chinaman and a Digger Indian to assist in driving for the first few days in the brushy foothills, and myself with notebook tied to my belt.

The home ranch from which we set out is on the south side of the Tuolumne River near French Bar, where the foothills of metamorphic gold-bearing slates dip below the stratified deposits of the Central Valley. We had not gone more than a mile before some of the old leaders of the flock showed by the eager, inquiring way they ran and looked ahead that they were thinking of the high pastures they had enjoyed last summer. Soon the whole flock seemed to be hopefully excited, the mothers calling their lambs, the lambs replying in tones wonderfully human, their fondly quavering calls interrupted now and then by hastily snatched mouthfuls of withered grass. Amid all this seeming babel of baas as they streamed over the hills every mother and child recognized each other's voice. In case a tired lamb, half asleep in the smothering dust, should fail to answer, its mother would come running back through the flock toward the spot whence its last response was heard, and refused to be comforted until she found it, the one of a thousand, though to our eyes and ears all seemed alike.

The flock traveled at the rate of about a mile an hour,

outspread in the form of an irregular triangle, about a hundred yards wide at the base, and a hundred and fifty yards long, with a crooked, ever-changing point made up of the strongest foragers, called the "leaders," which, with the most active of those scattered along the ragged sides of the "main body," hastily explored nooks in the rocks and bushes for grass and leaves; the lambs and feeble old mothers dawdling in the rear were called the "tail end."

About noon the heat was hard to bear; the poor sheep panted pitifully and tried to stop in the shade of every tree they came to, while we gazed with eager longing through the dim burning glare toward the snowy mountains and streams, though not one was in sight. The landscape is only wavering foothills roughened here and there with bushes and trees and out-cropping masses of slate. The trees, mostly the blue oak (*Quercus douglasii*), are about thirty to forty feet high, with pale blue-green leaves and white bark, sparsely planted on the thinnest soil or in crevices of rocks beyond the reach of grass fires. The slates in many places rise abruptly through the tawny grass in sharp lichen covered slabs like tombstones in deserted burying-grounds. With the exception of the oak and four or five species of manzanita and ceanothus, the vegetation of the foot-hills is mostly the same as that of the plains. I saw this region in the early spring, when it was a charming land-scape garden full of birds and bees and flowers. Now the scorching weather makes everything dreary. The ground is full of cracks, lizards glide about on the rocks, and ants in amazing numbers, whose tiny sparks of life only burn the brighter with the heat, fairly quiver with unquenchable energy as they run in long lines to fight and gather food. How it comes that they do not dry to a crisp in a few seconds' exposure to such sun-fire is marvelous. A few rattlesnakes lie coiled in out-of-the-way places, but are seldom seen. Magpies and crows, usually so noisy, are silent now, standing in mixed flocks on the ground beneath the best shade trees, with bills wide open and wings drooped, too breathless to speak; the quails also are trying to keep in the shade about the few tepid alkaline water holes; cottontail rabbits are running from shade to shade among the ceanothus brush, and occasionally the long-eared hare is seen cantering gracefully across the wider openings.

After a short noon rest in a grove, the poor dust-choked flock was again driven ahead over the brushy hills, but the dim roadway we had been following faded away just where it was most needed, compelling us to stop to look about us and get our bearings. The Chinaman seemed to think we were lost, and chattered in pidgin English concerning the abundance of "litty stick" (chaparral), while the Indian silently scanned the billowy ridges and gulches for openings. Pushing through the thorny jungle, we at length discovered a road trending toward Coulterville, which we followed until an hour before sunset, when we reached a dry ranch and camped for the night.

Camping in the foothills with a flock of sheep is simple and easy, but far from pleasant. The sheep were allowed to pick what they could find in the neighborhood until after sunset, watched by the shepherd, while the others gathered wood, made a fire, cooked, unpacked and fed the horses, etc. About dusk the weary sheep were gathered on the highest open spot near camp, where they willingly bunched close together, and after each mother had found her lamb and suckled it, all lay down and required no attention until morning.

(From *My First Summer in the Sierra*, Ch. 1)

In Camp

June 13. —Another glorious Sierra day in which one seems to be dissolved and absorbed and sent pulsing onward we know not where. Life seems neither long nor short, and we take no more heed to save time or make haste than do the trees and stars. This is true freedom, a good practical sort of immortality. Yonder rises another white skyland. How sharply the yellow pine spires and the palm-like crowns of the sugar pines are outlined on its smooth white domes. And hark! the grand thunder billows booming, rolling from ridge to ridge, followed by the faithful shower.

A good many herbaceous plants come thus far up the mountains from the plains, and are now in flower, two months later than their lowland relatives. Saw a few columbines today. Most of the ferns are in their prime, —rock ferns on the sunny hillsides, cheilanthes, pellaea, gymnogramme; woodwardia, aspidium, woodsia along the stream banks, and the common *Pteris aquilina* on sandy flats. This last, however common, is here making shows of strong, exuberant, abounding beauty to set the botanist wild with admiration. I measured some scarce full grown that are more than seven feet high. Though the commonest and most widely distributed of all the ferns, I might almost say that I never saw it before. The broad-shouldered fronds held high on smooth stout stalks growing close together, overleaning and overlapping, make a complete ceiling, beneath which one may walk erect over several acres without being seen, as if beneath a roof. And how soft and lovely the light streaming through this living ceiling, revealing the arching branching ribs and veins of the fronds as the framework of countless panes of pale green and yellow plant-glass nicely fitted together—a fairyland created out of the commonest fern-stuff.

The smaller animals wander about as if in a tropical forest. I saw the entire flock of sheep vanish at one side of a patch and reappear a hundred yards farther on at the other, their progress betrayed only by the jerking and trembling of the fronds; and strange to say very few of the stout woody stalks were broken. I sat a long time beneath the tallest fronds, and never enjoyed anything in the way of a bower of wild leaves more strangely impressive. Only spread a fern frond over a man's head and worldly cares are cast out, and freedom and beauty and peace come in. The waving of a pine tree on the top of a mountain, —a magic wand in Nature's hand, —every devout mountaineer knows its power; but the marvelous beauty value of what the Scotch call a breckan in a still dell, what poet has sung this? It would seem impossible that any one, however incrusted with care, could escape the Godful influence of these sacred fern forests. Yet this very day I saw a shepherd pass through one of the finest of them without betraying more feeling than his sheep. "What do you think of these grand ferns?" I asked. "Oh, they're only d-—d big brakes," he replied.

Lizards of every temper, style, and color dwell here, seemingly as happy and companionable as the birds and squirrels. Lowly, gentle fellow mortals, enjoying God's sunshine, and doing the best they can in getting a living, I like to watch them at their work and play. They bear acquaintance well, and one likes them the better the longer one looks into their beautiful, innocent eyes. They are easily tamed, and one soon learns to love them, as they dart about on the hot rocks, swift as dragon-flies. The eye can hardly follow them; but they never make long-sustained runs, usually only about ten or twelve feet, then a sudden stop, and as sudden a start again; going all their journeys by quick, jerking impulses. These many stops I find are necessary as rests, for they are short-winded, and when pursued steadily are soon out of breath, pant pitifully, and are easily caught. Their bodies are more than half tail, but these tails are well managed, never heavily dragged nor curved up as if hard to carry; on the contrary, they seem to follow the body lightly of their own will. Some are colored like the sky, bright as bluebirds, others gray like the lichened rocks on which they hunt and bask. Even the horned toad of the plains is a mild, harmless creature, and so are the snake-like species which glide in curves with true snake motion, while their small, undeveloped limbs drag as useless appendages. One specimen fourteen inches long which I observed closely made no use whatever of its tender, sprouting limbs, but glided with all the soft, sly ease and grace of a snake. Here comes a little, gray, dusty fellow who seems to know and trust me, running about my feet, and looking up cunningly into my face. Carlo is watching, makes a quick pounce on him, for the fun of the thing I suppose; but Liz has shot away from his paws like an arrow, and is safe in the recesses of a clump of chaparral. Gentle saurians, dragons, descendants of an ancient and mighty race, Heaven bless you all and make your virtues known! for few of us know as yet that scales may cover fellow creatures as gentle and lovable as feathers, or hair, or cloth.

Mastodons and elephants used to live here no great geological time ago, as shown by their bones, often discovered by miners in washing gold-gravel. And bears of at least two species are here now, besides the California lion or panther, and wild cats, wolves, foxes, snakes, scorpions, wasps, tarantulas; but one is almost tempted at times to regard a small savage black ant as the master existence of this vast mountain world. These fearless, restless, wandering imps, though only about a quarter of an inch long, are fonder of fighting and biting than any beast I know. They attack every living thing around their homes, often without cause as far as I can see. Their bodies are mostly jaws curved like ice-hooks, and to get work for these weapons seems to be their chief aim and pleasure. Most of their colonies are established in living oaks somewhat decayed or hollowed, in which they can conveniently build their cells. These are chosen probably because of their strength as opposed to the attacks of animals and storms. They work both day and night, creep into dark caves, climb the highest trees, wander and hunt through cool ravines as well as on hot, unshaded ridges, and extend their highways and byways over everything but water and sky. From the foothills to a mile above the level of the sea nothing can stir without their knowledge; and alarms are spread in an incredibly short time, without any howl or cry that we can hear. I can't understand the need of their ferocious courage; there seems to be no common sense in it. Some-times, no doubt, they fight in defense of their homes, but they fight anywhere and always wherever they can find anything to bite. As soon as a vulnerable spot is discovered on man or beast, they stand on their heads and sink their jaws, and though torn limb from limb, they will yet hold on and die biting deeper. When I contemplate this fierce creature so widely distributed and strongly intrenched, I see that much remains to be done ere the world is brought under the rule of universal peace and love. . . .

June 14. —The pool-basins below the falls and cascades hereabouts, formed by the heavy down-plunging currents, are kept nicely clean and clear of detritus. The heavier parts of the material swept over the falls are heaped up a short distance in front of the basins in the form of a dam, thus tending, together with erosion, to increase their size. Sudden changes, however, are effected during the spring floods, when the snow is melting and the upper tributaries are roaring loud from "bank to brae." Then boulders that have fallen into the channels, and which the ordinary summer and winter currents were unable to move, are suddenly swept forward as by a mighty besom, hurled over the falls into these pools, and piled up in a new dam together with part of the old one, while some of the smaller boulders are carried further down stream and variously lodged according to size and shape, all seeking rest where the force of the current is less than the resistance they are able to offer. But the greatest changes made in these relations of fall, pool, and dam are caused, not by the ordinary spring floods, but by extraordinary ones that occur at irregular intervals. The testimony of trees growing on flood boulder deposits shows that a century or more has passed since the last master flood came to awaken everything movable to go swirling and dancing on wonderful journeys. These floods may occur during the summer, when heavy thunder-showers, called "cloud-bursts," fall on wide, steeply inclined stream basins furrowed by converging channels, which suddenly gather the waters together into the main trunk in booming torrents of enormous transporting power, though short lived.

One of these ancient flood boulders stands firm in the middle of the stream channel, just below the lower edge of the pool dam at the foot of the fall nearest our camp. It is a nearly cubical mass of granite about eight feet high, plushed with mosses over the top and down the sides to ordinary high-water mark. When I climbed on top of it to-day and lay down to rest, it seemed the most romantic spot I had yet found, —the one big stone with its mossy level top and smooth sides standing square and firm and solitary, like an altar, the fall in front of it bathing it lightly with the finest of the spray, just enough to keep its moss cover fresh; the clear green pool beneath, with its foam-bells and its half circle of lilies leaning forward like a band of admirers, and flowering dogwood and alder trees leaning over all in sun-sifted arches. How soothingly, restfully cool it is beneath that leafy, translucent ceiling, and how delightful the water music—the deep bass tones of the fall, the clashing, ringing spray, and infinite variety of small low tones of the current gliding past the side of the boulder-island, and glinting against a thousand smaller stones down the ferny channel! All this shut in; every one of these influences acting at short range as if in a quiet room. The place seemed holy, where one might hope to see God.

After dark, when the camp was at rest, I groped my way back to the altar boulder and passed the night on it, —above the water, beneath the leaves and stars, —everything still more impressive than by day, the fall seen dimly white, singing Nature's old love song with solemn enthusiasm, while the stars peering through the leaf-roof seemed to join in the white water's song. Precious night, precious day to abide in me forever. Thanks be to God for this immortal gift.

June 16. —One of the Indians from Brown's Flat got right into the middle of the camp this morning, unobserved. I was seated on a stone, looking over my notes and sketches, and happening to look up, was startled to see him standing grim and silent within a few steps of me, as motionless and weather-stained as an old tree-stump that had stood there for centuries. All Indians seem to have learned this wonderful way of walking unseen, —making themselves invisible like certain spiders I have been observing here, which, in case of alarm, caused, for example, by a bird alighting on the bush their webs are spread upon, immediately bounce themselves up and down on their elastic threads so rapidly that only a blur is visible. The wild Indian power of escaping observation, even where there is little or no cover to hide in, was probably slowly acquired in hard hunting and fighting lessons while trying to approach game, take enemies by surprise, or get safely away when compelled to retreat. And this experience transmitted through many generations seems at length to have become what is vaguely called instinct.

How smooth and changeless seems the surface of the mountains about us! Scarce a track is to be found beyond the range of the sheep except on small open spots on the sides of the streams, or where the forest carpets are thin or wanting. On the smoothest of these open strips and patches deer tracks may be seen, and the great suggestive footprints of bears, which, with those of the many small animals, are scarce enough to answer as a kind of light ornamental stitching or embroidery. Along the main ridges and larger branches of the river Indian trails may be traced, but they are not nearly as distinct as one would expect to find them. How many centuries Indians have roamed these woods nobody knows, probably a great many, extending far beyond the time that Columbus touched our shores, and it seems strange that heavier marks have not been made. Indians walk softly and hurt the landscape hardly more than the birds and squirrels, and their brush and bark huts last hardly longer than those of wood rats, while their more enduring monuments, excepting those wrought on the forests by the fires they made to improve their hunting grounds, vanish in a few centuries.

How different are most of those of the white man, especially on the lower gold region, —roads blasted in the solid rock, wild streams dammed and tamed and turned out of their channels and led along the sides of cañons and valleys to work in mines like slaves. Crossing from ridge to ridge, high in the air, on long straddling trestles as if flowing on stilts, or down and up across valleys and hills, imprisoned in iron pipes to strike and wash away hills and miles of the skin of the mountain's face, riddling, stripping every gold gully and flat. These are the white man's marks made in a few feverish years, to say nothing of mills, fields, villages, scattered hundreds of miles along the flank of the Range. Long will it be ere these marks are effaced, though Nature is doing what she can, replanting, gardening, sweeping away old dams and flumes, leveling gravel and boulder piles, patiently trying to heal every raw scar. The main gold storm is over. Calm enough are the gray old miners scratching a bare living in waste diggings here and there. Thundering underground blasting is still going on to feed the pounding quartz mills, but their influence on the landscape is light as compared with that of the pick-and-shovel storms waged a few years ago. Fortunately for Sierra scenery the gold-bearing slates are mostly restricted to the foothills. The region about our camp is still wild, and higher lies the snow about as trackless as the sky.

Only a few hills and domes of cloudland were built yesterday and none at all to-day. The light is peculiarly white and thin, though pleasantly warm. The serenity of this mountain weather in the spring, just when Nature's pulses are beating highest, is one of its greatest charms. There is only a moderate breeze from the summits of the Range at night, and a slight breathing from the sea and the lowland hills and plains during the day, or stillness so complete no leaf stirs. The trees hereabouts have but little wind history to tell.

Sheep, like people, are ungovernable when hungry. Excepting my guarded lily gardens, almost every leaf that these hoofed locusts can reach within a radius of a mile or two from camp has been devoured. Even the bushes are stripped bare, and in spite of dogs and shepherds the sheep scatter to all points of the compass and vanish in dust. I fear some are lost, for one of the sixteen black ones is missing. . .

June 19. —Pure sunshine all day. How beautiful a rock is made by leaf shadows! Those of the live oak are particularly clear and distinct, and beyond all art in grace and delicacy, now still as if painted on stone, now gliding softly as if afraid of noise, now dancing, waltzing in swift, merry swirls, or jumping on and off sunny rocks in quick dashes like wave embroidery on seashore cliffs. How true and substantial is this shadow beauty, and with what sublime extravagance is beauty thus multiplied! The big orange lilies are now arrayed in all their glory of leaf and flower. Noble plants, in perfect health, Nature's darlings.

June 20. —Some of the silly sheep got caught fast in a tangle of chaparral this morning, like flies in a spider's web, and had to be helped out. Carlo found them and tried to drive them from the trap by the easiest way. How far above sheep are intelligent dogs! No friend and helper can be more affectionate and constant than Carlo. The noble St. Bernard is an honor to his race.

The air is distinctly fragrant with balsam and resin and mint, —every breath of it a gift we may well thank God for. Who could ever guess that so rough a wilderness should yet be so fine, so full of good things. One seems to be in a majestic domed pavilion in which a grand play is being acted with scenery and music and and incense, —all the furniture and action so interesting we are in no danger of being called on to endure one dull moment. God himself seems to be always doing his best here, working like a man in a glow of enthusiasm.

(From *My First Summer in the Sierra,* Ch. 2)

The Shepherd and His Dog

Our shepherd is a queer character and hard to place in this wilderness. His bed is a hollow made in red dry-rot punky dust beside a log which forms a portion of the south wall of the corral. Here he lies with his wonderful everlasting clothing on, wrapped in a red blanket, breathing not only the dust of the decayed wood but also that of the corral, as if determined to take ammoniacal snuff all night after chewing tobacco all day. Following the sheep he carries a heavy six-shooter swung from his belt on one side and his luncheon on the other. The ancient cloth in which the meat, fresh from the frying-pan, is tied serves as a filter through which the clear fat and gravy juices drip down on his right hip and leg in clustering stalactites. This oleaginous formation is soon broken up, however, and diffused and rubbed evenly into his scanty apparel, by sitting down, rolling over, crossing his legs while resting on logs, etc., making shirt and trousers water-tight and shiny. His trousers, in particular, have become so adhesive with the mixed fat and resin that pine needles, thin flakes and fibres of bark, hair, mica scales and minute grains of quartz, hornblende, etc., feathers, seed wings, moth and butterfly wings, legs and antennae of innumerable insects, or even whole insects such as the small beetles, moths and mosquitoes, with flower petals, pollen dust and indeed bits of all plants, animals, and minerals of the region adhere to them and are safely imbedded, so that though far from being a naturalist he collects fragmentary specimens of everything and becomes richer than he knows. His specimens are kept passably fresh, too, by the purity of the air and the resiny bituminous beds into which they are pressed. Man is a microcosm, at least our shepherd is, or rather his trousers. These precious overalls are never taken off, and nobody knows how old they are, though one may guess by their thickness and concentric structure. Instead of wearing thin they wear thick, and in their stratification have no small geological significance....

... Shepherd Billy is in a peck of trouble about the sheep; he declares that they are possessed with more of the evil one than any other flock from the beginning of the invention of mutton and wool to the last batch of it. No matter how many are missing, he will not, he says, go a step to seek them, because, as he reasons, while getting back one wanderer he would probably lose ten. Therefore runaway hunting must be Carlo's and mine. Billy's little dog Jack is also giving trouble by leaving camp every night to visit his neighbors up the mountain at Brown's Flat. He is a common-looking cur of no particular breed, but tremendously enterprising in love and war. He has cut all the ropes and leather straps he has been tied with, until his master in desperation, after climbing the brushy mountain again and again to drag him back, fastened him with a pole attached to his collar under his chin at one end, and to a stout sapling at the other. But the pole gave good leverage, and by constant twisting during the night, the fastening at the sapling end was chafed off, and he set out on his usual journey, dragging the pole through the brush, and reached the Indian settlement in safety. His master followed, and making no allowance, gave him a beating, and swore in bad terms that next evening he would "fix that infatuated pup" by anchoring him unmercifully to the heavy cast-iron lid of our Dutch oven, weighing about as much as the dog. It was linked directly to his collar close up under the chin, so that the poor fellow seemed unable to stir. He stood quite discouraged until after dark, unable to look about him, or even to lie down unless he stretched himself out with his front feet across the lid, and his head close down between his paws. Before morning, however, Jack was heard far up the height howling Excelsior, cast-iron anchor to the contrary notwithstanding. He must have walked, or rather climbed, erect on his hind legs, clasping the heavy lid like a shield against his breast, a formidable iron-clad condition in which to meet his rivals. Next night, dog, pot-lid, and all, were tied up in an old bean-sack, and thus at last angry Billy gained the victory.

(From *My First Summer in the Sierra,* Ch. 2 and 5)

The Grasshopper

A queer fellow and a jolly fellow is the grasshopper. Up the mountains he comes on excursions, how high I don't know, but at least as far and high as Yosemite tourists. I was much interested with the hearty enjoyment of the one that danced and sang for me on the Dome this afternoon. He seemed brimful of glad, hilarious energy, manifested by springing into the air to a height of twenty or thirty feet, then diving and springing up again and making a sharp musical rattle just as the lowest point in the descent was reached. Up and down a dozen times or so he danced and sang, then alighted to rest, then up and at it again. The curves he described in the air in diving and rattling resembled those made by cords hanging loosely and attached at the same height at the ends, the loops nearly covering each other. Braver, heartier, keener, care-free enjoyment of life I have never seen or heard in any creature, great or small. The life of this comic redlegs, the mountain's merriest child, seems to be made up of pure, condensed gayety. The Douglas squirrel is the only living creature that I can compare him with in exuberant, rollicking, irrepressible jollity. Wonderful that these sublime mountains are so loudly cheered and brightened by a creature so queer.

Nature in him seems to be snapping her fingers in the face of all earthly dejection and melancholy with a boyish hip-hip-hurrah. How the sound is made I do not understand. When he was on the ground he made not the slightest noise, nor when he was simply flying from place to place, but only when diving in curves, the motion seeming to be required for the sound; for the more vigorous the diving the more energetic the corresponding outbursts of jolly rattling. I tried to observe him closely while he was resting in the intervals of his performances; but he would not allow a near approach, always getting his jumping legs ready to spring for immediate flight, and keeping his eyes on me. A fine sermon the little fellow danced for me on the Dome, a likely place to look for sermons in stones, but not for grasshopper sermons. A large and imposing pulpit for so small a preacher. No danger of weakness in the knees of the world while Nature can spring such a rattle as this. Even the bear did not express for me the mountain's wild health and strength and happiness so tellingly as did this comical little hopper. No cloud of care in his day, no winter of discontent in sight. To him every day is a holiday; and when at length his sun sets, I fancy he will cuddle down on the forest floor and die like the leaves and flowers, and like them leave no unsightly remains calling for burial.

(From *My First Summer in the Sierra,* Ch. 5)

A Grand Page of Mountain Manuscript

July 11. — We are now about seven thousand feet above the sea, and the nights are so cool we have to pile coats and extra clothing on top of our blankets. Tamarack Creek is icy cold, delicious, exhilarating champagne water. It is flowing bank full in the meadow with silent speed, but only a few hundred yards below our camp the ground is bare gray granite strewn with boulders, large spaces being without a single tree or only a small one here and there anchored in narrow seams and cracks. The boulders, many of them very large, are not in piles or scattered like rubbish among loose crumbling debris as if weathered out of the solid as boulders of disintegration; they mostly occur singly, and are lying on a clean pavement on which the sunshine falls in a glare that contrasts with the shimmer of light and shade we have been accustomed to in the leafy woods. And, strange to say, these boulders lying so still and deserted, with no moving force near them, no boulder carrier anywhere in sight, were nevertheless brought from a distance, as difference in color and composition shows, quarried and carried and laid down here each in its place; nor have they stirred, most of them, through calm and storm since first they arrived. They look lonely here, strangers in a strange land, —huge blocks, angular mountain chips, the largest twenty or thirty feet in diameter, the chips that Nature has made in modeling her landscapes, fashioning the forms of her mountains and valleys. And with what tool were they quarried and carried? On the pavement we find its marks. The most resisting unweathered portion of the surface is scored and striated in a rigidly parallel way, indicating that the region has been overswept by a glacier from the northeastward, grinding down the general mass of the mountains, scoring and polishing, producing a strange, raw, wiped appearance, and dropping whatever boulders it chanced to be carrying at the time it was melted at the close of the Glacial Period. A fine discovery this. As for the forests we have been passing through, they are probably growing on deposits of soil most of which has been laid down by this same ice agent in the form of moraines of different sorts, now in great part disintegrated and out-spread by post-glacial weathering.

Out of the grassy meadow and down over this ice-planed granite runs the glad young Tamarack Creek, rejoicing, exulting, chanting, dancing in white, glowing, irised falls and cascades on its way to the Merced Cañon, a few miles below Yosemite, falling more than three thousand feet in a distance of about two miles.

All the Merced streams are wonderful singers, and Yosemite is the centre where the main tributaries meet. From a point about half a mile from our camp we can see into the lower end of the famous valley, with its wonderful cliffs and groves, a grand page of mountain manuscript that I would gladly give my life to be able to read. How vast it seems, how short human life when we happen to think of it, and how little we may learn, however hard we try! Yet why bewail our poor inevitable ignorance? Some of the external beauty is always in sight, enough to keep every fibre of us tingling, and this we are able to gloriously enjoy though the methods of its creation may lie beyond our ken. Sing on, brave Tamarack Creek, fresh from your snowy fountains, plash and swirl and dance to your fate in the sea; bathing, cheering every living thing along your way.

Have greatly enjoyed all this huge day, sauntering and seeing, steeping in the mountain influences, sketching, noting, pressing flowers, drinking ozone and Tamarack water. Found the white fragrant Washington lily, the finest of all the Sierra lilies. Its bulbs are buried in shaggy chaparral tangles, I suppose for safety from pawing bears; and its magnificent panicles sway and rock over the top of the rough snow-pressed bushes, while big, bold, blunt-nosed bees drone and mumble in its polleny bells. A lovely flower, worth going hungry and footsore endless miles to see. The whole world seems richer now that I have found this plant in so noble a landscape.

A log house serves to mark a claim to the Tamarack

meadow, which may become valuable as a station in case travel to Yosemite should greatly increase. Belated parties occasionally stop here. A white man with an Indian woman is holding possession of the place.

Sauntered up the meadow about sundown, out of sight of camp and sheep and all human mark, into the deep peace of the solemn old woods, everything glowing with Heaven's unquenchable enthusiasm.

(From *My First Summer in the Sierra*, Ch. 4)

Mountains are Fountains

July 26. —Ramble to the summit of Mt. Hoffman, eleven thousand feet high, the highest point in life's journey my feet have yet touched. And what glorious landscapes are about me, new plants, new animals, new crystals, and multitudes of new mountains far higher than Hoffman, towering in glorious array along the axis of the range, serene, majestic, snow-laden, sundrenched, vast domes and ridges shining below them, forests, lakes, and meadows in the hollows, the pure blue bell-flower sky brooding them all, —a glory day of admission into a new realm of wonders as if Nature had wooingly whispered, "Come higher." What questions I asked, and how little I know of all the vast show, and how eagerly, tremulously hopeful of some day knowing more, learning the meaning of these divine symbols crowded together on this wondrous page.

Mt. Hoffman is the highest part of a ridge or spur about fourteen miles from the axis of the main range, perhaps a remnant brought into relief and isolated by unequal denudation. The southern slopes shed their waters into Yosemite Valley by Tenaya and Dome Creeks, the northern in part into the Tuolumne River, but mostly into the Merced by Yosemite Creek. The rock is mostly granite, with some small piles and crests rising here and there in picturesque pillared and castellated remnants of red metamorphic slates. Both the granite and slates are divided by joints, making them separable into blocks like the stones of artificial masonry, suggesting the Scripture "He hath builded the mountains." Great banks of snow and ice are piled in hollows on the cool precipitous north side forming the highest perennial sources of Yosemite Creek. The southern slopes are much more gradual and accessible. Narrow slot-like gorges extend across the summit at right angles, which look like lanes, formed evidently by the erosion of less resisting beds. They are usually called "devil's slides," though they lie far above the region usually haunted by the devil; for though we read that he once climbed an exceeding high mountain, he cannot be much of a mountaineer, for his tracks are seldom seen above the timberline.

The broad gray summit is barren and desolate-looking in general views, wasted by ages of gnawing storms; but looking at the surface in detail, one finds it covered by thousands and millions of charming plants with leaves and flowers so small they form no mass of color visible at a distance of a few hundred yards. Beds of azure daisies smile confidingly in moist hollows, and along the banks of small rills, with several species of eriogonum, silky-leaved ivesia, pentstemon, orthocarpus, and patches of *Primula suffruticosa*, a beautiful shrubby species. Here also I found bryanthus, a charming heathwort covered with purple flowers and dark green foliage like heather, and three trees new to me, —a hemlock and two pines. The hemlock (*Tsuga mertensiana*) is the most beautiful conifer I have ever seen; the branches and also the main axis droop in a singularly graceful way, and the dense foliage covers the delicate, sensitive, swaying branchlets all around. It is now in full bloom, and the flowers, together with thousands of last season's cones still clinging to the drooping sprays, display wonderful wealth of color, brown and purple and blue. Gladly I climbed the first tree I found to revel in the midst of it. How the touch of the flowers makes one's flesh tingle! The pistillate are dark, rich purple, and almost translucent, the staminate blue, —a vivid, pure tone of blue like the mountain sky, —the most uncommonly beautiful of all the Sierra tree flowers I have seen. How wonderful that, with all its delicate feminine grace and beauty of form and dress and behavior, this lovely tree up here, exposed to the wildest blasts, has already endured the storms of centuries of winters!

The two pines also are brave storm-enduring trees, the mountain pine (*Pinus monticola*) and the dwarf pine (*Pinus albicaulis*). The mountain pine is closely related to the sugar pine, though the cones are only about four to six inches long. The largest trees are from five to six feet in diameter at four feet above the ground, the bark rich brown. Only a few storm-beaten adventurers approach the summit of the mountain. The dwarf or white-bark pine is the species that forms the timber-line, where it is so completely dwarfed that one may walk over the top of a bed of it as over snow-pressed chaparral.

How boundless the day seems as we revel in these storm-beaten sky gardens amid so vast a congregation of onlooking mountains! Strange and admirable it is that the more savage and chilly and storm-chafed the mountains, the finer the glow on their faces and the finer the plants they bear. The myriads of flowers tingeing the mountain-top do not seem to have grown out of the dry, rough gravel of disintegration, but rather they appear as visitors, a cloud of witnesses to Nature's love in what we in our timid ignorance and unbelief call howling desert. The surface of the ground, so dull and forbidding at first sight, besides being rich in plants, shines and sparkles with crystals: mica, hornblende, feldspar, quartz, tourmaline. The radiance in some places is so great as to be fairly dazzling, keen lance rays of every color flashing, sparkling in glorious abundance, joining the plants in their fine, brave beauty-work, —every crystal, every flower a window opening into heaven, a mirror reflecting the Creator.

From garden to garden, ridge to ridge, I drifted enchanted, now on my knees gazing into the face of a daisy, now climbing again and again among the purple and azure flowers of the hemlocks, now down into the treasuries of the snow, or gazing afar over domes and peaks, lakes and woods, and the billowy glaciated fields of the upper Tuolumne, and trying to sketch them. In the midst of such beauty, pierced with its rays, one's body is all one tingling palate. Who wouldn't be a mountaineer! Up here all the world's prizes seem nothing....

July 27. —Up and away to Lake Tenaya, —another big day, enough for a lifetime. The rocks, the air, everything speaking with audible voice or silent; joyful, wonderful, enchanting, banishing weariness and sense of time. No longing for anything now or hereafter as we go home into the mountain's heart. The level sunbeams are touching the fir-tops, every leaf shining with dew. Am holding an easterly course, the deep cañon of Tenaya Creek on the right hand, Mt. Hoffman on the left, and the lake straight ahead about ten miles distant, the summit of Mt. Hoffman about three thousand feet above me, Tenaya Creek four thousand feet below and separated from the shallow, irregular valley, along which most of the way lies, by smooth domes and wave-ridges. Many mossy emerald bogs, meadows, and gardens in rocky hollows to wade and saunter through, —and what fine plants they give me, what joyful streams I have to cross, and how many views are displayed of the Hoffman and Cathedral Peak masonry, and what a wondrous breadth of shining granite pavement to walk over for the first time about the shores of the lake! On I sauntered in freedom complete; body without weight as far as I was aware; now wading through starry parnassia bogs, now through gardens shoulder deep in larkspur and lilies, grasses and rushes, shaking off showers of dew; crossing piles of crystalline moraine boulders, bright mirror pavements, and cool, cheery streams going to Yosemite; crossing bryanthus carpets and the scoured pathways of avalanches, and thickets of snow-pressed ceanothus; then down a broad, majestic stairway into the ice-sculptured lake-basin.

The snow on the high mountains is melting fast, and the streams are singing bankfull, swaying softly through the level meadows and bogs, quivering with sun-spangles, swirling in pot-holes, resting in deep pools, leaping, shouting in wild, exulting energy over rough boulder dams, joyful, beautiful in all their forms. No Sierra landscape that I have seen holds anything truly dead or dull, or any trace of what in manufactories is called rubbish or waste; everything is perfectly clean and pure and full of divine lessons. This quick, inevitable interest attaching to everything seems marvelous until the hand of God becomes visible; then it seems reasonable that what interests Him may well interest us. When we try to pick out anything by itself, we find it hitched to everything else in the universe. One fancies a heart like our own must be beating in every crystal and cell, and we feel like stopping to speak to the plants and animals as friendly fellow-mountaineers. Nature as a poet, an enthusiastic workingman, becomes more

and more visible the farther and higher we go; for the
mountains are fountains—beginning places, however
related to sources beyond mortal ken.

(From *My First Summer in the Sierra,* Ch. 6)

A Strange Experience

*James Davie Butler had written to Muir that he would be coming
to California sometime during the summer of 1869, but Muir had
no knowledge of his former professor's itinerary when this incident
took place.*

༺ེ⚬ཻ⚬ཻ⚬ཻ⚬ེ༻

August 2. —Clouds and showers, about the same as yesterday.
Sketching all day on the North Dome until four or five
o'clock in the afternoon, when, as I was busily employed
thinking only of the glorious Yosemite landscape, trying
to draw every tree and every line and feature of the rocks,
I was suddenly, and without warning, possessed with the
notion that my friend, Professor J.D. Butler, of the State
University of Wisconsin, was below me in the valley, and I
jumped up full of the idea of meeting him, with almost as
much startling excitement as if he had suddenly touched
me to make me look up. Leaving my work without the
slightest deliberation, I ran down the western slope of the
Dome and along the brink of the valley wall, looking for
a way to the bottom, until I came to a side cañon, which,
judging by its apparently continuous growth of trees and
bushes, I thought might afford a practical way into the
valley, and immediately began to make the descent, late as
it was, as if drawn irresistibly. But after a little, common
sense stopped me and explained that it would be long after

dark ere I could possibly reach the hotel, that the visitors would be asleep, that nobody would know me, that I had no money in my pockets, and moreover was without a coat. I therefore compelled myself to stop, and finally succeeded in reasoning myself out of the notion of seeking my friend in the dark, whose presence I only felt in a strange, telepathic way. I succeeded in dragging myself back through the woods to camp, never for a moment wavering, however, in my determination to go down to him next morning. This I think is the most unexplainable notion that ever struck me. Had some one whispered in my ear while I sat on the Dome, where I had spent so many days, that Professor Butler was in the valley, I could not have been more surprised and startled. When I was leaving the university he said, "Now, John, I want to hold you in sight and watch your career. Promise to write me at least once a year." I received a letter from him in July, at our first camp in the Hollow, written in May, in which he said that he might possibly visit California some time this summer, and therefore hoped to meet me. But inasmuch as he named no meeting-place, and gave no directions as to the course he would probably follow, and as I should be in the wilderness all summer, I had not the slightest hope of seeing him, and all thought of the matter had vanished from my mind until this afternoon, when he seemed to be wafted bodily almost against my face. Well, to-morrow I shall see; for, reasonable or unreasonable, I feel I must go.

August 3. —Had a wonderful day. Found Professor Butler as the compass-needle finds the pole. So last evening's telepathy, transcendental revelation, or whatever else it may be called, was true; for, strange to say, he had just entered the valley by way of the Coulterville Trail and was coming up the valley past El Capitan when his presence struck me. Had he then looked toward the North Dome with a good glass when it first came in sight, he might have seen me jump up from my work and run toward him. This seems the one well-defined marvel of my life of the kind called supernatural; for, absorbed in glad Nature, spirit-rappings, second sight, ghost stories, etc., have never interested me since boyhood, seeming comparatively useless and infinitely less wonderful than Nature's open, harmonious, songful, sunny, every-day beauty.

This morning, when I thought of having to appear among tourists at a hotel, I was troubled because I had no suitable clothes, and at best am desperately bashful and shy. I was determined to go, however, to see my old friend after two years among strangers; got on a clean pair of overalls, a cashmere shirt, and a sort of jacket, —the best my camp wardrobe afforded, —tied my note-book on my belt, and strode away on my strange journey, followed by Carlo. I made my way through the gap discovered last evening, which proved to be Indian Cañon. There was no trail in it, and the rocks and brush were so rough that Carlo frequently called me back to help him down precipitous places. Emerging from the cañon shadows, I found a man making hay on one of the meadows, and asked him whether Professor Butler was in the valley. "I don't know," he replied; "but you can easily find out at the hotel. There are but few visitors in the valley just now. A small party came in yesterday afternoon, and I heard some one called Professor Butler, or Butterfield, or some name like that."

In front of the gloomy hotel I found a tourist party adjusting their fishing tackle. They all stared at me in silent wonderment, as if I had been seen dropping down through the trees from the clouds, mostly, I suppose, on account of my strange garb. Inquiring for the office, I was told it was locked, and that the landlord was away, but I might find the landlady, Mrs. Hutchings, in the parlor. I entered in a sad state of embarrassment, and after I had waited in the big, empty room and knocked at several doors the landlady at length appeared, and in reply to my question said she rather thought Professor Butler was in the valley, but to make sure, she would bring the register from the office. Among the names of the last arrivals I soon discovered the Professor's familiar handwriting, at the sight of which bashfulness vanished; and having learned that his party had gone up the valley, —probably to the Vernal and Nevada Falls, —I pushed on in glad pursuit, my heart now sure of its prey. In less than an hour I reached the head of the Nevada Cañon at the Vernal Fall, and just outside of the spray discovered a distinguished-looking gentleman, who, like everybody else I have seen to-day, regarded me curiously as I approached. When I made bold to inquire if he knew where Professor Butler was, he seemed yet more curious to know what could possibly have happened that required a messenger for the Professor, and instead of answering my question he asked with military sharpness, "Who wants him?" "I want him," I replied with equal sharpness. "Why? Do *you* know him?" "Yes," I said. "Do *you* know him?" Astonished that anyone in the mountains could possibly know Professor Butler and find him as soon as he had reached the valley, he came down to meet the strange mountaineer on equal terms, and courteously replied, "Yes, I know Professor Butler very well. I am General Alvord, and we were fellow students in Rutland, Vermont, long ago, when we were both young." "But where is he now?" I persisted, cutting short his story. "He has gone beyond the falls with a companion, to try to climb that big rock, the top of which you see from here." His guide now volunteered the information that it was the Liberty Cap Professor Butler and his companion had gone to climb, and that if I waited at the head of the fall I should be sure to find them on their way down. I therefore climbed the ladders alongside the Vernal Fall, and was pushing forward, determined to go to the top of Liberty Cap rock in my hurry, rather than wait, if I should not meet my friend sooner. So heart-hungry at times may one be to see a friend in the flesh, however happily full and care-free one's life may be. I had gone but a short distance, however, above the brow of the Vernal Fall when I caught sight of him in the brush and rocks, half erect, groping his way, his sleeves rolled up, vest open, hat in his hand, evidently very hot and tired. When he saw me coming he sat down on a boulder to wipe the perspiration from his brow and neck, and taking me for one of the valley guides, he inquired the way to the fall ladders. I pointed out the path marked with little piles of stones, on seeing which he called his companion, saying that the way was found; but he did not yet recognize me. Then I stood directly in front of him, looked him in the face, and held out my hand. He thought I was offering to assist him in rising. "Never mind," he said. Then I said, "Professor Butler, don't you know me?" "I think not," he replied; but catching my eye, sudden recognition followed, and astonishment that I should have found him just when he was lost in the brush and did not know that I was within hundreds of miles of him. "John Muir, John Muir, where have you come from?" Then I told him the story of my feeling his presence when he entered the valley last evening, when he was four or five miles distant, as I sat sketching on the North Dome. This, of course, only made him wonder the more. Below the foot of the Vernal Fall the guide was waiting with his saddle-horse, and I walked along the trail, chatting all the way back to the hotel, talking of school days, friends in Madison, of the students, how each had prospered, etc., ever and anon gazing at the stupendous rocks about us, now growing indistinct in the gloaming, and again quoting from the poets, —a rare ramble.

It was late ere we reached the hotel, and General Alvord was waiting the Professor's arrival for dinner. When I was introduced he seemed yet more astonished than the Professor at my descent from cloudland and going straight to my friend without knowing in any ordinary way that he was even in California. They had come on direct from the East, had not yet visited any of their friends in the state, and considered themselves undiscoverable. As we sat at dinner, the General leaned back in his chair, and looking down the table, thus introduced me to the dozen guests or so, including the staring fisherman mentioned above: "This man, you know, came down out of these huge, trackless mountains, you know, to find his friend Professor Butler here, the very day he arrived; and how did he know he was here? He just felt him, he says. This is the queerest case of Scotch farsightedness I ever heard of," etc., etc. While my friend quoted Shakespeare: "More things in heaven and earth, Horatio, than are dreamt of in your philosophy," "As the sun, ere he has risen, sometimes paints his image in the firmament, e'en so the shadows of events precede the events, and in today already walks to-morrow."

Had a long conversation, after dinner, over Madison days. The Professor wants me to promise to go with him, sometime, on a camping trip in the Hawaiian Islands, while I tried to get him to go back with me to camp in the high Sierra. But he says, "Not now." He must not leave the General; and I was surprised to learn they are to leave the valley tomorrow or next day. I'm glad I'm not great enough to be missed in the busy world.

(From *My First Summer in the Sierra,* Ch. 7)

Every Rock, Mountain, Stream...

September 1. —Clouds .05, —motionless, of no particular color, —ornaments with no hint of rain or snow in them. Day all calm, —another grand throb of Nature's heart, ripening late flowers and seeds for next summer, full of life and the thoughts and plans of life to come, and full of ripe and ready death beautiful as life, telling divine wisdom and goodness and immortality. Have been up Mt. Dana, making haste to see as much as I can now that the time of departure is drawing nigh. The views from the summit reach far and wide, eastward over the Mono Lake and Desert; mountains beyond mountains looking strangely barren and gray and bare like heaps of ashes dumped from the sky. The lake, eight or ten miles in diameter, shines like a burnished disk of silver, no trees about its gray, ashy, cindery shores. Looking westward, the glorious forests are seen sweeping over countless ridges and hills, girdling domes and subordinate mountains, fringing in long curving lines the dividing ridges, and filling every hollow where the glaciers have spread soil-beds however rocky or smooth. Looking northward and southward along the axis of the range, you see the glorious array of high mountains, crags and peaks and snow, the fountain-heads of rivers that are flowing west to the sea through the famous Golden Gate, and east to hot salt lakes and deserts to evaporate and hurry back into the sky. Innumerable lakes are shining like eyes beneath heavy rock brows, bare or tree fringed, or imbedded in black forests. Meadow openings in the woods seem as numerous as the lakes or perhaps more so. Far up the moraine-covered slopes and among crumbling rocks I found many delicate hardy plants, some of them still in flower. The best gains of this trip were the lessons of unity and inter-relation of all the features of the landscape revealed in general views. The lakes and meadows are located just where the ancient glaciers bore heaviest at the foot of the steepest parts of their channels, and of course their longest diameters are approximately parallel with each other and with the belts of forests growing in long curving lines on the lateral and medial moraines, and in broad outspreading fields on the terminal beds deposited toward the end of the ice period when the glaciers were receding. The domes, ridges, and spurs also show the influence of glacial action in their forms, which approximately seem to be the forms of greatest strength with reference to the stress of oversweeping, past-sweeping, down-grinding ice-streams; survivals of the most resisting masses, or those most favorably situated. How interesting everything is! Every rock, mountain, stream, plant, lake, lawn, forest, garden, bird, beast, insect seems to call and invite us to come and learn something of its history and relationship. But shall the poor ignorant scholar be allowed to try the lessons they offer? It seems too great and good to be true. Soon I'll be going to the lowlands. The bread camp must soon be removed. If I had a few sacks of flour, an axe, and some matches, I would build a cabin of pine logs, pile up plenty of firewood about it and stay all winter to see the grand fertile snow-storms, watch the birds and animals that winter thus high, how they live, how the forests look snow-laden or buried, and how the avalanches look and sound on their way down the mountains. But now I'll have to go, for there is nothing to spare in the way of provisions. I'll surely be back, however, surely I'll be back. No other place has ever so overwhelmingly attracted me as this hospitable, Godful wilderness.

(From *My First Summer in the Sierra*, Ch. 10)

Emerson

Jeanne Carr, the wife of Muir's former University of Wisconsin professor Ezra S. Carr, was a significant friend and mentor to Muir throughout his adult life. The Carrs moved in social circles that included the likes of Ralph Waldo Emerson. When Emerson visited Yosemite in the spring of 1871, Jeanne arranged for him to meet the talented young naturalist.

❧❧❧

The coniferous forests of the Yosemite Park, and of the Sierra in general, surpass all others of their kind in America or indeed in the world, not only in the size and beauty of the trees, but in the number of species assembled together, and the grandeur of the mountains they are growing on. Leaving the workaday lowlands, and wandering into the heart of the mountains, we find a new world, and stand beside the majestic pines and firs and sequoias silent and awe-stricken, as if in the presence of superior beings new arrived from some other star, so calm and bright and godlike they are.

Going to the woods is going home; for I suppose we came from the woods originally. But in some of nature's forests the adventurous traveler seems a feeble, unwelcome creature; wild beasts and the weather trying to kill him, the rank, tangled vegetation, armed with spears and stinging needles, barring his way and making life a hard struggle. Here everything is hospitable and kind, as if planned for your pleasure, ministering to every want of body and soul. Even the storms are friendly and seem to regard you as a brother, their beauty and tremendous fateful earnestness charming alike. But the weather is mostly sunshine, both winter and summer, and the clear sunny brightness of the park is one of its most striking characteristics. Even the heaviest portions of the main forest belt, where the trees are tallest and stand closest, are not in the least gloomy. The sunshine falls in glory through the colossal spires and crowns, each a symbol of health and strength, the noble shafts faithfully upright like the pillars of temples, upholding a roof of infinite leafy interlacing arches and fretted skylights. The more open portions are like spacious parks, carpeted with small shrubs, or only with the fallen needles sprinkled here and there with flowers. In some places, where the ground is level or slopes gently, the trees are assembled in groves, and the flowers and underbrush in trim beds and thickets as in landscape gardens or the lovingly planted grounds of homes; or they are drawn up in orderly rows around meadows and lakes and along the brows of cañons....

...But the noble oaks and all these rock-shading, stream-embowering trees are as nothing amid the vast abounding billowy forests of conifers. During my first years in the Sierra I was ever calling on everybody within reach to admire them, but I found no one half warm enough until Emerson came. I had read his essays, and felt sure that of all men he would best interpret the sayings of these noble mountains and trees. Nor was my faith weakened when I met him in Yosemite. He seemed as serene as a sequoia, his head in the empyrean; and forgetting his age, plans, duties, ties of every sort, I proposed an immeasurable camping trip back in the heart of the mountains. He seemed anxious to go, but considerately mentioned his party. I said: "Never mind. The mountains are calling; run away, and let plans and parties and dragging lowland duties all gang tapsal-teerie. We'll go up a cañon singing your own song, "Good-by, proud world! I'm going home, in divine earnest. Up there lies a new heaven and a new earth; let us go to the show." But alas, it was too late,—too near the sundown of his life. The shadows were growing long, and he leaned on his friends. His party, full of indoor philosophy, failed to see the natural beauty and fullness of promise of my wild plan, and laughed at it in good-natured ignorance, as if it were necessarily amusing to imagine that Boston people might be led to accept Sierra manifestations of God at the price of rough camping. Anyhow, they would have none of it, and held Mr. Emerson to the hotels and trails.

After spending only five tourist days in Yosemite he was led away, but I saw him two days more; for I was kindly invited to go with the party as far as the Mariposa big trees. I told Mr. Emerson that I would gladly go to the sequoias with him, if he would camp in the grove. He consented heartily, and I felt sure that we would have at least one good wild memorable night around a sequoia camp-fire. Next day we rode through the magnificent forests of the Merced basin, and I kept calling his attention to the sugar pines, quoting his wood-notes, "Come listen what the pine tree saith," etc., pointing out the noblest as kings and high priests, the most eloquent and commanding preachers of all the mountain forests, stretching forth their century-old arms in benediction over the worshiping congregations crowded about them. He gazed in devout admiration, saying but little, while his fine smile faded away.

Early in the afternoon, when we reached Clark's Station, I was surprised to see the party dismount. And when I asked if we were not going up into the grove to camp they said: "No; it would never do to lie out in the night air. Mr. Emerson might take cold; and you know, Mr. Muir, that would be a dreadful thing." In vain I urged, that only in homes and hotels were colds caught, that nobody ever was known to take cold camping in these woods, that there was not a single cough or sneeze in all the Sierra. Then I pictured the big climate-changing, inspiring fire I would make, praised the beauty and fragrance of sequoia flame, told how the great trees would stand about us transfigured in the purple light, while the stars looked down between the great domes; ending by urging them to come on and make an immortal Emerson night of it. But the house habit was not to be overcome, nor the strange dread of pure night air, though it is only cooled day air with a little dew in it. So the carpet dust and unknowable reeks were preferred. And to think of this being a Boston choice! Sad commentary on culture and the glorious transcendentalism.

Accustomed to reach whatever place I started for, I was going up the mountain alone to camp, and wait the coming of the party next day. But since Emerson was so soon to vanish, I concluded to stop with him. He hardly spoke a word all the evening, yet it was a great pleasure simply to be near him, warming in the light of his face as at a fire. In the morning we rode up the trail through a noble forest of pine and fir into the famous Mariposa Grove, and stayed an hour or two, mostly in ordinary tourist fashion,—looking at the biggest giants, measuring them with a tape line, riding through prostrate fire-bored trunks, etc., though Mr. Emerson was alone occasionally, sauntering about as if under a spell. As we walked through a fine group, he quoted, "There were giants in those days," recognizing the antiquity of the race. To commemorate his visit, Mr. Galen Clark, the guardian of the grove, selected the finest of the unnamed trees and requested him to give it a name. He named it Samoset, after the New England sachem, as the best that occurred to him.

The poor bit of measured time was soon spent, and while the saddles were being adjusted I again urged Emerson to stay. "You are yourself a sequoia," I said. "Stop and get acquainted with your big brethren." But he was past his prime, and was now as a child in the hands of his affectionate but sadly civilized friends, who seemed as full of old-fashioned conformity as of bold intellectual independence. It was the afternoon of the day and the afternoon of his life, and his course was now westward down all the mountains into the sunset. The party mounted and rode away in wondrous contentment, apparently, tracing the trail through ceanothus and dogwood bushes, around the bases of the big trees, up the slope of the sequoia basin, and over the divide. I followed to the edge of the grove. Emerson lingered in the rear of the train, and when he reached the top of the ridge, after all the rest of the party were over and out of sight, he turned his horse, took off his hat and waved me a last good-by. I felt lonely, so sure had I been that Emerson of all men would be the quickest to see the mountains and sing them. Gazing awhile on the spot where he vanished, I sauntered back into the heart of the grove, made a bed of sequoia plumes and ferns by the side of a stream, gathered a store of firewood, and then walked about until sundown. The birds, robins, thrushes, warblers, etc., that had kept out of sight, came about me, now that all was quiet, and made cheer. After sundown I built a great fire, and as usual had it all to myself. And though lonesome for the first time in these forests, I quickly took heart again,—the trees had not gone to Boston, nor the birds; and as I sat by the fire, Emerson was still with me in spirit, though I never again saw him in the flesh. He sent books and wrote, cheering me on; advised me not to stay too long in solitude. Soon he hoped that my guardian angel would intimate that my probation was at a close. Then I was to roll up my herbariums, sketches, and poems (though I never knew I had any poems), and come to his house; and when I tired of him and his humble surroundings, he would show me to better people.

But there remained many a forest to wander through, many a mountain and glacier to cross, before I was to see his Wachusett and Monadnock, Boston and Concord. It was seventeen years after our parting on the Wawona ridge that I stood beside his grave under a pine tree on the hill above Sleepy Hollow. He had gone to higher Sierras, and, as I fancied, was again waving his hand in friendly recognition.

(From *Our National Parks,* Ch. 4)

Living Glaciers of California

Through careful observation and study, Muir came up with an original theory of how Yosemite Valley had been carved by the activity of ancient glaciers. Ridiculed by leading scientists of the day, his ideas were eventually accepted into the mainstream.

⁂

On one of the yellow days of October, 1871, when I was among the mountains of the "Merced group," following the foot-prints of the ancient glaciers that once flowed grandly from their ample fountains, reading what I could of their history as written in moraines, cañons, lakes, and carved rocks, I came upon a small stream that was carrying mud of a kind I had never seen. In a calm place, where the stream widened, I collected some of this mud, and observed that it was entirely mineral in composition, and fine as flour, like the mud from a fine-grit grindstone. Before I had time to reason, I said, "Glacier mud— mountain meal!"

Then I observed that this muddy stream issued from a

bank of fresh-quarried stones and dirt, that was sixty or seventy feet in height. This I at once took to be a moraine. In climbing to the top of it, I was struck with the steepness of its slope, and with its raw, unsettled, plantless, new-born appearance. The slightest touch started blocks of red and black slate, followed by a rattling train of smaller stones and sand, and a cloud of dry dust of mud, the whole moraine being as free from lichens and weather-stains as if dug from the mountain that very day.

When I had scrambled to the top of the moraine, I saw what seemed to be a huge snow-bank, four or five hundred yards in length, by half a mile in width. Imbedded in its stained and furrowed surface were stones and dirt like that of which the moraine was built. Dirt-stained lines curved across the snowbank from side to side, and when I observed that these curved lines coincided with the curved moraine, and that the stones and dirt were most abundant near the bottom of the bank, I shouted, *"A living glacier!"*

These bent dirt-lines show that the ice is following in its different parts with unequal velocity, and these imbedded stones are journeying down, to be built into the moraine, and they gradually become more abundant as they approach the moraine, because there the motion is slower.

On traversing my new-found glacier, I came to a crevasse, down a wide and jagged portion of which I succeeded in making my way, and discovered that my so-called snow-bank was clear, green ice, and, comparing the form of the basin which it occupied with similar adjacent basins that were empty, I was led to the opinion that this glacier was several hundred feet in depth.

Then I went to the "snow-banks" of Mts. Lyell and McClure, and, on examination, was convinced that they also were true glaciers, and that a dozen other snow-banks seen from the summit of Mt. Lyell, crouching in shadow, were glaciers, living as any in the world, and busily engaged in completing that vast work of mountain-making accomplished by their giant relations now dead, which, united and continuous, covered all the range from summit to sea.

But, although I was myself thus fully satisfied concerning the real nature of these ice masses, I found that my friends regarded my deductions and statements with distrust; therefore, I determined to collect proofs of the common, measured, arithmetical kind.

On the twenty-first of August last, I planted five stakes in the glacier of Mt. McClure, which is situated east of Yosemite Valley, near the summit of the range. Four of these stakes were extended across the glacier, in a straight line, from the east side to a point near the middle of the glacier. The first stake was planted about twenty-five yards from the east bank of the glacier; the second, ninety-four yards; the third, 152, and the fourth, 225 yards. The positions of these stakes were determined by sighting across from bank to bank, past a plumb-line, made of a stone and a black horse-hair.

On observing my stakes on the sixth of October, or in forty-six days after being planted, I found that stake No. 1 had been carried down stream eleven inches; No. 2, eighteen inches: No. 3, thirty-four, and No. 4, forty-seven inches. As stake No. 4 was near the middle of the glacier, perhaps it was not far from the point of maximum velocity —forty-seven inches in forty-six days, or one inch per day. Stake No. 5 was planted about midway between the head of the glacier and stake No. 4. Its motion I found to be, in forty-six days, forty inches. Thus these ice-masses are seen to possess the true glacial motion. Their surfaces are striped with bent dirt-bands, and are bulged and undulated by inequalities in the bottom of their basins, causing an upward and downward swedging, corresponding to the horizontal swedging as indicated by the curved dirt-bands.

The Mt. McClure glacier is about one-half of a mile in length, and the same in width at the broadest place. It is crevassed on the south-east corner. The crevasse runs about south-west and north-east, and is several hundred yards in length. It is nowhere more than one foot in width.

The Mt. Lyell glacier, separated from that of McClure by a narrow crest, is about a mile in width by a mile in length. I have planted stakes in the glaciers of "Red Mountain" also, but have not yet observed them.

The Sierras adjacent to the Yosemite Valley are composed of slate and granite, set on edge at right angles to the direction of the range, or about north 300 east, and south 300 west. Lines of cleavage cross these, running nearly parallel with the main range; and the granite of this region has a horizontal cleavage or stratification. The first-mentioned of these lines have the fullest development, and give direction and character to many valleys and cañons, and determine the principal features of many rock-forms. No matter how hard, how domed or homogeneous the granite may be, it still possesses these lines of cleavage, which require only simple conditions of moisture, time, etc., for their development.

But I am not ready to discuss the origin of these planes of cleavage, which make this granite so easily denudable, nor their full significance with regard to mountain structure in general. I will only say here, that oftentimes the granite contained between two of these north 300 east planes is softer than the rock outside, and has been denuded, leaving vertical walls, as determined by the direction of the cleavage, thus giving rise to those narrow-slotted *cañons*, called "devil's slides," "devil's lanes," "devil's gateways," etc.

In many places, in the higher portions of the Sierras,

these slotted cañons are filled with "snow," which I thought might prove to be ice; might prove to be living glaciers, still engaged in cutting into the mountains, like endless saws. To decide this question, on the twenty-third of August last, I set two stakes in the narrow-slot glacier of Mt. Hoffman, marking their position by sighting across from wall to wall, as I did on the McClure glacier; but on visiting them, a month afterward, they had been melted out, and I was unable to decide anything with any great degree of accuracy.

On the fourth of October last, I stretched a small trout-line across the glacier, fastening both ends in the solid banks, which at this place were only sixteen feet apart. I set a short, inflexible stake in the ice, so as just to touch the tightly drawn line, by which means I was enabled to measure the flow of the glacier with great exactness. Examining the stake in twenty-four hours after setting it, I found that it had been carried down about three-sixteenths of an inch. At the end of four days, I again examined it, and found that the whole downward motion was thirteen-sixteenths of an inch, showing that the flow of this glacier was perfectly regular.

In accounting for those narrow-lane *cañons*, so common here, I always referred them to ice-action in connection with special conditions of cleavage, and I was gratified to find that their formation was still going on. This Hoffman glacier is about 1,000 feet long by fifteen to thirty feet wide, and perhaps 100 feet deep in the deepest places.

I go back to the mountains to complete these observations. These are the first fruits, and the rest of the crop I will bring in when I come to study in the Coast Range.

(*The Overland Monthly*, December 1, 1872)

Flood

Many a joyful stream is born in the Sierras, but not one can sing like the Merced. In childhood, high on the mountains, her silver thread is a moving melody; of sublime Yosemite she is the voice; the blooming *chaparral* or the flowery plains owe to her fullness their plant-wealth of purple and gold, and to the loose dipping willows and broad green oaks she is bounteous in blessing. I think she is the most absorbing and readable of rivers. I have lived with her for three years, sharing all her life and fortunes, dreaming that I appreciated her; but I never have so much as imagined the sublimity, the majesty of her music, until seeing and listening at every pore I stood in her temple to-day.

December brought to Yosemite, first of all, a cluster of ripe, golden days and silvery nights—a radiant company of the sweetest winter children of the sun. The blue sky had Sabbath and slept in its high dome, and down in its many mansions of cañon and cave, crystals grew in the calm nights, and fringed the rocks like mosses. The November torrents were soothed, and settled tranquillity beamed from every feature of rock and sky.

In the afternoon of December 16th, 1871, an immense crimson cloud grew up in solitary grandeur above Cathedral Rocks. It resembled a fungus, with a bulging base like a sequoia, a smooth, tapering stalk, and a round, bossy, down-curled head like a mushroom—stalk, head, and root, in equal, glowing, half-transparent crimson: one of the most gorgeous and symmetrical clouds I ever beheld. Next morning, I looked eagerly at the weather, but all seemed tranquil; and whatever was being done in the deep places of the sky, little stir was visible below. An ill-defined dimness consumed the best of the sunbeams, and toward noon well-developed grayish clouds appeared, having a close, curly grain, like bird's-eye maple. Late in the night some rain fell, which changed to snow, and, in the morning, about ten inches remained unmelted on the meadows, and was still falling—a fine, cordial snow-storm; but the end was not yet.

On the night of the 18th rain fell in torrents, but, as it had a temperature of 34° Fahrenheit, the snow-line was only a few feet above the meadows, and there was no promise of flood; yet sometime after eleven o'clock the temperature was suddenly raised by a south wind to 42°, carrying the snow-line to the top of the wall and far beyond—out on the upper basins, perhaps, to the very summit of the range— and morning saw Yosemite in the glory of flood. Torrents of warm rain were washing the valley walls, and melting the upper snows of the surrounding mountains; and the liberated waters held jubilee. On both sides the Sentinel foamed a splendid cascade, and across the valley by the Three Brothers, down through the pine grove, I could see fragments of an unaccountable outgush of snowy cascades. I ran for the open meadow, that I might hear and see the whole glowing circumference at once, but the tinkling brook was an unfordable torrent, bearing down snow and boulders like a giant. Farther up on the débris I discovered a place where the stream was broken up into three or four strips among the boulders, where I crossed easily, and ran for the meadows. But, on emerging from the bordering bushes, I found them filled with green lakes, edged and islanded with floating snow. I had to keep along the débris as far as Hutchings', where I crossed the river, and reached a wadable meadow in the midst of the most glorious congregation of water-falls ever laid bare to mortal eyes. Between Black's and Hutchings' there were ten snowy, majestic, loud-voiced cascades and falls; in the neighborhood of Glacier Point, six; from Three Brothers to Yosemite Falls, nine; between Yosemite and Arch Falls, ten; between Washington Column and Mount Watkins, ten; on the slopes of South Dome, facing Mirror Lake, eight; on the shoulder of South Dome, facing the main valley, three. Fifty-six newborn falls occupying this upper end of the valley; besides a countless host of silvery-netted arteries gleaming everywhere! I did not go down to the Ribbon or Pohono; but in the whole valley there must have been upward of a hundred. As if inspired with some great water purpose, cascades and falls had come thronging, in Yosemite costume, from every grove and *cañon* of the mountains; and be it remembered, that these falls and cascades were not small, dainty, momentary gushes, but broad, noble-mannered water creations; sublime in all their attributes, and well worthy Yosemite rocks, shooting in arrowy foam from a height of near three thousand feet; the very smallest of which could be heard several miles away: a perfect storm of water-falls throbbing out their lives in one stupendous song. I have criticised Hill's painting for having two large falls between the Sentinel and Cathedral rocks; now I would not be unbelieving against fifty. From my first stand-point on the meadow toward Lamon's only one fall is usually seen; now there are forty. A most glorious convention this of vocal waters—not remote and dim, as only half present, but with forms and voices wholly seen and felt, each throbbing out rays of beauty warm and palpable as those of the sun.

All who have seen Yosemite in summer will remember the comet forms of upper Yosemite Falls, and the laces of Nevada. In these waters of the jubilee, the lace tissue predominates; but there is also a plentiful mingling of arrowy comets. A cascade back of Black's is composed of two white shafts set against the dark wall about thirty feet apart, and filled in with chained and beaded gauze of splendid pattern, among the living meshes of which the dark, purple granite is dimly seen. A little above Glacier Point there is a half-woven, half-divided web of cascades, with warp and woof so similar in song and in gestures, that they appear as one existence: living and rejoicing by the pulsings of one heart. The row of cascades between Washington Column and the Arch Falls are so closely side by side that they form an almost continuous sheet; and those about Indian Cañon and the Brothers are not a whit less noble. Tissiack is crowned with surpassing glory. Her sculptured walls and bosses and her great dome are nobly adorned with clouds and waters, and her thirteen cascades give her voice of song.

The upper Yosemite is queen of all these mountain waters; nevertheless, in the first half-day of jubilee, her voice was scarce heard. Ever since the coming of the first November storms, Yosemite has flowed with a constant stream, although far from being equal to the high water in May and June. About three o'clock this afternoon I heard a sudden crash and booming, mixed with heavy gaspings and rocky, angular explosions, and I ran out, sure that a rock-avalanche had started near the top of the wall, and hoping to see some of the huge blocks journeying down; but I quickly discovered that these craggy, sharp-angled notes belonged to the flood-wave of the upper fall. The great wave, gathered from many a glacier-cañon of the Hoffman spurs, had just arrived, sweeping logs and ice before it, and, plunging over the tremendous verge, was blended with the storm-notes of crowning grandeur.

During the whole two days of storm no idle, unconscious water appeared, and the clouds, and winds, and rocks were inspired with corresponding activity and life. Clouds rose hastily, upon some errand, to the very summit of the walls, with a single effort, and as suddenly returned; or, sweeping horizontally, near the ground, draggled long-bent streamers through the pine-tops; while others traveled up and down Indian Cañon, and overtopped the highest brows, then suddenly drooped and condensed, or, thinning to gauze, veiled half the valley, leaving here and there a summit looming alone. These clouds, and the crooked cascades, raised the valley-rocks to double their usual height, for the eye, mounting from cloud to cloud, and from angle to angle upon the cascades, obtained a truer measure of their sublime stature.

The warm wind still poured in from the south, melting the snows far out on the highest mountains. Thermometer, at noon, 45°. The smaller streams of the valley edge are waning, by the slackening of the rain; but the far-reaching streams, coming in by the Tenaya, Nevada, and Illilouette cañons, are still increasing. The Merced, in some places, overflows its banks, having risen at once from a shallow, prattling, ill-proportioned stream, to a deep, majestic river. The upper Yosemite is in full, gushing, throbbing glory of prime; still louder spring its shafts of song; still deeper grows the intense whiteness of its mingled meteors; fearlessly blow the winds among its dark, shadowy chambers, now softly bearing away the outside sprays, now swaying and bending the whole massive column. So sings Yosemite, with her hundred fellow-falls, to the trembling bushes, and solemn-waving pines, and winds, and clouds, and living, pulsing rocks—one stupendous unit of mountain power—one harmonious storm of mountain love.

On the third day the storm ceased. Frost killed the new falls; the clouds are withered and empty; a score of light is drawn across the sky, and our chapter of flood is finished. Visions like these do not remain with us as mere maps and pictures—flat shadows cast upon our minds, to brighten, at times, when touched by association or will, and fade again from our view, like landscapes in the gloaming. They saturate every fibre of the body and soul, dwelling in us and with us, like holy spirits, through all of our after-deaths and after-lives.

(*The Overland Monthly*, April 1, 1872)

Yosemite in Spring

By 1872, Muir was writing articles for the tourist trade to help support his Yosemite studies. A massive earthquake in March, centered in Southern California's Owens Valley, caused a literal and figurative stir. Josiah Whitney, the California state geologist, believed that Yosemite had been formed by cataclysmic earth-shaking activity—putting him at odds with Muir and his glacier theory of the valley's origins.

≈≈≈

YOSEMITE VALLEY, MAY 7

The solons of our State Capitol have disbanded—disintegrated from the awful majesty of Senate and House to common men, who have betaken themselves to their taverns and ranchos without giving us one Yosemite law, save a paltry $1,000 appropriation for salary of Guardian. A great deal of chatter took place at different times during the Session, about smooth mountain highways and solid appropriations for the settlement of "claims," but the several bills, after being tossed from House to Senate, from Senate to Committees, were nibbled to death, and we are left to Providence for another year, roadless and moneyless, with only a thousand dollar drop of legislation for the burning thirst of our rights and wrongs.

There be some who would shed the salt tear for the unmitigated soreness of our Sierra Eden woes, not for the distracting uncertainties of private claimants, which are deplorable enough, but for our rugged unapproachableness and improvement discouragements. To such mourners these earthquake storms may seem sympathetic—Yosemite sighing through all her works, giving signs of woe that all is lost. But the billed laws of Sacramento, and paper compulsions and prohibitions of our managing commissioners, do us little harm or good. Human sparrows of improvement will not ruffle El Capitan, and he needs no legal props; he can stand alone. The Falls will manage their harmonies well enough, and the birds will sing, and meadows grow green notwithstanding any quantity of the hush or buzz of Sacramento flies. Xerxes made laws for the sea; we make laws for the mountains—make "Commissioners to manage Yosemite Valley." As well make commissioners for the management of the moon....

The Manners of the Earthquake

Since March 26, we have enjoyed, on the average, about a dozen shocks per day; most of these consisted of a few moderate thrusts or jars, kept up for 15 or 20 seconds, with rarely a mingling of twisting motions and blows from underneath. They have occurred at all hours of night and day, and in all kinds of weather, snow, rain, or sun. There was no preceding murkiness of sky observable, nor extraordinary quietude, and however bird and beast may read foretelling signs of upper storms, they seem ignorant as man of those below. While the varied stream of life flows confidingly on, and our mountains repose in blue sky or storm, smooth, rumbling sounds are heard from below, which are followed by gentle or swift shattering oscillations, mostly from north to south, or parallel with the range. The regularity of these initial oscillations is disturbed by similar less intense oscillations from east to west, perhaps finishing up by a sudden twisting or upjolting. As soon as the mountains are let alone, they undulate gently back to rest with smooth, slow motion, like the calming waters of a lake.

Earthquakes have provoked lively discussions concerning the formation of the valley, and most believe beyond, or rather behind, the regions of doubt, that Yosemite is an earthquake crack produced by a hard crack of an earthquake. A severe earthquake storm occurred in Yosemite Valley two or three hundred years ago. Unmistakable history of this storm is written in huge avalanche slopes a thousand-fold greater than those of the present storm, but corresponding with them in minutest particulars of structure. There is evidence of the simultaneous formation of the different portions of the same slopes, and also of the simultaneous occurrence of all the principle slopes on both sides of the valley. A fair approximation to the period of the formation of these slopes may be possible by ascertaining the age of the oldest trees growing upon them, because the first generation of forest has not yet passed away.

But the severity of the earthquake which made these slopes cannot be correctly measured by the size of the slopes. We have all become philosophers, deep thinkers. Instead of wasting breath when we meet on the green of meadows or brightness of the sky, we salute by great shakes, solemnly comparing numbers and intensities. What care we for the surface of things? Our thoughts go far below to the underground country, where roll the strange thunders, and the waves to which our mountains are a liquid ocean and sky. Half-believing, we paint hypothetic landscapes of the earth beneath, volcanic fountains, lakes, and seas of molten rock, fed by a thousand glowing rivers. Amazons of gurgling, rippling fire flowing in beveled valleys, or deep Yosemite cañons, with a glare of red falls and cascades, with which our upper valley, in all its glory, will not compare.

The Waterfalls

These forty days of earthquake ague have made no visible alteration in the health of the valley. Now is the birth-time of leaves; the pines are retasseled, and the oaks are sprayed with young purple. Spring is fully committed. Ferns are a foot high, willows are letting fly drifts of ripe seeds, Balm of Gilead poplars, after weeks of caution, have launched their buds full of red and leaves of tender glossy yellow. Cherries, honeysuckles, violets, bluettes, buttercups, larkspurs, gillias, are in full bloom of leaf and flower. Plant-odor fills the valley in light floating clouds and mists; it covers the ground and trees, and chapparal and tabled rocks, coming in small flakes from the impartial snow. Standing on the smooth, plushed meadows, bossed here and there with willows, and browned along the edge with dead ferns, the yellow spray of white-stemmed poplars is seen against the purple of oaks and the high, green groves of pine, back of which rise the purple and gray rock-walls fringed with glossy green live-oak, spotted with the yellow and orange of mistletoe.

The scents and sounds and forms of Yosemite Spring-time are as exquisitely compounded as her colors. The weather is warm. The noonday temperature is 65° Fahrenheit in shade; night temperature, about 45°; and the abundant snows of our compassing mountains are freely melted into flooded streams. Beside the five principal falls of the Valley: Pohono, Illilouette, Vernal, Nevada, and Yosemite, there are at present fed from the universal snows a large number of smaller cascades and falls, which come down on steps from a few feet to thousands of feet in height. The best known of these are the Big and Little Sentinel Cascades, the Bachelor's Tears, and the Virgin's Tears—magnificent weepers both of them. El Capitan is softened with a most graceful little stream that steals confidingly over his massive brow in a clear fall of more than a thousand feet. Seen at the right time the whole breadth of this fall is irised almost from top to bottom.

But of all the white outgush of Yosemite waters, the Upper Yosemite Fall is greatest. It is on the north side of the valley, and is about 1,600 feet in height. Its waters gather from a basin filled with domes, which reaches back to the edge of the main Tuolomne River cañon, a distance in a straight line of ten or twelve miles. The size of Yosemite Creek, near the brink of the valley, in the months of May and June, in a snow season like the present, is, where the current runs at the rate of three miles an hour, about twenty-five feet in width and four feet in depth. Those who have not visited this fall can have but little conception of the forms and sounds that water can develop when, after being churned and foamed, it is launched free in air, and left for 1,600 feet to its own devices. Few persons see this fall at a distance less than a mile, and very little intimation is granted at so uncordial a distance of its surprising glory. It is easily approached on the east side by a climb up the rocks to an altitude of 1,200 feet. Seen from up the valley near Lamon's, about 8 o'clock a.m., a cross-section five or six hundred feet in length is most gorgeously irised throughout—not as a motionless arc, but as a living portion of the fall with ordinary forms and motions of shooting rockets and whirling sprays of endless variety of texture transformed to the substance of rainbow melted and flowing. At this Upper Yosemite Fall, and also at the Middle Yosemite Fall, magnificent lunar bows may be found for half a dozen nights in the months of April, May, June, and sometimes in July.

If the weather continues sunful, the falls will speedily attain to highest development. May and June are usually branded best for visits to this region; but those who would behold the legions of Yosemites that are encamped around and beyond Yosemite so-called, should come any time from the end of June to the end of October. The Spring visiting campaign has just been opened by a half-dozen skirmishing parties, who reached the valley by forced marches, mostly from Mariposa; but all of the three war trails will soon be opened, although Tamarac and Crane Flat, on the Big Oak Flat and Coulterville Roads, are still deeply snowclad. Tourists will find no difficulty in procuring bread and smiles—bread at three dollars a day, smiles free—both articles in abundance, and excellent in quality.

(From *New York Daily Tribune*, July 11, 1872)

Hetch Hetchy Valley (1873)

This description of Muir's first visit to Hetch Hetchy Valley in the fall of 1871 differs from his later writings with the same title.

ঊৣৣ৵৵৵ঌৣ৵৵ঌৣৣ৵

YOSEMITE, CALIFORNIA, MARCH 1872

Hetch Hetchy is one of a magnificent brotherhood of Yosemite Valleys, distant from Yosemite Valley, so-called, eighteen or twenty miles in a northwesterly direction, but by the only trail the distance is not less than forty miles.

In the first week of last November, I set out from here on an excursion of this wonderful valley. My "proper route" was by the Big Oak Flat road as far as Hardin's Mills, thence by a trail which mazes among rocks and chaparral, past "Wade's and the Hog Ranch," but as I never follow trails when I may walk the living granite, and as I was moreover anxious to see as much as possible of the cañons of

Cascade Creek on my way, I set out straight across the mountains leaving Yosemite by Indian Cañon. There was some little danger of being caught in snow thus late in the season, but as I was afoot and had no companion to fear for, I felt confident that I could force my way out of any common storm. I carried one pair of woolen blankets and three loaves of bread—I reckoned that two loaves would be sufficient for the trip, provided all went sunnily, the third was a big round extra that I called my storm loaf. In case of being snowed in, it would last me three days, or, if necessary, six days. Besides those "breads," I carried their complementary coffee and a two-ounce mug of the Fray Bentos Extractum Carnis of Baron Liebig. Thus grandly allowanced, I was ready to enjoy my ten days' journey of any kind of calm or storm.

On reaching the top of Indian Cañon I bore off to the left, crossed Yosemite Creek about a mile back of the falls, and slanted up the side of El Capitan Mountain towards the gap, through which the Mono trail passes. By the time I reached the summit it was sundown, and as I found an old friend of a brooklet still living, and plenty of dry logs, I concluded to camp, that is, to set fire to a log and cut an armful of pine or fir branches for a bed.

Most of the next day was spent in crossing parallel rows of ice-polished cañons belonging to the basin of Cascade Creek. Night overtook me in a magnificent grove of silver fir, in which I camped.

Next morning, after climbing a long timbered slope and crossing a few groove-shaped valleys I came upon the precipitous rim of the great Tuolumne Cañon, a mile or two above Hetch Hetchy. I had explored a few miles of the central portion of this stupendous cañon in one of my former excursions. It is a Yosemite Valley in depth and in width, and is over twenty miles in length, abounding in falls and cascades, and glacial rock forms. Hetch Hetchy is only an expanded lower portion of this vast Yosemite. The view from my first standpoint is one of the very grandest I ever beheld. From the great cañon as a sort of base line, extends a most sublime map of mountains rising gradually higher, dome over dome, crest over crest, to the summit of the range, and the whole glorious engraving is reposed at such an angle that you look full upon its surface near and far. To one unacquainted with the hidden life and tenderness of the high Sierra, the first impression is one of intense soul-crushing desolation. Robert Burns described the Scottish Highlands as "a country where savage streams tumble over savage mountains," and nothing but the same (outside) savageness and confusion is apparent here. Castaway heaps of dead, broken mountains outspread, cold and gray, like a storm sky of winter. But, venture to the midst of these bleached mountain bones—dwell with them, and every death taint will disappear, you will find them living joyously, with lakes, and forests, and a thousand flowers, their hardest domes pulsing with life, breathing in atmospheres of beauty and love.

After I had carefully scanned a mile or two of the cañon wall I discovered a curve that seemed climbable all the way to the bottom, which I concluded to test. After I had descended two or three hundred yards, I struck a well-worn trail that mazed down to the cañon just where I wished to go. At first I took it to be an Indian trail, but after following it a short distance, I discovered certain hieroglyphics which suggested the possibility of its belonging to the bears. It was plain that a broad-footed mother and a family of cubs had been the last to pass over it.

It is dangerous to come suddenly upon an affectionate family of bears, but this seldom happens, if one walks noisily, for bears have excellent ears, and they are acquainted with caves and thickets, to which they gladly retire for the sake of peace.

A little below this discovery of paws, I was startled by a noise close in front. Of course in so grizzly a place, the noise was speedily clothed upon by a bear skin, but it was only the bounding of a frightened deer which I had cornered, and compelled to make a desperate leap in order to pass me. In its hurried flight up the mountain, it started several heavy boulders, that came crashing and thumping uncomfortably near.

A little further on, I came to a most interesting group of glacial records, which led me away from the trail to the edge of a sheer precipice, which, by comparison with my recollections of those of Yosemite, must be betwixt two and three thousand feet in depth. Peering cautiously over the wall, I noticed a narrow ledge fringed with dwarf live oaks, which I made out to reach; my hope was, that by following this ledge along the face of the wall I would strike my neighbor's highway, in which I had full confidence, believing that I could climb any rock that a bear could. But it soon proved that this was not unconditionally true, for in scrambling through the brush fringe of my narrow way, I observed a solitary bear track; the rugged author of those broad prints had gone in the same direction as I was going, and there was no return track. This made me more hopeful than before of being able to creep along the wall to the main traveled road, but the track appeared fresh, and the possibility of meeting long claws upon so conquer-or-die a place made me uneasy. I moved forward with great caution until I came to a recess where a few trees were anchored. Here I found that my pioneer had climbed to a sloping place on the wall above, by a dead pine that leaned against it like a ladder. Had I been empty handed like him I would have followed by the same way, but my blankets encumbered my limbs and kept them out of balance. A little farther on I was positively halted by a sheer wall, and my hour's scramble in this direction, so far as getting to the bottom was concerned, was worse than useless. Escaping from this rigid bench by the same way as I found it, I made out to zigzag down a fissured portion of the wall to another bushy seam, still hoping to reach the bear road by creeping along the face of the rock, but this second shelf terminated like the first. I was now tired of cut-offs, and decided to seek my way back up the mountain to where I first wandered from the trail. In groping through brush and fissures I found a rock cup which contained a few quarts of water, and as it was now past noon, and there was a flat place close by where I could unroll my blankets, I made a fire with chaparral twigs, and boiled a tin cupful of coffee. After dining and resting upon this lofty rock table, I continued my return climb up the rocks at a slow pace, careful to avoid thirst, in case I might be compelled to pass the night on the mountain without water. However, I encountered no extraordinary difficulties, and by two or three o'clock was safe in Bear Cañon, with fair prospects of reaching the bottom before dark. I was not on a good road and I made fast time, careful always to make abundance of admonitory noise for the benefit of Mother Bruin and her muffy cubs.

They followed the windings of the trail, in Indian file, with great fidelity, scraping it clear of sticks and pine needles, at steep places, where they had been compelled to adopt a shuffling gait to keep from rolling head over heels. Thin crumbs of dirt, around the edges of their tracks, were still moist. I could not help thinking, at times, that so remarkably well worn and well directed a trail must formerly have belonged to the Indians; but on reaching a long slope of debris, near the bottom of the cañon, it suddenly branched and melted out in all directions into densest thickets of chaparral, as Indian trails never do, and when at length I touched bottom on the level cañon floor, so good a highway was easily accounted for. Here are fine groves of black oak, and the ground was brown with acorns. At the upper end of the road are extensive fields of manzanita bushes, which yield the berries of which they are so fond; a manzanita orchard at one terminus, an acorn orchard at the other. It was plain that I had near neighbors, but they caused no alarm, as they never choose to eat men where acorns are plentiful.

I selected a camping ground near the river, in the middle of a close group of cedars, whose lower boughs drooped to the ground. I cut off some of their flat, spicy plumes for a bed, gathered a store of wood, and made a cordial fire, and was at home in this vast unhandselled Yosemite. Night gathered, in most impressive repose; my blazing fire illumined the grand brown columns of my compassing cedars and a few withered briers and gold-enrods that leaned forward between them, as if eager to drink the light. Stars glinted here and there through the rich plumes of my ceiling, and in front I could see a portion of the mighty cañon walls, dark against the sky, making me feel as if at the bottom of a sea. Few sounds reached me, excepting a few broken scraps of song from distant cascades. My weariness and the near soothing hush of the river made me drowsy. The breath of my cedar pillow was delicious, and I quickly drifted deep into the land of sleep.

Next morning I was up betimes, ate my usual crust, and started down the river bank to Hetch Hetchy, which I reached in about an hour. Hetch Hetchy bears are early risers, for they had been out in the open valley printing the hoar frost before I arrived.

This valley is situated on the main Tuolumne River, just as Yosemite is on the Merced. It is about three miles in length, with a width varying from an eighth to half a mile; most of its surface is level as a lake, and lies at an elevation of 3800 feet above the sea. Its course is mostly from east to west, but it is bent northward in the middle like Yosemite. At the end of the valley the river enters a narrow cañon which cannot devour spring floods sufficiently fast to prevent the lower half of the valley from becoming a lake. Beginning at the west end of the valley where the Hardin trail comes in, the first conspicuous rocks on the right are a group like the Cathedral Rocks of Yosemite, and occupying the same relative position to the valley. The lowest member of the group which stands out well isolated above, exactly like the corresponding rock of the Yosemite group, is, according to the State geological survey, about 2270 feet in height. The two higher members are not so separate as those of Yosemite. They are best seen from the top of the wall a mile or two farther east. On the north side of the valley there is a vast perpendicular rock front 1800 feet high, which resembles El Capitan of Yosemite. In spring a large stream pours over its brow with a clear fall of at least one thousand feet. East of this, on the same side, is the Hetch Hetchy Fall, occupying a position relative to the valley like that of Yosemite Fall. It is about seventeen hundred feet in height, but not in one unbroken fall. It is said to have a much larger body of water than the Yosemite Fall, but at the time of my visit (November), it was nearly dry. The wall of the valley above this fall has two benches fringed with live oak, which correspond with astonishing minuteness to the benches of the same relative portion of the Yosemite wall.

At the upper end of the valley a stream comes in from the northwest which is large enough to be considered a fork of the river. Its cañon is exceedingly rich in rock forms, of which a good view may be had from the south side of the valley. The surface of Hetch Hetchy is diversified with groves and meadows in the same manner as Yosemite, and the trees are identical in species. The dryer and warmer portions have fine groves of the black oak (*Quercus sonomensis*) with a few sugar pines (*P. lambertiania*). The Sabine pine (*P. sabiniana*) which grows on the north side of the valley in sun-beaten rocks, is not found in Yosemite. Upon the debris slopes, and in the small side cañons of the south wall, dwell the two silver firs (*Picea amabilis* and *grandis*). The white cedar (*Libocedrus decurrens*) and Douglas spruce (*Abies douglasii*) are noble trees and pretty generally distributed throughout the valley. Thickets of azalea and the brier rose are common and extensive tracts along the edges of the meadows are covered with the common bracken (*Pteris aquilina*). I measured several specimens of this fern that exceeded eight feet in height, and the fissured walls of the valley, from top to bottom, abound in tufted rock ferns of rare beauty, which we have not space to enumerate. The crystal river glides between sheltering groves of alder and poplar and flowering dogwood. Where there is a few inches of fall it ripples and sparkles songfully, but it flows gently in most places, often with a lingering expression, as if half inclined to become a lake. Many of these river nooks are gloriously bordered with ferns and sedges and drooping willows; some were enlivened with ducks that blended charmingly into the picture, only it seemed wonderful that mountain water, so pure and so light like, could be sufficiently substantial to float a duck.

It is estimated that about 7000 persons have seen Yosemite. If this multitude were to be gathered again, and set down in Hetch Hetchy, perhaps less than one percent of the whole number would doubt their being in Yosemite. They would see rocks and waterfalls, meadows and groves, of Yosemite size and kind, and grouped in Yosemite style.

Amid so vast an assemblage of sublime mountain forms, only the more calm and careful observers would be able to fix upon special differences.

The trail from Hardin's enters the valley on the south side, upon a slope which corresponds to that upon which the Mariposa trail enters Yosemite. It was made by the well-known hunter "Joe Screech" for the purpose of driving stock into the meadow. The whole valley is at present claimed by the "Smith brothers" as a summer sheep range. Sheep are driven into Hetch Hetchy every spring, about the same time that a nearly equal number of tourists are driven into Yosemite; another coincident which is remarkably suggestive.

We have no room here to discuss the formation of this valley; we will only state as our opinion that it is an inseparable portion of the great Glacier Cañon of the Tuolumne, and that its level bottom is one of a chain of lake basins extending throughout the cañon, which have been no great time ago filled up with glacial drift. The Yosemite Valley is a cañon of exactly the same origin.

Mr. Screech first visited this valley in the year 1850, one year before Yosemite was entered by Captain Boling and his party. At present there are a couple of shepherds' cabins and a group of Indian huts in the valley, which I believe is all that will come under the head of improvements.

In returning to Yosemite, I left the valley by the trail, which I followed a few miles, then turned southward, intending to cross the head cañons of the south and middle forks of the Tuolumne to Tamarac, thence to drift along the north side of Yosemite and dive to the lower world of home by some one of the side cañons.

Shortly after I had gained the summit of the divide between the main river and the middle fork, the sky, which had been growing dark and opaque all the forenoon, began to yield snowflakes. I at once hastened to a sheltered hollow which was groved with firs and watered by a tiny brook. I searched until I found a place where a number of large trees had fallen, which in case the storm should be severe would afford abundance of fire. At the stump of one of these trees, which had splintered in falling, I found plenty of laths from two to ten feet long, with which I could make a hut, but I had not sufficient time, as the snow began to fall fast. Beneath one of my fire logs I hastily burrowed a sort of bear's nest, and lined it with branchlets of fir—that was home. Then I gathered up a large pile of dry limbs in my front yard, and made a fire before the door, and boiled a cup of coffee, and went into the house. The storm was earnest, and I most intensely enjoyed its growing magnificence.

Towards night the wind, which had been making grand songs in the fir tops and upon the edges of the hollow, began to slacken, the flakes came softly, in a sauntering mood. It seemed as if snow dust were falling from the forest ceiling, and that I had crept beneath a straw on the floor.

It was delightful to lie and look out from my ample windows to the forest. Scores of firs in my front yard were over 200 feet in height. How nobly and unreservedly they gave themselves to the storm. Heart and voice, soul and body, sang to the flowering sky, each frond tip seemed to bestow a separate welcome to every ward of the wind, and to every snowflake as they arrived. How perfectly would the pure soul of Thoreau have mingled with those glorious trees, and he would have been content with my log house. I did not expect company in such unfavorable weather; nevertheless I was visited towards evening by a brown nugget of a wren. He came in, without knocking, by the back door, which, happily, he found high enough for his upslanted tail. He nodded, mannerly enough, when he reached the middle of the floor, and I invited him to stay over night. He made no direct reply; but judging from his fussy gestures around my boots, I thought he intended lodging beneath them, or in one of the legs. I crumbled bread for him, but he had already dined in his own home, and required none of my clumsy cares.

The night became cold, and I had frequently to rise to mend my fire. Towards midnight the stars shone out, and I no longer planned concerning a snowbound. Only a few inches of snow had fallen, just sufficient to droop the whorled branches of the firs, and felt a smooth cloth for the ground.

Morning came to the snow-blossomed mountains in most surpassing splendor. The forest was one dazzling field of snow-flowers, and the ground was silvered and printed like a photographer's plate, with trees and groves and all their life. Before I had gone a hundred and fifty yards from my fire I came upon the tracks of a herd of deer that had been feeding on the branches of the ceanothus. Deer were exceedingly abundant all the way to Tamarac. In many places the ground was broidered with the footprints of foxes, squirrels, coyotes, etc.

I found that the cañons of the middle and south forks of the Tuolumne were very deep and numerous, and by the time I reached Tamarac I was glad to camp. On the sixth day of this excursion I rambled along the edge of Yosemite, and at night swooped to the bottom and home. Thus easily and safely may we mingle ourselves with the so-called frightful rocks and bears of the two Yosemites of Tuolumne and Merced.

Tourists who can afford the time ought to visit Hetch Hetchy on their way to or from Yosemite. The trail from

Hardin's will be found as good as mountain trails usually are, and it certainly is worth while riding a few miles out of a direct course to assure one's self that the world is so rich as to possess at least two Yosemites instead of one.

(*Boston Weekly Transcript*, March 25, 1873)

A Geologist's Winter Walk

Muir's friend and mentor Jeanne Carr submitted this excerpt from one of his letters to her for publication in a popular San Francisco literary magazine.

࿇࿇࿇࿇࿇

After reaching Turlock, I sped afoot over the stubble fields and through miles of brown hemizonia and purple erigeron, to Hopeton, conscious of little more than that the town was behind and beneath me, and the mountains above and before me; on through the oaks and chaparral of the foothills to Coulterville; and then ascended the first great mountain step upon which grows the sugar pine. Here I slackened pace, for I drank the spicy, resiny wind, and beneath the arms of this noble tree I felt that I was safely home. Never did pine trees seem so dear. How sweet was their breath and their song, and how grandly they winnowed the sky! I tingled my fingers among their tassels, and rustled my feet among their brown needles and burrs, and was exhilarated and joyful beyond all I can write.

When I reached Yosemite, all the rocks seemed talk-ative, and more telling and lovable than ever. They are dear friends, and seemed to have warm blood gushing through their granite flesh; and I love them with a love intensified by long and close companionship. After I had bathed in the bright river, sauntered over the meadows, conversed with the domes, and played with the pines, I still felt blurred and weary, as if tainted in some way with the sky of your streets. I determined, therefore, to run out for a while to say my prayers in the higher mountain temples. "The days are sunful," I said, "and, though now winter, no great danger need be encountered, and no sudden storm will block my return, if I am watchful."

The morning after this decision, I started up the canyon of Tenaya, caring little about the quantity of bread I carried; for, I thought, a fast and a storm and a difficult canyon were just the medicine I needed. When I passed Mirror Lake, I scarcely noticed it, for I was absorbed in the great Tissiack — her crown a mile away in the hushed azure; her purple granite drapery flowing in soft and graceful folds down to my feet, embroidered gloriously around with deep, shadowy forest. I have gazed on Tissiack a thousand times — in days of solemn storms, and when her form shone divine with the jewelry of winter, or was veiled in living clouds; and I have heard her voice of winds, and snowy, tuneful waters when floods were falling; yet never did her soul reveal itself more impressively than now. I hung about her skirts, lingering timidly, until the higher mountains and glaciers compelled me to push up the canyon.

This canyon is accessible only to mountaineers, and I was anxious to carry my barometer and clinometer through it, to obtain sections and altitudes, so I chose it as the most attractive highway. After I had passed the tall groves that stretch a mile above Mirror Lake, and scrambled around the Tenaya Fall, which is just at the head of the lake groves, I crept through the dense and spiny chaparral that plushes the roots of the mountains here for miles in warm green, and was ascending a precipitous rock front, smoothed by glacial action, when I suddenly fell — for the first time since I touched foot to Sierra rocks. After several somersaults, I became insensible from the shock, and when consciousness returned I found myself wedged among short, stiff bushes, trembling as if cold, not injured in the slightest.

Judging by the sun, I could not have been insensible very long; probably not a minute, possibly an hour; and I could not remember what made me fall, or where I had fallen from; but I saw that if I had rolled a little further, my mountain climbing would have been finished, for just beyond the bushes the canyon wall steepened and I might have fallen to the bottom. "There," said I, addressing my feet, to whose separate skill I had learned to trust night and day on any mountain, "that is what you get by intercourse with stupid town stairs, and dead pavements." I felt degraded and worthless. I had not yet reached the most difficult portion of the canyon, but I determined to guide my humbled body over the most nerve-trying places I could find; for I was now awake, and felt confident that the last of the town fog had been shaken from both head and feet.

I camped at the mouth of a narrow gorge which is cut into the bottom of the main canyon, determined to take earnest exercise next day. No plushy boughs did my ill-behaved bones enjoy that night, nor did my bumped head get a spicy cedar plume pillow mixed with flowers. I slept on a naked boulder, and when I awoke all my nervous trembling was gone.

The gorged portion of the canyon, in which I spent all the next day, is about a mile and a half in length; and I passed the time in tracing the action of the forces that determined this peculiar bottom gorge, which is an abrupt, ragged-walled, narrow-throated canyon, formed in the bottom of the wide-mouthed, smooth, and beveled main canyon. I will not stop now to tell you more; some day you may see it, like a shadowy line, from Cloud's Rest. In high water, the stream occupies all the bottom of the gorge, surging and chafing in glorious power from wall to wall. But the sound of the grinding was low as I entered the gorge, scarcely hoping to be able to pass through its entire length. By cool efforts, along glassy, ice-worn slopes, I reached the upper end in a little over a day, but was compelled to pass the second night in the gorge, and in the moonlight I wrote you this short pencil-letter in my notebook: —

The moon is looking down into the canyon, and how marvelously the great rocks kindle to her light! Every dome, and brow, and swelling boss touched by her white rays, glows as if lighted with snow. I am now only a mile from last night's camp; and have been climbing and sketching all day in this difficult but instructive gorge. It is formed in the bottom of the main canyon, among the roots of Cloud's Rest. It begins at the filled-up lake basin where I camped last night, and ends a few hundred yards above, in another basin of the same kind. The walls everywhere are craggy and vertical, and in some places they overlean. It is only from twenty to sixty feet wide, and not, though black and broken enough, the thin, crooked mouth of some mysterious abyss; but it was eroded, for in many places I saw its solid, seamless floor.

I am sitting on a big stone, against which the stream divides, and goes brawling by in rapids on both sides; half of my rock is white in the light, half in shadow. As I look from the opening jaws of this shadowy gorge, South Dome is immediately in front — high in the stars, her face turned from the moon, with the rest of her body gloriously muffled in waved folds of granite. On the left, sculptured from the main Cloud's Rest ridge, are three magnificent rocks, sisters of the great South Dome. On the right is the massive, moonlit front of Mount Watkins, and between, low down in the furthest distance, is Sentinel Dome, girdled and darkened with forest. In the near foreground Tenaya Creek is singing against boulders that are white with snow and moonbeams. Now look back twenty yards, and you will see a waterfall fair as a spirit; the moonlight just touches it, bringing it into relief against a dark background of shadow. A little to the left, and a dozen steps this side of the fall, a flickering light marks my camp — and a precious camp it is. A huge, glacier-polished slab, falling from the smooth, glossy flank of Cloud's Rest, happened to settle on edge against the wall of the gorge. I did not know that this slab was glacier-polished until I lighted my fire. Judge of my delight. I think it was sent here by an earthquake. It is about twelve feet square. I wish I could take it home for a hearthstone. Beneath this slab is the only place in this torrent-swept gorge where I could find sand sufficient for a bed.

I expected to sleep on the boulders, for I spent most of the afternoon on the slippery wall of the canyon, endeavoring to get around this difficult part of the gorge, and was compelled to hasten down here for water before dark. I shall sleep soundly on this sand; half of it is mica. Here, wonderful to behold, are a few green stems of prickly rubus, and a tiny grass. They are here to meet us. Ay, even here in this darksome gorge, "frightened and tormented" with raging torrents and choking avalanches of snow. Can it be? As if rubus and the grass leaf were not enough of God's tender prattle words of love, which we so much need in these mighty temples of power, yonder in the "benmost bore" are two blessed adiantums. Listen to them! How wholly infused with God is this one big word of love that we call the world! Good-night. Do you see the fire-glow on my ice-smoothed slab, and on my two ferns and the rubus and grass panicles? And do you hear how sweet a sleep-song the fall and cascades are singing?

The water-ground chips and knots that I found fastened between the rocks kept my fire alive all through the night. Next morning I rose nerved and ready for another day of sketching and noting, and any form of climbing. I escaped from the gorge about noon, after accomplishing some of the most delicate feats of mountaineering I ever attempted; and here the canyon is all broadly open again — the floor luxuriantly forested with pine, and spruce, and silver fir, and brown-trunked libocedrus. The walls rise in Yosemite forms, and Tenaya Creek comes down seven hundred feet in a white brush of foam. This is a little Yosemite valley. It is about two thousand feet above the level of the main Yosemite, and about twenty-four hundred below Lake Tenaya.

I found the lake frozen, and the ice was so clear and unruffled that the surrounding mountains and the groves that look down upon it were reflected almost as perfectly as I ever beheld them in the calm evening mirrors of summer. At a little distance, it was difficult to believe the lake frozen at all; and when I walked out on it, cautiously stamping at short intervals to test the strength of the ice, I seemed to walk mysteriously, without adequate faith, on the surface of the water. The ice was so transparent that I could see through it the beautifully wave-rippled, sandy bottom, and the scales of mica glinting back the down-pouring light. When I knelt down with my face close to the ice, through which the sunbeams were pouring, I was delighted to discover myriads of Tyndall's six-rayed water flowers, magnificently colored.

A grand old mountain mansion is this Tenaya region! In the glacier period it was a *mer de glace*, far grander than the *mer de glace* of Switzerland, which is only about half a mile broad. The Tenaya *mer de glace* was not less than two miles broad, late in the glacier epoch, when all the principal dividing crests were bare; and its depth was not less than fifteen hundred feet. Ice streams from Mounts Lyell and Dana, and all the mountains between, and from the nearer Cathedral Peak, flowed hither, welded into one, and worked together. After eroding this Tenaya Lake basin, and all the splendidly sculptured rocks and mountains that surround and adorn it, and the great Tenaya Canyon, with its wealth of all that makes mountains sublime, they were welded with the vast South, Lyell, and Illilouette glaciers on one side, and with those of Hoffman on the other — thus forming a portion of a yet grander *mer de glace* in Yosemite Valley.

I reached the Tenaya Canyon, on my way home, by coming in from the northeast, rambling down over the shoulders of Mount Watkins, touching bottom a mile above Mirror Lake. From thence home was but a saunter in the moonlight.

After resting one day, and the weather continuing calm, I ran up over the left shoulder of South Dome and down in front of its grand split face to make some measurements, completed my work, climbed to the right shoulder, struck off along the ridge for Cloud's Rest, and reached the topmost heave of her sunny wave in ample time to see the sunset.

Cloud's Rest is a thousand feet higher than Tissiack. It is a wavelike crest upon a ridge, which begins at Yosemite with Tissiack, and runs continuously eastward to the thicket of peaks and crests around Lake Tenaya. This lofty granite wall is bent this way and that by the restless and weariless action of glaciers just as if it had been made of dough. But the grand circumference of mountains and forests are coming from far and near, densing into one close assemblage; for the sun, their god and father, with love ineffable, is glowing a sunset farewell. Not one of all the assembled rocks or trees seemed remote. How impressively their faces shone with responsive love!

I ran home in the moonlight with firm strides; for the

sun-love made me strong. Down through the junipers; down through the firs; now in jet shadows, now in white light; over sandy moraines and bare, clanking rocks; past the huge ghost of South Dome rising weird through the firs; past the glorious fall of Nevada, the groves of Illilouette; through the pines of the valley; beneath the bright crystal sky blazing with stars. All of this mountain wealth in one day! — one of the rich ripe days that enlarge one's life; so much of the sun upon one side of it, so much of the moon and stars on the other.

(*The Overland Monthly*, April 1, 1873)

Shasta in Winter

Sisson's Station, November 24, 1874

Shasta Storms

Snow is falling on icy Shasta. Its rugged glaciers, steep lava-slopes, and broad, swelling base are all gloriously snow-covered, and day and night snow is still falling—snow on snow. The October storms that began a month ago and extended so generally throughout the State, fell with special emphasis upon the lofty cone of Shasta, weaving and felting its lavish cross of snow-crystals, fold over fold, and clothing the whole massive mountain in richest winter white. The big dark cluster of November storms was separated from those of October by a week of brilliant sunshine, during which I sauntered leisurely Shasta-ward, allowing time for the snow, that I knew had fallen, to settle somewhat, with a view to making the ascent of the mountain. This bright lane of cloudless weather was exceedingly buoyant and delightful; every mountain and valley seemed exhilarated with their magnificent storm-bath. The Indian summer disappeared, leaving the atmosphere intensely clear, yet not without a racy autumnal mellowness. The washed colors of the dogwood and the maple shone out gorgeously along every watercourse. The pine-needles thrilled and sparkled as if tuned anew; flies danced in the warm sunbeams; the bent and dripping grasses rose again, and the dainty squirrels came out, with every hair of their tails dry and electric, as if they had never known a single rain-drop; even the teamsters, dragging toilsomely through the turn-pike mud, began to swear in lower tones and look hopeful.

A Pedestrian in the Mountains—A Rough Trip

I followed the main Oregon and California stage-road from Redding to Sisson's, and besides trees, squirrels, and beautiful mountain-streams, I came upon some interesting men, rugged, weather-beaten fellows, who, in hunting and mining, had been brought face to face with many a Shasta storm. Most of them were a kind of almanac, stored with curious facts and dates and ancient weather-notes, extending through a score of stormy mountain years. Whether the coming winter was to be mild or severe was the question of questions, and the diligence and fervor with which it was discussed was truly admirable. A picturesque series of prognostications were offered, based by many different methods upon the complexion of the sky, the fall of leaves, the flight of wild geese, etc., each of which seemed wholly satisfactory only to its author.

A pedestrian upon these mountain-roads is sure to excite curiosity, and many were the interrogations put concerning my little ramble. When told that I came from town for an airing and a walk, and that icy Shasta was my mark, I was invariably informed that I had come the wrong time of year. The snow was too deep, the wind too violent, and the danger of being lost in blinding drifts too great. And when I hinted that clean snow was beautiful, and that storms were not so bad as they were called, they closed the argument by directing attention to their superior experiences, declaring most emphatically that the ascent of "Shasta Butte" through the snow was impossible. Nevertheless, I watched the robins eating wild cherries, and rejoiced in brooding over the miles of lavish snow that I was to meet. Sisson gave me bread and venison, and before noon of the 2nd of November I was in the frosty azure of the summit.

Mount Shasta—A Glorious Picture

In journeying up the valley of the Sacramento one obtains frequent glimpses of Mt. Shasta through the pine-trees from the tops of hills and ridges, but at Sisson's there is a grand out-opening both of the mountains and the forests, and Shasta stands revealed at just the distance to be seen most comprehensively and impressively. It was in the middle of the last day of October that I first beheld this glorious picture. Gorgeous thickets of the thorn, cherry, birch, and alder flamed around the meadow. There were plenty of bees and golden-rods, and the warm air was calm as the bottom of a lake. Standing on the hotel-veranda, and looking only at outlines, there, first of all, is a brown meadow with its crooked stream, then a zone of dark forest—its countless spires of fir and pine rising above one another, higher, higher in luxuriant ranks, and above all the great white Shasta cone sweeping far into the cloudless blue; meadow, forest and mountain inseparably blended and framed in by the arching sky. I was in the heart of this beauty next day. Sisson, who is a capital mountaineer, fitted me out for calms or storms as only a mountaineer could, with a week's provisions so generous in kind and quantity it could easily be made to last a month in case of a fortunate snow-bound. Of course I knew the weariness of snow-climbing, and the stinging frosts, and the so-called dangers of mountaineering so late in the year, therefore I could not ask any guide to go with me. All I wanted was to have blankets and provisions deposited as far up in the timber as the snow would allow a pack-horse to go. Here I could make a storm-nest and lie warm, and make raids up or around the mountain whenever the weather would allow. On setting out from Sisson's my barometer as well as the sky gave notice of the approach of another storm, the wind sighed in the pines, filmy, half-transparent clouds began to dim the sunshine. It was one of those brooding days that Keith so well knows how to paint, in which every tree of the forest and every mountain seems conscious of the approach of some great blessing, and stands hushed and waiting.

Ascending Shasta in Winter

The ordinary and proper way to ascend Shasta is to ride from Sisson's to the upper edge of the timber line,—a distance of some eight or ten miles—the first day, and camp, and rising early push on to the summit, and return the second day. But the deep snow prevented the horses from reaching the camping-ground, and after stumbling and wallowing in the drifts and lava blocks we were glad to camp as best we could, some eight or ten hundred feet lower. A pitch-pine fire speedily changed the climate and shed a blaze of light on the wild lava slope and the straggling storm-bent pines around us. Melted snow answered for coffee-water and we had plenty of delicious venison to roast.

Toward midnight I rolled myself in my blankets and slept until half-past one, when I arose and ate more venison, tied two days' provisions to my belt, and set out for the summit. After getting above the highest flexilis pines it was fine practice pushing up the magnificent snow-slopes alone in the silence of the night. Half the sky was clouded; in the other half the stars sparkled icily in the thin, frosty air, while everywhere the glorious snow fell away from the summit of the cone in flowing folds more extensive and unbroken than any I had ever yet beheld. When the day dawned the clouds were crawling slowly and massing themselves, but gave no intimation of immediate danger. The snow was dry as meal, and drifted freely, rolling over and over in angular fragments like sand, or rising in the air like dust. The frost was intense, and the wind full of crystal dust, making breathing at times rather difficult. In pushing upwards I frequently sank to my arm-pits between buried lava-blocks, but most of the way only to my knees. When tired of walking I still wallowed forward on all fours. The steepness of the slope—thirty-five degrees in many places—made any species of progress very fatiguing, but the sublime beauty of the snowy expanse and of the land-scapes that began to rise around, and the intense purity of the icy azure overhead thrilled every fibre with wild enjoy-ment and rendered absolute exhaustion impossible. Yet I watched the sky with great caution, for it was easy to see that a storm was approaching. Mount Shasta rises 10,000 feet above the general level in blank exposure to the deep gulf-streams of air, and I have never been in a labyrinth of peaks and canyons where the dangers of a storm seemed so formidable as here. I was, therefore, in constant readiness to retreat into the timber. However, by half past 10 o'clock I reached the utmost summit.

Among the Glaciers and the Lava—The Descent

I have seen Montgomery Street, and I know that
California is in a hurry, therefore I have no intention of
saying anything here concerning the building of this grand
fire-mountain, nor of the sublime circumference of landscapes of which it is the centre. I spent a couple of hours
tracing the outlines of its ancient lava-streams, extending
far into the surrounding plains and the path-ways of its
ancient glaciers, but the wind constantly increased in
violence, raising the snow in magnificent drifts, and
forming it into long, wavering banners that flowed in the
sun. A succession of small storm-clouds struck against the
summit pinnacles, like icebergs, darkening the air as they
passed, and producing a chill as definite and sudden as if
ice-water were dashed in one's face. This is the kind of
cloud in which snow-flowers grow, and I was compelled to
begin a retreat, which, after spending a few minutes upon
the main Shasta glacier and the side of the "Crater Butte,"
I accomplished more than an hour before dark, so that I
had time to hollow a strip of ground for a nest in the lee of
a block of red lava, where firewood was abundant.

Among the Storm-clouds

Next morning, breaking suddenly out of profound sleep,
my eyes opened upon one of the most sublime scenes I
ever beheld. A boundless wilderness of storm-clouds of
different age and ripeness were congregated over all the
landscape for thousands of square miles, colored gray,
and purple, and pearl and glowing white, among which I
seemed to be floating, while the cone of Shasta above and
the sky was tranquil and full of the sun. It seemed not so
much an ocean as a land of clouds, undulating hill and dale,
smooth purple plains, and silvery mountains of cumuli,

range over range, nobly diversified with peaks and domes, with cool shadows between, and with here and there a wide trunk canyon, smooth and rounded as if eroded by glaciers. I gazed enchanted, but cold gray masses drifting hither and thither like rack on a wind-swept plain began to shut out the light, and it was evident that they would soon be marshalled for storm. I gathered as much wood as possible, and snugged it shelteringly around my storm-nest. My blankets were arranged, and the topmost fastened down with stakes, and my precious bread-sack tucked in at my head, I was ready when the first flakes fell. All kinds of clouds began to fuse into one, the wind swept past in hissing floods, and the storm closed down on all things, producing a wild exhilaration.

My fire blazed bravely, I had a week's wood, a sack full of bread, and a nest that the wildest wind could not demolish, and I had, moreover, plenty of material for the making of snow-shoes if the depth of the snow should render them necessary.

The storm lasted about a week, and I had plenty to do listening to its tones and watching the gestures of the flexilis pine, and in catching snow-crystals and examining them under a lens and observing the methods of their deposition as summer fountains.

Back to Sisson's

On the third day Sisson sent up two horses for me, and his blankets, notwithstanding I had expressed a wish to be let alone in case it stormed. The horses succeeded in breaking through on the trail they made in coming up. In a few hours more this would have been impossible. The ride down through the forest of silver firs was truly enchanting, the thick flakes falling aslant the noble columns decorated with yellow lichen, and their rich, fronded branches drooped and laden in universal bloom. Farther down, the sugar-pines with sublime gestures were feeding on the storm and waving their giant arms as if in ecstasy. At an elevation of 4,000 feet above the sea the snow became rain, and all the chaparral, cherry, manzanita and ceanothus were bright and dripping.

A Good Centre for Storm News

Sisson's Station seems to be a favorite resort of teamsters as well as of tourists, and one could hardly be more advantageously situated for the reception of storm news. Drivers from Oregon and California meet here almost every night, and while gathered—steaming and mud-bedraggled—around the bar-room fire compare road and weather notes in terms more picturesque than exact. California storms seem at present to be about as continuous as those of Oregon, for they are alike described as "never letting up," and I can hear of but two species, namely, "dam'd" and "damndest." Meanwhile, the grand storm continues. The wind sings gloriously in the pine-trees. Snow is still falling on icy Shasta, snow on snow, treasuring up food for forests and glaciers and for the thousand springs that gush out around its base.

(*San Francisco Daily Evening Bulletin*, Dec. 2, 1874)

Shasta Bee-Pastures

Of all the upper flower fields of the Sierra, Shasta is the most honeyful, and may yet surpass in fame the celebrated honey hills of Hybla and hearthy Hymettus. Regarding this noble mountain from a bee point of view, encircled by its many climates, and sweeping aloft from the torrid plain into the frosty azure, we find the first 5000 feet from the summit generally snow-clad, and therefore about as honeyless as the sea. The base of this arctic region is girdled by a belt of crumbling lava measuring about 1000 feet in vertical breadth, and is mostly free from snow in summer. Beautiful lichens enliven the faces of the cliffs with their bright colors, and in some of the warmer nooks there are a few tufts of alpine daisies, wall-flowers and pentstemons; but, notwithstanding these bloom freely in the late summer, the zone as a whole is almost as honeyless as the icy summit, and its lower edge may be taken as the honey-line. Immediately below this comes the forest zone, covered with a rich growth of conifers, chiefly Silver Firs, rich in pollen and honey-dew, and diversified with countless garden openings, many of them less than a hundred yards across. Next, in orderly succession, comes the great bee zone. Its area far surpasses that of the icy summit and both the other zones combined, for it goes sweeping majestically around the entire mountain, with a breadth of six or seven miles and a circumference of nearly a hundred miles.

Shasta, as we have already seen, is a fire-mountain created by a succession of eruptions of ashes and molten lava, which, flowing over the lips of its several craters, grew outward and upward like the trunk of a knotty exogenous tree. Then followed a strange contrast. The glacial winter came on, loading the cooling mountain with ice, which flowed slowly outward in every direction, radiating from the summit in the form of one vast conical glacier—a down-crawling mantle of ice upon a fountain of smoldering fire, crushing and grinding for centuries its brown, flinty lavas with incessant activity, and thus degrading and remodeling the entire mountain. When, at length, the glacial period began to draw near its close, the ice-mantle was gradually melted off around the bottom, and, in receding and breaking into its present fragmentary condition, irregular rings and heaps of moraine matter were stored upon its flanks. The glacial erosion of most of the Shasta lavas produces detritus, composed of rough, sub-angular boulders of moderate size and of porous gravel and sand, which yields freely to the transporting power of running water. Magnificent floods from the ample fountains of ice and snow working with sublime energy upon this prepared glacial detritus, sorted it out and carried down immense quantities from the higher slopes, and reformed it in smooth, delta-like beds around the base; and it is these flood-beds joined together that now form the main honey-zone of the old volcano.

Thus, by forces seemingly antagonistic and destructive, has Mother Nature accomplished her beneficent designs—now a flood of fire, now a flood of ice, now a flood of water; and at length an outburst of organic life, a milky way of snowy petals and wings, girdling the rugged mountain like a cloud, as if the vivifying sunbeams beating against its sides had broken into a foam of plant-bloom and bees, as sea-waves break and bloom on a rock shore.

In this flowery wilderness the bees rove and revel, rejoicing in the bounty of the sun, clambering eagerly through bramble and hucklebloom, ringing the myriad bells of the manzanita, now humming aloft among polleny willows and firs, now down on the ashy ground among gilias and buttercups, and anon plunging deep into snowy banks of cherry and buckthorn. They consider the lilies and roll into them, and, like lilies, they toil not, for they are impelled by sun-power, as water-wheels by water power; and when the one has plenty of high-pressure water, the other plenty of sunshine, they hum and quiver alike. Sauntering in the Shasta bee-lands in the sun-days of summer, one may readily infer the time of day from the comparative energy of bee-movements alone—drowsy and moderate in the cool of the morning, increasing in energy with the ascending sun, and, at high noon, thrilling and quivering in wild ecstasy, then gradually declining again to the stillness of night. In my excursions among the glaciers I occasionally meet bees that are hungry, like mountaineers who venture too far and remain too long above the bread-line; then they droop and wither like autumn leaves. The Shasta bees are perhaps better fed than any others in the Sierra. Their field-work is one perpetual feast; but, however exhilarating the sunshine or bountiful the supply of flowers, they are always dainty feeders. Humming-moths and humming-birds seldom set foot upon a flower, but poise on the wing in front of it, and reach forward as if they were sucking through straws. But bees, though as dainty as they, hug their favorite flowers with profound cordiality, and push their blunt, polleny faces against them, like babies on their mother's bosom. And fondly, too, with eternal love, does Mother Nature clasp her small bee-babies, and suckle them, multitudes at once, on her warm Shasta breast.

Besides the common honey-bee there are many other species here—fine mossy, burly fellows, who were nourished on the mountains thousands of sunny seasons before the advent of the domestic species. Among these are the bumblebees, mason-bees, carpenter-bees, and leaf-cutters. Butterflies, too, and moths of every size and pattern; some broad-winged like bats, flapping slowly, and sailing in easy curves; others like small, flying violets, shaking about loosely in short, crooked flights close to the flowers, feasting luxuriously night and day. Great numbers of deer also delight to dwell in the brushy portions of the bee-pastures.

Bears, too, roam the sweet wilderness, their blunt, shaggy forms harmonizing well with the trees and tangled bushes, and with the bees, also, notwithstanding the disparity in size. They are fond of all good things, and enjoy them to the utmost, with but little troublesome discrimination—flowers and leaves as well as berries, and the bees themselves as well as their honey. Though the California bears have as yet had but little experience with honey-bees, they often succeed in reaching their bountiful stores, and it seems doubtful whether bees themselves enjoy honey with so great a relish. By means of their powerful teeth and claws they can gnaw and tear open almost any hive conveniently accessible. Most honey-bees, however, in search of a home are wise enough to make choice of a hollow in a living tree, a considerable distance above the ground, when such places are to be had; then they are pretty secure, for though the smaller black and brown bears climb well, they are unable to break into strong hives while compelled to exert themselves to keep from falling, and at the same time to endure the stings of the fighting bees without having their paws free to rub them off. But woe to the black bumblebees discovered in their mossy nests in the ground! With a few strokes of their huge paws the bears uncover the entire establishment, and, before time is given for a general buzz, bees old and young, larvæ, honey, stings, nest, and all are taken in one ravishing mouthful.

Not the least influential of the agents concerned in the superior sweetness of the Shasta flora are its storms—storms I mean that are strictly local, bred and born on the mountain. The magical rapidity with which they are grown on the mountain-top, and bestow their charity in rain and snow, never fails to astonish the inexperienced lowlander. Often in calm, glowing days, while the bees are still on the wing, a storm-cloud may be seen far above in the pure ether, swelling its pearl bosses, and growing silently, like a plant. Presently a clear, ringing discharge of thunder is heard, followed by a rush of wind that comes sounding over the bending woods like the roar of the ocean, mingling raindrops, snow-flowers, honey-flowers, and bees in wild storm harmony.

Still more impressive are the warm, reviving days of spring in the mountain pastures. The blood of the plants throbbing beneath the life-giving sunshine seems to be heard and felt. Plant growth goes on before our eyes, and every tree in the woods, and every bush and flower is seen as a hive of restless industry. The deeps of the sky are mottled with singing wings of every tone and color; clouds of brilliant chrysididæ dancing and swirling in exquisite rhythm, golden-barred vespidæ, dragon-flies, butterflies, grating cicadas, and jolly, rattling grasshoppers, fairly enameling the light.

On bright, crisp mornings a striking optical effect may frequently be observed from the shadows of the higher mountains while the sunbeams are pouring past over-head. Then every insect, no matter what may be its own proper color, burns white in the light. Gauzy-winged hymenoptera, moths, jet-black beetles, all are transfigured alike in pure, spiritual white, like snowflakes.

(From *The Mountains of California*, Ch. 16)

Ascent of Mount Whitney

INDEPENDENCE, INYO COUNTY, AUGUST 17, 1875

Men ascend mountains as instinctively as squirrels ascend trees, and, of course, the climbing of Mount Whitney was a capital indulgence, apart from the enjoyment drawn from landscapes and scientific pursuits. We set out from the little village of Independence with plenty of excelsior determination, Bayley, as usual, rejoicing in war-whoops, much to the wonderment of sober passers-by. The massive sun-beaten Sierra rose before us out of the gray sagebrush levels like one vast wall 9,000 feet high, adorned along the top with a multitude of peaks that seem to have been nicked out in all kinds of fanciful forms for the sake of beauty. Mount Whitney is one of those wall-top peaks, having no special geological significance beyond the scores of nameless peaks amid which it stands, and possessing so little appreciable individuality that we did not meet a single person living here who was able to point it out. Where is Mount Whitney? we would ask the teamsters and farmers we met between Independence and Lone Pine. "Don't know exactly," was the common reply. "One of them topmost peaks you see yonder," at the same time waving their hands indefinitely toward the wilderness of summits.

For those travelers who dislike climbing, the proper way to the top of Whitney lies from Lone Pine around the southern extremity of the High Sierra to the Upper Kern river valley, by way of Cottonwood Creek. The mountain is thus approached from the west where the slopes are lowest, and where one may easily ride to an elevation of 12,000 feet above sea-level, leaving only a light foot scramble of between 2,500 and 8,000 feet to be made in reaching the utmost summit; whereas, by the quick direct route discovered by me two years ago, leading up the east flank of the range opposite Lone Pine, the elevation to be overcome by foot climbing amounts to about 9,000 feet.

The Ascent

With the exception of our one young student, our party were mountaineers, and we chose the eastern route, the mountain influences bearing us buoyantly aloft without leaving us any gross weight to overcome by ordinary conscious effort. On the first day we rode our mules some eighteen miles, through a fine, evenly-planted growth of sage-brush to the foot of the range, immediately west of Lone Pine. Here we "found *a man*," a whole-souled Welshman, by the name of Thomas, with whom we camped for the night, and where all was made ready for an early start up the mountain next morning. Each carried a loaf of bread, a handful of tea and a tin cup, and a block of beef about four inches in diameter, cut from the lean heartwood of a steer; the whole compactly bundled in half a blanket, and carried by a strap passed over the shoulder, and beside these common necessaries, Bayley carried a small bottle of spirits for healing, sustaining, and forti- fying uses, in case of encounters with triangular headed snakes, bears, Indians, mountain rams, noxious night airs, snow storms, etc.; and in case of vertigo and difficult breathing at great heights, together with broken bones, flesh wounds, skin erosions, abrasions, contusions. For in prudence, is it not well to realize that "something might happen," and well to have a helpful spirit—a guardian angel in a bottle ever near?

The highway by which we ascended was constructed by an ancient glacier that drew its sources from the eastern flank of Mount Whitney and the adjacent summits, and poured its icy floods into Owens Valley, which during the glacial epoch was a sea of ice. Of this mighty, rock- crushing ice-river, scarce a vestige remains, and its channel is now occupied by a dashing crystal stream that kept us good company all the way to the summit. The day was warm, and many were the delicious lavings we enjoyed among its pools beneath the cooling shadows of its leafy border groves. The great declivity of the cañon gives rise to numerous rapids and cascades, along the edges of which, soil of sufficient depth for the best wild gardens and thickets cannot be made to lie; but small oval flats of rich alluvium occur between the rocky inclines, rising one above another in almost regular order like stairs. Here the alder and the birch grow close together in luxuriant masses, crossing their topmost branches above the streams, and weaving a bowery root.

A Minor Yosemite

At an elevation of about 8,000 feet above the sea we come to a fine Yosemite Valley, where a large tributary glacier from the southwest had united with the main trunk. The sheer granite walls rise loftily into the pure azure to the height of from two to three thousand feet, sculptured in true Yosemitic style, and presenting a most lavish abundance of spires and gothic gables along the top, with huge buttresses and free and interlacing arches down the face, with numerous caves and niches for ornamental groups of pines. Nor is there any lack of white falling water, nor of tender joyous plant beauty, to complement every manifestation of stern, enduring rockiness. For a distance of two or three miles above the head of this wild Yosemite the ascent is rather steep and difficult, because the canyon walls come sheer down in many places to the brink of the rushing stream, leaving no free margin for a walk, and in many places a dense growth of alder and willow, crushed and felted with the pressure of winter snow, renders the gorge all but impassable, the dead limbs all sloping downward, meeting the up-struggling mountaineer like clusters of presented bayonets.

The difficulties I encountered in forcing my way through this portion of the gorge during my first ascent caused me to scan the gaps and terraces of the south wall, with a view to avoiding the bottom of the gorge altogether. Coming to the conclusion that the thing was at least practicable, I led the party over a rough earthquake talus, beneath an over-hanging cliff, and up an extremely steep and narrow gully to the edge of the main canyon wall.

An Accident—Glacier Meadows—A Glimpse of Whitney

Here occurred the only accident worth mentioning connected with the trip. Washburn, who climbs slowly, was soon a considerable distance in the rear, and I sat down at the head of the narrow gully to wait for him. Bayley soon came up somewhat breathless with exertion, and without thinking of consequences, loosened a big boulder that went bounding down the narrow lane with terrible energy, followed by a train of small stones and dust. Washburn was about a hundred feet below, and his destruction seemed inevitable, as he was hemmed in between two sheer walls not five feet apart. We shouted to give him warning, and listened breathlessly until his answering shout assured us of his escape. On coming up weary and nerve-shaken with fright, he reported that the dangerous mass shot immedi-ately over him as he lay crouched in a slight hollow. Falling rocks, single or in avalanches, form the greatest of all the perils that beset the mountaineer among the summit peaks.

By noon we reached a genuine glacier meadow, where we disturbed a band of wild sheep that went bounding across the stream and up the precipitous rocks out of sight. We were now 10,000 feet above sea level, and were in the Alps; having passed in half a day from the torrid plains of Owens Valley to an Arctic climate, cool and distant in all its sounds and aspects as Greenland or Labrador.

Here we caught our first fair view of the jagged, storm-worn crest of Mount Whitney, yet far above and beyond, looming gray and ruin-like from a multitude of shattered ridges and spires. Onward we pushed, unwearied, waking hosts of new echoes with shouts of emphatic excelsior. Along the green, plushy meadow, following its graceful margin curves, then up rugged slopes of gray boulders that had thundered from the shattered heights in an earthquake, then over smooth polished glacier pavements to the utmost limits of the timber line, and our first day's climbing was done.

Camping on the Mountain

Our elevation was now eleven thousand five hundred feet, and as the afternoon was less than half done, we had ample time to prepare beds, make tea, and gather a store of pitchy pine roots for our night fire. We chose the same camping ground I had selected two years before on the edge of a sedgy meadow enamelled with buttercups and daises, near a waterfall and snowbank, and surrounded with ranks of majestic alps. There were the withered pine tassels on which I had slept, and circling heap of stones built as a shelter from the down rushing night wind, and the remains of my wood-pile gathered in case of a sudden snow-storm. Each made his own tin cupful of tea, and dinner was speedily accomplished. Then bed-building was vigorously carried on, each selecting willow shoots, pine tassels or withered grass with a zeal and naturalness whose sources must lie somewhere among our ancient grandfathers, when "wild in woods," etc. I have experimented with all kinds of plant pillows with especial reference to softness and fragrance, and here I was so happy as to invent a new one, composed of the leaves and flowers of the alpine dodeca-theon, elastic, fragrant and truly beautiful. Here we rested as only mountaineers can. The wind fell to soft whispers, keen spiky shadows stole over the meadow, and pale rosy light bathed the savage peaks, making a picture of Nature's repose that no words can ever describe. Darkness came, and the night wind began to flow like a deep and gentle river; the cascades nearby sounded all its notes with most impressive distinctness, and the sky glowed with living stars. Then came the moon, awakening the giant peaks that seemed to return her solemn gaze. The grand beauty of our chamber walls came out in wonderfully clear relief, white light and jet shadows revealing their wild fountain architecture, divested of all distracting details.

Still Upward—Glacier Lakes—Vegetation

We rose early and were off in the first flash of dawn, passing first over a rounded ice-polished brow, then along the north shore of a glacier lake whose simple new-born beauty enchanted us all. It lay imbedded in the rocks like a dark blue green—a perfect mountain eye. Along its northern shore we sped joyously, inspired with the fresh unfolding beauties of the morning, leaping huge blocks of porphyry laid down by an ancient earthquake, and over morainal embankments and slopes of crystalline gravel; every muscle in harmonious accord, thrilled and toned and yielding us the very highest pleasures of the flesh. Speedily we meet the glances of another crystal lake, and of our dearest alpine flowers; azure daisies and primulas, cassiope and bryanthus, the very angels of mountain flora. Now the sun rose, and filled the rocks with beamless spiritual light. The Clark crow was on the wing, and the frisky tamias and marmo came out to bask on favorite boulder, and the daisies spread their rays and were glad. Above the second lake basin we found a long up-curving field of frozen snow, across which we scampered, with our breasts filled with exhilarating azure, leaping with excess of strength and rolling over and over on the clean snow-ground, like dogs.

Scaling the Dividing Ridge—At the Summit

We followed the snow nearly to its upper limit, where it leaned against the dividing axis of the range, placing our feet in hollows melted by radiated heat from stones shot down from the crumbling heights. To scale the dividing ridge in front was impossible, for it swept aloft in one colossal wave with a vertical shattered crest. We were therefore compelled to swerve to the north; then carefully picking our way from ledge to ledge, gained the summit about 8 A.M. There stood Mount Whitney now without a single ridge between; its spreading base within a stone's throw; its pointed, helmet-shaped summit 2,000 feet above us. We gazed but a moment on the surrounding grandeur: the mighty granite battlements; the dark pine woods far below, and the glistening streams and lakes; then dashed down the western slope into the valley of the Kern. On my first ascent I pushed direct to the summit up the north flank, but the memories of steep slopes of ice and snow over which I had to pick my way, holding on by small points of stones frozen more or less surely into the surface, where a single slip would result in death, made me determine that no one would ever be led by me through the same dangers. I therefore led around the north base of the mountain to the westward, much to Bayley's disgust, who declared that he could, or at least *would* follow wherever I was able to lead. Cautious Washburn wisely gave in his adhesion for the longer and safer route; and I remained firm in avoiding the dangerous ice slopes. We passed along the rocky shores of a lake whose surface was still (July 21st) covered with cakes of winter ice, around the edges of which the color of the water was a beautiful emerald green. Beyond the lake we gradually climbed higher, mounting in a spiral around the northwest shoulder of the mountain, crossing many a strong projecting buttress and fluting hollow, then bearing to the left urged our way directly to the summit. Higher, higher, we climbed with muscles in excellent poise, the landscape becoming more and more glorious as the wild Alps rose in the tranquil sky. Bayley followed closely, lamenting the absence of danger, whenever in this attenuated air he could command sufficient breath. Washburn seldom ventured to leap from rock to rock, but moved mostly on all fours, hugging projecting angles and boulders in a sprawled, outspread fashion, like a child clinging timidly to its mother, often calling for directions around this or that precipice, and careful never to look down for fear of giddiness, yet from first to last evincing a most admirable determination and persistence of the slow and sure kind. Shortly after 10 o'clock A.M. we gained the utmost summit—a fact duly announced by Bayley as soon as he was rested into a whooping condition, and before any note was taken of the wilderness of landscapes by which we were zoned. Undemonstrative Washburn examined the records of antecedent visitors, then remarked with becoming satisfaction, "I'm the first and only student visitor to this highest land in North America."

Successive Ascents—Clarence King's Mistake

This mountain was first ascended in the summer of 1873 by a party of farmers and stock raisers from Owens Valley, who were taking exercise. It was ascended a few weeks later by Clarence King, myself and a few others, and this summer by one party besides our own. The first climbers of the mountain named it Fisherman's Peak. The mountain climbed by Clarence King several years previous, and supposed by him to be the highest in the range, and on which he then bestowed the name of Whitney, lies some six or seven miles to the south of the present Mount Whitney, alias Fisherman's Peak. The old Mount Whitney, though upward of 14,000 feet in height, may easily be ascended to the very summit on horseback, and, in general, every mountain in the range may easily be ascended by climbers of ordinary nerve and skill. Mount Whitney has not yet been accurately measured, although fair approximations have been reached, making its height about 14,800 feet above the sea. Mount Shasta, situated near the northern extremity of the range, is a few hundred feet lower; yet its individual height, measured from its own proper base, is from nine to eleven thousand feet, while that of Whitney is only from two to three thousand. The former is a colossal cone rising in solitary grandeur and might well be regarded as an object of religious worship; the latter is one of the many peaks of an irregular and fragmentary form. Shasta was built *upward* by fire, Whitney was built *downward* by ice. I would gladly try to write a few words concerning the landscapes that lay manifest in all their glory beneath and around us, but there is no room here. We left the summit about noon and swooped to the torrid plains before sundown, as if dropping out of the sky.

(*San Francisco Daily Evening Bulletin,* August 24, 1875)

The San Gabriel Mountains

In the mountains of San Gabriel, overlooking the lowland vines and fruit groves, Mother Nature is most ruggedly, thornily savage. Not even in the Sierra have I ever made the acquaintance of mountains more rigidly inaccessible. The slopes are exceptionally steep and insecure to the foot of the explorer, however great his strength or skill may be, but thorny chaparral constitutes their chief defense. With the exception of little park and garden spots not visible in comprehensive views, the entire surface is covered with it, from the highest peaks to the plain. It swoops into every hollow and swells over every ridge, gracefully complying with the varied topography, in shaggy, ungovernable exuberance, fairly dwarfing the utmost efforts of human culture out of sight and mind.

But in the very heart of this thorny wilderness, down in the dells, you may find gardens filled with the fairest flowers, that any child would love, and unapproachable linns lined with lilies and ferns, where the ousel builds its mossy hut and sings in chorus with the white falling water. Bears, also, and panthers, wolves, wildcats; wood rats, squirrels, foxes, snakes, and innumerable birds, all find grateful homes here, adding wildness to wildness in glorious profusion and variety.

Where the coast ranges and the Sierra Nevada come together we find a very complicated system of short ranges, the geology and topography of which is yet hidden, and many years of laborious study must be given for anything like a complete interpretation of them. The San Gabriel is one or more of these ranges, forty or fifty miles long, and half as broad, extending from the Cajon Pass on the east, to the Santa Monica and Santa Susanna ranges on the west. San Antonio, the dominating peak, rises towards the eastern extremity of the range to a height of about six thousand feet, forming a sure landmark throughout the valley and all the way down to the coast, without, however, possessing much striking individuality. The whole range, seen from the plain, with the hot sun beating upon its southern slopes, wears a terribly forbidding aspect. There is nothing of the grandeur of snow, or glaciers, or deep forests, to excite curiosity or adventure; no trace of gardens or waterfalls. From base to summit all seems gray, barren, silent — dead, bleached bones of mountains, overgrown with scrubby bushes, like gray moss. But all mountains are full of hidden beauty, and the next day after my arrival at Pasadena I supplied myself with bread and eagerly set out to give myself to their keeping.

Hot Weather—A Mountain Character

On the first day of my excursion I went only as far as the mouth of Eaton Canyon, because the heat was oppressive, and a pair of new shoes were chafing my feet to such an extent that walking began to be painful. While looking for a camping ground among the boulder beds of the canyon, I came upon a strange, dark man of doubtful parentage. He kindly invited me to camp with him, and led me to his little hut. All my conjectures as to his nationality failed, and no wonder, since his father was Irish and mother Spanish, a mixture not often met even in California. He happened to be out of candles, so we sat in the dark while he gave me a sketch of his life, which was exceedingly picturesque. Then he showed me his plans for the future. He was going to settle among these canyon boulders, and make money, and marry a Spanish woman. People mine for irrigating water along the foothills as for gold. He is now driving a prospecting tunnel into a spur of the mountains back of his cabin. "My prospect is good," he said, "and if I strike a strong flow, I shall soon be worth five or ten thousand dollars. That flat out there," he continued, referring to a small, irregular patch of gravelly detritus that had been sorted out and deposited by Eaton Creek during some flood season, "is large enough for a nice orange grove, and, after watering my own trees, I can sell water down the valley; and then the hillside back of the cabin will do for vines, and I can keep bees, for the white sage and black sage up the mountains is full of honey. You see, I've got a good thing." All this prospective affluence in the sunken, boulder-choked flood-bed of Eaton Creek! Most home-seekers would as soon think of settling on the summit of San Antonio.

Beautiful Waterfall

Half an hour's easy rambling up the canyon brought me to the foot of "The Fall," famous throughout the valley settlements as the finest yet discovered in the range. It is a charming little thing, with a voice sweet as a songbird's, leaping some thirty-five or forty feet into a round, mirror pool. The cliff back of it and on both sides is completely covered with thick, furry mosses, and the white fall shines against the green like a silver instrument in a velvet case. Here come the Gabriel lads and lassies from the commonplace orange groves, to make love and gather ferns and dabble away their hot holidays in the cool pool. They are fortunate in finding so fresh a retreat so near their homes. It is the Yosemite of San Gabriel. The walls, though not of the true Yosemite type either in form or sculpture, rise to a height of nearly two thousand feet. Ferns are abundant on all the rocks within reach of the spray, and picturesque maples and sycamores spread a grateful shade over a rich profusion of wild flowers that grow among the boulders, from the edge of the pool a mile or more down the dell-like bottom of the valley, the whole forming a charming little poem of wildness—the vestibule of these shaggy mountain temples.

A Hard Climb—Chaparral

The foot of the fall is about a thousand feet above the level of the sea, and here climbing begins. I made my way out of the valley on the west side, followed the ridge that forms the western rim of the Eaton Basin to the summit of one of the principal peaks, thence crossed the middle of the basin, forcing a way over its many subordinate ridges, and out over the eastern rim, and from first to last during three days spent in this excursion, I had to contend with the richest, most self-possessed and uncompromising chaparral I have ever enjoyed since first my mountaineering began.

For a hundred feet or so the ascent was practicable only by means of bosses of the club moss that clings to the rock. Above this the ridge is weathered away to a slender knife-edge for a distance of two or three hundred yards, and thence to the summit it is a bristly mane of chaparral. Here and there small openings occur, commanding grand views of the valley and beyond to the ocean. These are favorite outlooks and resting places for bears, wolves, and wildcats. In the densest places I came upon woodrat villages whose huts were from four to eight feet high, built in the same style of architecture as those of the muskrats.

A Beautiful View

The day was nearly done. I reached the summit and I had time to make only a hasty survey of the topography of the wild basin now outspread maplike beneath, and to drink in the rare loveliness of the sunlight before hastening down in search of water. Pushing through another mile of chaparral, I emerged into one of the most beautiful park-like groves of live oak I ever saw. The ground beneath was planted only with aspidiums and brier roses. At the foot of the grove I came to the dry channel of one of the tributary streams, but, following it down a short distance, I descried a few specimens of the scarlet mimulus; and I was assured that water was near. I found about a bucketful in a granite bowl, but it was full of leaves and beetles, making a sort of brown coffee that could be rendered available only by filtering it through sand and charcoal. This I resolved to do in case the night came on before I found better. Following the channel a mile farther down to its confluence with another, larger tributary, I found a lot of boulder pools, clear as crystal, and brimming full, linked together by little glistening currents just strong enough to sing. Flowers in full bloom adorned the banks, lilies ten feet high, and luxuriant ferns arching over one another in lavish abundance, while a noble old live oak spread its rugged boughs over all, forming one of the most perfect and most secluded of Nature's gardens. Here I camped, making my bed on smooth cobblestones.

Next morning, pushing up the channel of a tributary that takes its rise on Mount San Antonio, I passed many lovely gardens watered by oozing currentlets, every one of which had lilies in them in the full pomp of bloom, and a rich growth of ferns, chiefly woodwardias and aspidiums and maidenhairs; but toward the base of the mountain the channel was dry, and the chaparral closed over from bank to bank, so that I was compelled to creep more than a mile on hands and knees.

Snakes—Bear Tracks

In one spot I found an opening in the thorny sky where I could stand erect, and on the further side of the opening discovered a small pool. "Now, *here*," I said, "I must be careful in creeping, for the birds of the neighborhood come here to drink, and the rattlesnakes come here to catch them." I then began to cast my eye along the channel, perhaps instinctively feeling a snaky atmosphere, and finally discovered one rattler between my feet. But there was a bashful look in his eye, and a withdrawing, deprecating kink in his neck that showed plainly as words could tell that he would not strike, and only wished to be let alone. I therefore passed on, lifting my foot a little higher than usual, and left him to enjoy his life in this his own home.

My next camp was near the heart of the basin, at the head of a grand system of cascades from ten to two hundred feet high, one following the other in close succession and making a total descent of nearly seventeen hundred feet. The rocks above me leaned over in a threatening way and were full of seams, making the camp a very unsafe one during an earthquake.

Next day the chaparral, in ascending the eastern rim of the basin, was, if possible, denser and more stubbornly bayoneted than ever. I followed bear trails, where in some places I found tufts of their hair that had been pulled out in squeezing a way through; but there was much of a very interesting character that far overpaid all my pains. Most of the plants are identical with those of the Sierra, but there are quite a number of Mexican species. One coniferous tree was all I found. This is a spruce of a species new to me, *Douglasii macrocarpa*.

My last camp was down at the narrow, notched bottom of a dry channel, the only open way for the life in the neighborhood. I therefore lay between two fires, built to fence out snakes and wolves.

From the summit of the eastern rim I had a glorious view of the valley out to the ocean, which would require a whole book for its description. My bread gave out a day before reaching the settlements, but I felt all the fresher and clearer for the fast.

(*San Francisco Daily Evening Bulletin,* September 11, 1877)

God's First Temples: How Shall We Preserve Our Forests?

By the mid-1870s, the conservation movement was on the rise and Muir's articles had begun appearing in nationally circulated magazines. It was a logical progression for him to begin writing about the need for government protection of natural resources.

≈≈≈≈≈≈≈

The forests of coniferous trees growing on our mountain ranges are by far the most destructible of the natural resources of California. Our gold, and silver, and cinnabar are stored in the rocks, locked up in the safest of all banks, so that notwithstanding the world has been making a run upon them for the last twenty-five years, they still pay out steadily and will probably continue to do so centuries hence, like rivers pouring from perennial mountain fountains. The riches of our magnificent soil beds are also comparatively safe, because even the most barbarous methods of wildcat farming cannot effect complete destruction, and however great the impoverishment produced, full restoration of fertility is always possible to the enlightened farmer. But our forest belts are being burned and cut down and wasted like a field of unprotected grain, and once destroyed can never be wholly restored, even by centuries of persistent and painstaking cultivation.

The practical importance of the preservation of our forests is augmented by their relations to climate, soil, and streams. Strip off the woods with their underbrush from the mountain flanks, and the whole state, the lowlands as well as the highlands, would gradually change into a desert.

During rainfalls, and when the winter snow was melting, every stream would become a destructive torrent, overflowing its banks, stripping off and carrying away the fertile soils, filling up the lower river channels, and over-spreading the lowland fields with detritus to a vastly more destructive degree than all the washings from hydraulic mines concerning which we now hear so much. Dripping forests give rise to moist sheets and currents of air, and the sod of grasses and underbrush thus fostered, together with the roots of trees themselves, absorb and hold back rains and melting snow, yet allowing them to ooze and percolate and flow gently in useful fertilizing streams. Indeed every pine needle and rootlet, as well as fallen trunks and large clasping roots, may be regarded as dams, hoarding the bounty of storm clouds and dispensing it as blessings all through the summer, instead of allowing it to gather and rush headlong in short-lived, devastating floods. Streams taking their rise in deep woods flow unfailingly as those derived from the eternal ice and snow of the Alps. So constant, indeed, and apparent is the relationship between forests and never-failing springs, that effect is frequently mistaken for cause, it being often asserted that line forests will grow only along streamsides where their roots are well watered, when in fact the forests themselves produce many of the streams flowing through them.

The main forest belt of the Sierra is restricted to the western flank, and extends unbrokenly from one end of the range to the other at an elevation of from three to eight thousand feet above sea level. The great master-existence of these noble woods is *Sequoia gigantea*, or big tree. Only two species of sequoia are known to exist in the world. Both belong to California, one being found only in the Sierra, the other (*Sequoia sempervirens*) in the Coast Ranges, although no less than five distinct fossil species have been discovered in the tertiary and cretaceous rocks of Greenland. I would like to call attention to this noble tree, with special reference to its preservation. The species extends from the well known Calaveras groves on the north, to the head of Deer Creek on the south, near the big bend of the Kern River, a distance of about two hundred miles, at an elevation above sea level of from about five to eight thousand feet. From the Calaveras to the south fork of the King's River, it occurs only in small isolated groves, and so sparsely and irregularly distributed that two gaps occur nearly forty miles in width, the one between the Calaveras and Tuolumne groves, the other between those of the Fresno and King's rivers. From King's River the belt extends across the broad, rugged basins of the Kaweah and Tule rivers to its southern boundary on Deer Creek, interrupted only by deep, rocky canyons, the width of this portion of the belt being from three to ten miles.

In the northern groves few young trees or saplings are found ready to take the places of the failing old ones, and because these ancient, childless sequoias are the only ones known to botanists, the species has been generally regarded as doomed to speedy extinction, as being nothing more than an expiring remnant of an ancient flora, and that therefore there is no use trying to save it or to prolong its few dying days. This, however, is in the main a mistaken notion, for the Sierra as it now exists never had an ancient flora. All the species now growing on the range have been planted since the close of the glacial period, and the Big Tree has never formed a greater part of these postglacial forests than it does today, however widely it may have been distributed throughout preglacial forests.

In tracing the belt southward, all the phenomena bearing upon its history goes to show that the dominion of *Sequoia gigantea*, as king of California trees, is not yet passing away. No tree in the woods seems more firmly established, or more safely settled in accordance with climate and soil. They fill the woods and form the principal tree, growing heartily on solid ledges, along water courses, in the deep, moist soil of meadows, and upon avalanche and glacial debris, with a multitude of thrifty seedlings and saplings crowding around the aged, ready to take their places and rule the woods.

Nevertheless, Nature in her grandly deliberate way keeps up a rotation of forest crops. Species develop and die like individuals, animal as well as plant. Man himself will as surely become extinct as sequoia or mastodon, and be at length known only as a fossil. Changes of this kind are, however, exceedingly slow in their movements, and, as far as the lives of individuals are concerned, such changes have no appreciable effect. Sequoia seems scarcely further past prime as a species than its companion firs (*Picea amabilis* and *P. grandis*), and judging from its present condition and its ancient history, as far as I have been able to decipher it, our sequoia will live and flourish gloriously until A.D. 15,000 at least—probably for longer—that is, if it be allowed to remain in the hands of nature.

But waste and pure destruction are already taking place at a terrible rate, and unless protective measures be speedily invented and enforced, in a few years this noblest tree-species in the world will present only a few hacked and scarred remnants. The great enemies of forests are fire and the ax. The destructive effects of these, as compared with those caused by the operations of nature, are instantaneous. Floods undermine and kill many a tree, storm winds bend and break, landslips and avalanches overwhelm whole groves, lightning shatters and burns, but the combined effects of all these amount only to a wholesome beauty-producing culture. Last summer I found some five sawmills located in or near the lower edge of the sequoia belt, all of which saw more or less of the big tree into lumber. One of these (Hyde's), situated on the north fork of the Kaweah, cut no less than two million feet of sequoia lumber last season. Most of the Fresno big trees are doomed to feed the mills recently erected near them, and a company has been formed by Chas. Converse to cut the noble forest on the south fork of King's River. In these milling operations, waste far exceeds use. After the choice young manageable trees have been felled, the woods are cleared of limbs and refuse by burning, and in these clearing fires, made with reference to further operations, all the young seedlings and saplings are destroyed, together with many valuable fallen trees and old trees, too large to be cut, thus effectually cutting off all hopes of a renewal of the forest.

These ravages, however, of mill-fires and mill-axes are small as compared with those of the "sheep men's" fires. Incredible numbers of sheep are driven to the mountain pastures every summer, and in order to make easy paths and to improve the pastures, running fires are set everywhere to burn off the old logs and underbrush. These fires are far more universal and destructive than would be guessed. They sweep through nearly the entire forest belt of the range from one extremity to the other, and in the dry weather, before the coming on of winter storms, are very destructive to all kinds of young trees, and especially to sequoia, whose loose fibrous bark catches and burns at once. Excepting the Calaveras, I, last summer, examined every sequoia grove in the range, together with the main belt extending across the basins of Kaweah and Tule, and found everywhere the most deplorable waste from this cause. Indians burn off underbrush to facilitate deer hunting. Campers of all kinds often permit fires to run, so also do mill-men, but the fires of sheep men probably form more than 90 percent of all destructive fires that sweep the woods.

Fire, then, is the arch destroyer of our forests, and sequoia forests suffer most of all. The young trees are most easily fire killed; the old are most easily burned, and the prostrate trunks, which never rot and would remain valuable until our tenth centennial, are reduced to ashes.

In European countries, especially in France, Germany, Italy, and Austria, the economies of forestry have been carefully studied under the auspices of government, with the most beneficial results. Whether our loose-jointed government is really able or willing to do anything in the matter remains to be seen. If our lawmakers were to discover and enforce any method tending to lessen even in a small degree the destruction going on, they would thus cover a multitude of legislative sins in the eyes of every tree lover. I am satisfied, however, that the question can be intelligently discussed only after a careful survey of our forests has been made, together with studies of the forces now acting upon them.

A law was constructed some years ago making the cutting down of sequoias over sixteen feet in diameter illegal. A more absurd and shortsighted piece of legislation could not be conceived. All the young trees might be cut and burned, and all the old ones might be burned but not cut.

(*Sacramento Daily Union*, February 5, 1876)

Alaska

To The Wild North

In 1879, shortly after becoming engaged to Louie Strentzel of Martinez, Muir left on his first trip to Alaska—a frontier that offered wild nature on a scale more grand and uncharted than anything he had yet encountered.

After eleven years of study and exploration in the Sierra Nevada of California and the mountain-ranges of the Great Basin, studying in particular their glaciers, forests, and wild life, above all their ancient glaciers and the influence they exerted in sculpturing the rocks over which they passed with tremendous pressure, making new landscapes, scenery, and beauty which so mysteriously influence every human being, and to some extent all life, I was anxious to gain some knowledge of the regions to the northward, about Puget Sound and Alaska. With this grand object in view I left San Francisco in May, 1879, on the steamer Dakota, without any definite plan, as with the exception of a few of the Oregon peaks and their forests all the wild north was new to me.

To the mountaineer a sea voyage is a grand, inspiring, restful change. For forests and plains with their flowers and fruits we have new scenery, new life of every sort; water hills and dales in eternal visible motion for rock waves, types of permanence.

It was curious to note how suddenly the eager countenances of the passengers were darkened as soon as the good ship passed through the Golden Gate and began to heave on the waves of the open ocean. The crowded deck was speedily deserted on account of seasickness. It seemed strange that nearly every one afflicted should be more or less ashamed.

Next morning a strong wind was blowing, and the sea was gray and white, with long breaking waves, across which the Dakota was racing half-buried in spray. Very few of the passengers were on deck to enjoy the wild scenery. Every wave seemed to be making enthusiastic, eager haste to the shore, with long, irised tresses streaming from its tops, some of its outer fringes borne away in scud to refresh the wind, all the rolling, pitching, flying water exulting in the beauty of rainbow light. Gulls and albatrosses, strong, glad life in the midst of the stormy beauty, skimmed the waves against the wind, seemingly without effort, oftentimes flying nearly a mile without a single wing-beat, gracefully swaying from side to side and tracing the curves of the briny water hills with the finest precision, now and then just grazing the highest.

And yonder, glistening amid the irised spray, is still more striking revelation of warm life in the so-called howling waste,—a half-dozen whales, their broad backs like glaciated bosses of granite heaving aloft in near view, spouting lustily, drawing a long breath, and plunging down home in colossal health and comfort. A merry school of porpoises, a square mile of them, suddenly appear, tossing themselves into the air in abounding strength and hilarity, adding foam to the waves and making all the wilderness wilder. One cannot but feel sympathy with and be proud of these brave neighbors, fellow citizens in the commonwealth of the world, making a living like the rest of us. Our good ship also seemed like a thing of life, its great iron heart beating on through calm and storm, a truly noble spectacle. But think of the hearts of these whales, beating warm against the sea, day and night, through dark and light, on and on for centuries; how the red blood must rush and gurgle in and out, bucketfuls, barrelfuls at a beat!

The cloud colors of one of the four sunsets enjoyed on the voyage were remarkably pure and rich in tone. There was a well-defined range of cumuli a few degrees above the horizon, and a massive, dark-gray rain-cloud above it, from which depended long, bent fringes overlapping the lower cumuli and partially veiling them; and from time to time sunbeams poured through narrow openings and painted the exposed bosses and fringes in ripe yellow tones, which, with the reflections on the water, made magnificent pictures. The scenery of the ocean, however sublime in vast expanse, seems far less beautiful to us dry-shod animals than that of the land seen only in comparatively small patches; but when we contemplate the whole globe as one great dewdrop, striped and dotted with continents and islands, flying through space with other stars all singing and shining together as one, the whole universe appears as an infinite storm of beauty.

The California coast-hills and cliffs look bare and uninviting as seen from the ship, the magnificent forests keeping well back out of sight beyond the reach of the sea winds; those of Oregon and Washington are in some places clad with conifers nearly down to the shore; even the little detached islets, so marked a feature to the northward, are mostly tree-crowned. Up through the Straits of Juan de Fuca the forests, sheltered from the ocean gales and favored with abundant rains, flourish in marvelous luxuriance on the glacier-sculptured mountains of the Olympic Range.

We arrived in Esquimault Harbor, three miles from Victoria, on the evening of the fourth day, and drove to the town through a magnificent forest of Douglas spruce,— with an undergrowth in open spots of oak, madrone, hazel, dogwood, alder, spiraea, willow, and wild rose,—and around many an upswelling *moutonné* rock, freshly glaciated and furred with yellow mosses and lichens.

Victoria, the capital of British Columbia, was in 1879 a small old-fashioned English town on the south end of Vancouver Island. It was said to contain about six thousand inhabitants. The government buildings and some of the business blocks were noticeable, but the attention of the traveler was more worthily attracted to the neat cottage homes found here, embowered in the freshest and floweriest climbing roses and honeysuckles conceivable. Californians may well be proud of their home roses loading sunny verandas, climbing to the tops of the roofs and falling over the gables in white and red cascades. But here, with so much bland fog and dew and gentle laving rain, a still finer development of some of the commonest garden plants is reached. English honeysuckle seems to have found here a most congenial home. Still more beautiful were the wild roses, blooming in wonderful luxuriance along the woodland paths, with corollas two and three inches wide. This rose and three species of spiraea fairly filled the air with fragrance after showers; and how brightly then did the red dogwood berries shine amid the green leaves beneath trees two hundred and fifty feet high.

Strange to say, all of this exuberant forest and flower vegetation was growing upon fresh moraine material scarcely at all moved or in any way modified by post-glacial agents. In the town gardens and orchards, peaches and apples fell upon glacier-polished rocks, and the streets were graded in moraine gravel; and I observed scratched and grooved rock bosses as unweathered and telling as those of the High Sierra of California eight thousand feet or more above sea-level. The Victoria Harbor is plainly glacial in origin, eroded from the solid; and the rock islets that rise here and there in it are unchanged to any appreciable extent by all the waves that have broken over them since first they came to light toward the close of the glacial period. The shores also of the harbor are strikingly grooved and scratched and in every way as glacial in all their characteristics as those of new-born glacial lakes. That the domain of the sea is being slowly extended over the land by incessant wave-action is well known; but in this freshly glaciated region the shores have been so short a time exposed to wave-action that they are scarcely at all wasted. The extension of the sea affected by its own action in post-glacial times is probably less than the millionth part of that affected by glacial action during the last glacier period. The direction of the flow of the ice-sheet to which all the main features of this wonderful region are due was in general southward.

From this quiet little English town I made many short excursions—up the coast to Nanaimo, to Burrard Inlet, now the terminus of the Canadian Pacific Railroad, to Puget Sound, up Fraser River to New Westminster and Yale at the head of navigation, charmed everywhere with the wild, new-born scenery. The most interesting of these and the most difficult to leave was the Puget Sound region, famous the world over for the wonderful forests of gigantic trees about its shores. It is an arm and many-fingered hand of the sea, reaching southward from the Straits of Juan de Fuca about a hundred miles into the heart of one of the noblest coniferous forests on the face of the globe. All its scenery is wonderful—broad river-like reaches sweeping in beautiful curves around bays and capes and jutting promontories, opening here and there into smooth, blue, lake-like expanses dotted with islands and feathered with tall, spiry evergreens, their beauty doubled on the bright mirror-water.

Sailing from Victoria, the Olympic Mountains are seen right ahead, rising in bold relief against the sky, with jagged crests and peaks from six to eight thousand feet high,—small residual glaciers and ragged snow-fields beneath them in wide amphitheatres opening down through the forest-filled valleys. These valleys mark the courses of the Olympic glaciers at the period of their greatest extension, when they poured their tribute into that portion of the great northern ice-sheet that overswept Vancouver Island and filled the strait between it and the mainland.

(From *Travels in Alaska*, Ch. 1)

Paradise of the Poets

To the lover of pure wildness Alaska is one of the most wonderful countries in the world. No excursion that I know of may be made into any other American wilderness where so marvelous an abundance of noble, newborn scenery is so charmingly brought to view as on the trip through the Alexander Archipelago to Fort Wrangell and Sitka. Gazing from the deck of the steamer, one is borne smoothly over calm blue waters, through the midst of countless forest-clad islands. The ordinary discomforts of a sea voyage are not felt, for nearly all the whole long way is on inland waters that are about as waveless as rivers and lakes. So numerous are the islands that they seem to have been sown broadcast; long tapering vistas between the largest of them open in every direction.

Day after day in the fine weather we enjoyed, we seemed

to float in true fairyland, each succeeding view seeming more and more beautiful, the one we chanced to have before us the most surprisingly beautiful of all. Never before this had I been embosomed in scenery so hopelessly beyond description. To sketch picturesque bits, definitely bounded, is comparatively easy—a lake in the woods, a glacier meadow, or a cascade in its dell; or even a grand master view of mountains beheld from some commanding outlook after climbing from height to height above the forests. These may be attempted, and more or less telling pictures made of them; but in these coast landscapes there is such indefinite, on-leading expansiveness, such a multitude of features without apparent redundance, their lines graduating delicately into one another in endless succession, while the whole is so fine, so tender, so ethereal, that all pen-work seems hopelessly unavailing. Tracing shining ways through fiord and sound, past forests and waterfalls, islands and mountains and far azure headlands, it seems as if surely we must at length reach the very paradise of the poets, the abode of the blessed.

Some idea of the wealth of this scenery may be gained from the fact that the coast-line of Alaska is about twenty-six thousand miles long, more than twice as long as all the rest of the United States. The islands of the Alexander Archipelago, with the straits, channels, canals, sounds, passages, and fiords, form an intricate web of land and water embroidery sixty or seventy miles wide, fringing the lofty icy chain of coast mountains from Puget Sound to Cook Inlet; and, with infinite variety, the general pattern is harmonious throughout its whole extent of nearly a thousand miles. Here you glide into a narrow channel hemmed in by mountain walls, forested down to the water's edge, where there is no distant view, and your attention is concentrated on the objects close about you— the crowded spires of the spruces and hemlocks rising higher and higher on the steep green slopes; stripes of paler green where winter avalanches have cleared away the trees, allowing grasses and willows to spring up; zigzags of cascades appearing and disappearing among the bushes and trees; short, steep glens with brawling streams hidden beneath alder and dogwood, seen only where they emerge on the brown algae of the shore; and retreating hollows, with lingering snow-banks marking the fountains of ancient glaciers. The steamer is often so near the shore that you may distinctly see the cones clustered on the tops of the trees, and the ferns and bushes at their feet.

But new scenes are brought to view with magical rapidity. Rounding some bossy cape, the eye is called away into far-reaching vistas, bounded on either hand by head-lands in charming array, one dipping gracefully beyond another and growing fainter and more ethereal in the distance. The tranquil channel stretching river-like between, may be stirred here and there by the silvery plashing of upspringing salmon, or by flocks of white gulls floating like water-lilies among the sun spangles; while mellow, tempered sunshine is streaming over all, blending sky, land, and water in pale, misty blue. Then, while you are dreamily gazing into the depths of this leafy ocean lane, the little steamer, seeming hardly larger than a duck, turning into some passage not visible until the moment of entering it, glides into a wide expanse—a sound filled with islands, sprinkled and clustered in forms and compositions such as nature alone can invent; some of them so small the trees growing on them seem like single handfuls culled from the neighboring woods and set in the water to keep them fresh, while here and there at wide intervals you may notice bare rocks just above the water, mere dots punctuating grand, outswelling sentences of islands.

(From *Travels in Alaska*, Ch. 2)

The Morning of Creation

When a river steamer chartered by a handful of mission-aries and white settlers for an excursion into native tribal country ran into engine trouble, Muir persuaded the traveling party to explore a glacier before turning back.

సందంగా ఈ సందంగా ఈ సందం

Arriving opposite the mouth of its fiord, we steered straight inland between beautiful wooded shores, and the grand glacier came in sight in its granite valley, glowing in the early sunshine and extending a noble invitation to come and see. After we passed between the two mountain rocks that guard the gate of the fiord, the view that was unfolded fixed every eye in wondering admiration. No words can convey anything like an adequate conception of its sublime grandeur—the noble simplicity and fineness of the sculpture of the walls; their magnificent proportions; their cascades, gardens, and forest adornments; the placid fiord between them; the great white and blue ice wall, and the snow-laden mountains beyond. Still more impotent are words in telling the peculiar awe one experiences in entering these mansions of the icy North, notwithstanding it is only the natural effect of appreciable manifestations of the presence of God.

Standing in the gateway of this glorious temple, and regarding it only as a picture, its outlines may be easily traced, the water foreground of a pale-green color, a smooth mirror sheet sweeping back five or six miles like one of the lower reaches of a great river, bounded at the head by a beveled barrier wall of blueish-white ice four or five hundred feet high. A few snowy mountain-tops appear beyond it, and on either hand rise a series of majestic, pale-gray granite rocks from three to four thousand feet high, some of them thinly forested and striped with bushes and flowery grass on narrow shelves, especially about half way up, others severely sheer and bare and built together into walls like those of Yosemite, extending far beyond the ice barrier, one immense brow appearing beyond another with their bases buried in the glacier. This is a Yosemite Valley in process of formation, the modeling and sculpture of the walls nearly completed and well planted, but no groves as yet or gardens or meadows on the raw and unfinished bottom. It is as if the explorer, in entering the Merced Yosemite, should find the walls nearly in their present condition, trees and flowers in the warm nooks and along the sunny portions of the moraine-covered brows, but the bottom of the valley still covered with water and beds of gravel and mud, and the grand glacier that formed it slowly receding but still filling the upper half of the valley.

Sailing directly up to the edge of the low, out spread, water-washed terminal moraine, scarce noticeable in a general view, we seemed to be separated from the glacier only by a bed of gravel a hundred yards or so in width; but on so grand a scale are all the main features of the valley, we afterwards found the distance to be a mile or more.

The captain ordered the Indian deck hands to get out the canoe, take as many of us ashore as wished to go, and accompany us to the glacier in case we should need their help. Only three of the company, in the first place, availed themselves of this rare opportunity of meeting a glacier in the flesh,—Mr. Young, one of the doctors, and myself. Paddling to the nearest and driest-looking part of the moraine flat, we stepped ashore, but gladly wallowed back into the canoe; for the gray mineral mud, a paste made of fine-ground mountain meal kept unstable by the tides, at once began to take us in, swallowing us feet foremost with becoming glacial deliberation. Our next attempt, made nearer the middle of the valley, was successful, and we soon found ourselves on firm gravelly ground, and made haste to the huge ice wall, which seemed to recede as we advanced. The only difficulty we met was a network of icy streams, at the largest of which we halted, not willing to get wet in fording. The Indian attendant promptly carried us over on his back. When my turn came I told him I would ford, but he bowed his shoulders in so ludicrously persuasive a manner I thought I would try the queer mount, the only one of the kind I had enjoyed since boyhood days in playing leapfrog. Away staggered my perpendicular mule over the boulders into the brawling torrent, and in spite of top-heavy predictions to the contrary, crossed without a fall. After being ferried in this way over several more of these glacial streams, we at length reached the foot of the glacier wall. The doctor simply played tag on it, touched it gently as if it were a dangerous wild beast, and hurried back to the boat, taking the portage Indian with him for safety, little knowing what he was missing. Mr. Young and I traced the glorious crystal wall, admiring its wonderful architecture, the play of light in the rifts and caverns, and the structure of the ice as displayed in the less fractured sections, finding fresh beauty everywhere and facts for study. We then tried to climb it, and by dint of patient zigzagging and doubling among the crevasses, and cutting steps here and there, we made our way up over the brow and back a mile or two to a height of about seven hundred feet. The whole front of the glacier is gashed and sculptured into a maze of shallow caves and crevasses, and a bewildering variety of novel architectural forms, clusters of glittering lance-tipped spires, gables, and obelisks, bold outstanding bastions and plain mural cliffs, adorned along the top with fretted cornice and battlement, while every gorge and crevasse, groove and hollow, was filled with light, shimmering and throbbing in pale-blue tones of ineffable tenderness and beauty. The day was warm, and back on the broad melting bosom of the glacier beyond the crevassed front, many streams were rejoicing, gurgling, ringing, singing, in frictionless channels worn down through the white disintegrated ice of the surface into the quick and living blue, in which they flowed with a grace of motion and flashing of light to be found only on the crystal hillocks and ravines of a glacier.

Along the sides of the glacier we saw the mighty flood grinding against the granite walls with tremendous pressure, rounding outswelling bosses, and deepening the retreating hollows into the forms they are destined to have when, in the fullness of appointed time, the huge ice tool shall be withdrawn by the sun. Every feature glowed with intention, reflecting the plans of God. Back a few miles from the front, the glacier is now probably but little more than a thousand feet deep; but when we examine the records on the walls, the rounded, grooved, striated, and polished features so surely glacial, we learn that in the earlier days of the ice age they were all over-swept, and that this glacier has flowed at a height of from three to four thousand feet above its present level, when it was at least a mile deep.

Standing here, with facts so fresh and telling and held up so vividly before us, every seeing observer, not to say geologist, must readily apprehend the earth-sculpturing, landscape-making action of flowing ice. And here, too, one learns that the world, though made, is yet being made; that this is still the morning of creation; that mountains long conceived are now being born, channels traced for coming rivers, basins hollowed for lakes; that moraine soil is being ground and outspread for coming plants,—coarse boulders and gravel for forests, finer soil for grasses and flowers,—while the finest part of the grist, seen hastening out to sea in the draining streams, is being stored away in darkness and builded particle on particle, cementing and crystallizing, to make the mountains and valleys and plains of other predestined landscapes, to be followed by still others in endless rhythm and beauty.

Gladly would we have camped out on this grand old landscape mill to study its ways and works; but we had no bread and the captain was keeping the Cassiar whistle screaming for our return. Therefore, in mean haste, we threaded our way back through the crevasses and down the blue cliffs, snatched a few flowers from a warm spot on the edge of the ice, flashed across the moraine streams, and were paddled aboard, rejoicing in the possession of so blessed a day, and feeling that in very foundational truth we had been in one of God's own temples and had seen Him and heard Him working and preaching like a man.

(From *Travels in Alaska*, Ch. 5)

Indian Lore

I greatly enjoyed the Indian's camp-fire talk this evening on their ancient customs, how they were taught by their parents ere the whites came among them, their religion, ideas connected with the next world, the stars, plants, the behavior and language of animals under different circumstances, manner of getting a living, etc. When our talk was interrupted by the howling of a wolf on the opposite side of the strait, Kadachan puzzled the minister with the question, "Have wolves souls?" The Indians believe that they have, giving as foundation for their belief that they are wise creatures who know how to catch seals and salmon by swimming slyly upon them with their heads hidden in a mouthful of grass, hunt deer in company, and always bring forth their young at the same and most favorable time of the year. I inquired how it was that with enemies so wise and powerful the deer were not all killed. Kadachan replied that wolves knew better than to kill them all and thus cut off their most important food-supply. He said they were numerous on all the large islands, more so than on the mainland, that Indian hunters were afraid of them and never ventured far into the woods alone, for these large gray and black wolves attacked man whether they were hungry or not. When attacked, the Indian hunter, he said, climbed a tree or stood with his back against a tree or rock as a wolf never attacks face to face. Wolves, and not bears, Indians regard as masters of the woods, for they sometimes attack and kill bears, but the wolverine they never attack, "for," said John, "wolves and wolverines are companions in sin and equally wicked and cunning."

(From *Travels in Alaska*, Ch. 9)

Celestial Fire

The next day being Sunday, the minister wished to stay in camp; and so, on account of the weather, did the Indians. I therefore set out on an excursion, and spent the day alone on the mountain-slopes above the camp, and northward, to see what I might learn. Pushing on through rain and mud and sludgy snow, crossing many brown, boulder-choked torrents, wading, jumping, and wallowing in snow up to my shoulders was mountaineering of the most trying kind. After crouching cramped and benumbed in the canoe, poulticed in wet or damp clothing night and day, my limbs had been asleep. This day they were awakened and in the hour of trial proved that they had not lost the cunning learned on many a mountain peak of the High Sierra. I reached a height of fifteen hundred feet, on the ridge that bounds the second of the great glaciers. All the landscape was smothered in clouds and I began to fear that as far as wide views were concerned I had climbed in vain. But at length the clouds lifted a little, and beneath their gray fringes I saw the berg-filled expanse of the bay, and the feet of the mountains that stand about it, and the imposing fronts of five huge glaciers, the nearest being immediately beneath me. This was my first general view of Glacier Bay, a solitude of ice and snow and newborn rocks, dim, dreary, mysterious. I held the ground I had so dearly won for an hour or two, sheltering myself from the blast as best I could, while with benumbed fingers I sketched what I could see of the landscape, and wrote a few lines in my notebook. Then, breasting the snow again, crossing the shifting avalanche slopes and torrents, I reached camp about dark, wet and weary and glad.

While I was getting some coffee and hardtack, Mr. Young told me that the Indians were discouraged, and had been talking about turning back, fearing that I would be lost, the canoe broken, or in some other mysterious way the expedition would come to grief if I persisted in going farther. They had been asking him what possible motive I could have in climbing mountains when storms were blowing; and when he replied that I was only seeking knowledge, Toyatte said, "Muir must be a witch to seek knowledge in such a place as this and in such miserable weather."

After supper, crouching about a dull fire of fossil wood, they became still more doleful, and talked in tones that accorded well with the wind and waters and growling torrents about us, telling sad old stories of crushed canoes, drowned Indians, and hunters frozen in snowstorms. Even brave old Toyatte, dreading the treeless, forlorn appearance of the region, said that his heart was not strong, and that he feared his canoe, on the safety of which our lives depended, might be entering a skookum-house (jail) of ice, from which there might be no escape; while the Hoona guide said bluntly that if I was so fond of danger, and meant to go close up to the noses of the ice-mountains, he would not consent to go any farther; for we should all be lost, as many of his tribe had been, by the sudden rising of bergs from the bottom. They seemed to be losing heart with every howl of the wind, and, fearing that they might fail me now that I was in the midst of so grand a congregation of glaciers, I made haste to reassure them, telling them that for ten years I had wandered alone among mountains and storms, and good luck always followed me; that with me, therefore, they need fear nothing. The storm would soon cease and the sun would shine to show us the way we should go, for God cares for us and guides us as long as we are trustful and brave, therefore all childish fear must be put away. This little speech did good. Kadachan, with some show of enthusiasm, said he liked to travel with good-luck people; and dignified old Toyatte declared that now his heart was strong again, and he would venture on with me as far as I liked for my "wawa" was "delait" (my talk was very good). The old warrior even became a little sentimental, and said that even if the canoe was broken he would not greatly care, because on the way to the other world he would have good companions.

Next morning it was still raining and snowing, but the south wind swept us bravely forward and swept the bergs from our course. In about an hour we reached the second of the big glaciers, which I afterwards named for Hugh Miller. We rowed up its fiord and landed to make a slight examination of its grand frontal wall. The berg-producing portion we found to be about a mile and a half wide, and broken into an imposing array of jagged spires and pyramids, and flat-topped towers and battlements, of many shades of blue, from pale, shimmering, limpid tones in the crevasses and hollows, to the most startling, chilling, almost shrieking vitriol blue on the plain mural spaces from which bergs had just been discharged. Back from the front for a few miles the glacier rises in a series of wide steps, as if this portion of the glacier had sunk in successive sections as it reached deep water, and the sea had found its way beneath it. Beyond this it extends indefinitely in a gently rising prairie like expanse, and branches along the slopes and cañons of the Fairweather Range.

From here a run of two hours brought us to the head of the bay, and to the mouth of the northwest fiord, at the head of which lie the Hoona sealing-grounds, and the great glacier now called the Pacific, and another called the Hoona. The fiord is about five miles long, and two miles wide at the mouth. Here our Hoona guide had a store of dry wood, which we took aboard. Then, setting sail, we were driven wildly up the fiord, as if the storm-wind were saying, "Go, then, if you will, into my icy chamber; but you shall stay in until I am ready to let you out." All this time sleety rain was falling on the bay, and snow on the mountains; but soon after we landed the sky began to open. The camp was made on a rocky bench near the front of the Pacific Glacier, and the canoe was carried beyond the reach of the bergs and berg-waves. The bergs were now crowded in a dense pack against the discharging front, as if the storm-wind had determined to make the glacier take back her crystal offspring and keep them at home....

... About daylight next morning we crossed the fiord and landed on the south side of the rock that divides the wall of the great glacier. The whiskered faces of seals dotted the open spaces between the bergs, and I could not prevent John and Charley and Kadachan from shooting at them. Fortunately, few, if any, were hurt. Leaving the Indians in charge of the canoe, I managed to climb to the top of the wall by a good deal of step-cutting between the ice and dividing rock, and gained a good general view of the glacier. At one favorable place I descended about fifty feet below the side of the glacier, where its denuding, fashioning action was clearly shown. Pushing back from here, I found the surface crevassed and sunken in steps, like the Hugh Miller Glacier, as if it were being undermined by the action of tide-waters. For a distance of fifteen or twenty miles the river-like ice-flood is nearly level, and when it recedes, the ocean water will follow it, and thus form a long extension of the fiord, with features essentially the same as those now extending into the continent farther south, where many great glaciers once poured into the sea, though scarce a vestige of them now exists. Thus the domain of the sea has been, and is being, extended in these ice-sculptured lands, and the scenery of their shores enriched. The brow of the dividing rock is about a thousand feet high, and is hard beset by the glacier. A short time ago it was at least two thousand feet below the surface of the over-sweeping ice; and under present climatic conditions it will soon take its place as a glacier-polished island in the middle of the fiord, like a thousand others in the magnificent archipelago. Emerging from its icy sepulchre, it gives a most telling illustration of the birth of a marked feature of a landscape. In this instance it is not the mountain, but the glacier, that is in labor, and the mountain itself is being brought forth.

The Hoona Glacier enters the fiord on the south side, a short distance below the Pacific, displaying a broad and far-reaching expanse, over which many lofty peaks are seen;

but the front wall, thrust into the fiord, is not nearly so interesting as that of the Pacific, and I did not observe any bergs discharged from it.

In the evening, after witnessing the unveiling of the majestic peaks and glaciers and their baptism in the down-pouring sunbeams, it seemed inconceivable that nature could have anything finer to show us. Nevertheless, compared with what was to come the next morning, all that was as nothing. The calm dawn gave no promise of anything uncommon. Its most impressive features were the frosty clearness of the sky and a deep, brooding stillness made all the more striking by the thunder of the newborn bergs. The sunrise we did not see at all, for we were beneath the shadows of the fiord cliffs; but in the midst of our studies, while the Indians were getting ready to sail, we were startled by the sudden appearance of a red light burning with a strange unearthly splendor on the topmost peak of the Fairweather Mountains. Instead of vanishing as suddenly as it had appeared, it spread and spread until the whole range down to the level of the glaciers was filled with the celestial fire. In color it was at first a vivid crimson, with a thick, furred appearance, as fine as the alpenglow, yet indescribably rich and deep—not in the least like a garment or mere external flush or bloom through which one might expect to see the rocks or snow, but every mountain apparently was glowing from the heart like molten metal fresh from a furnace. Beneath the frosty shadows of the fiord we stood hushed and awe-stricken, gazing at the holy vision; and had we seen the heavens opened and God made manifest, our attention could not have been more tremen-dously strained. When the highest peak began to burn, it did not seem to be steeped in sunshine, however glorious, but rather as if it had been thrust into the body of the sun itself. Then the supernal fire slowly descended, with a sharp line of demarcation separating it from the cold, shaded region beneath; peak after peak, with their spires and ridges and cascading glaciers, caught the heavenly glow, until all the mighty host stood transfigured, hushed, and thoughtful, as if awaiting the coming of the Lord. The white, rayless light of morning, seen when I was alone amid the peaks of the California Sierra, had always seemed to me the most telling of all the terrestrial manifestations of God. But here the mountains themselves were made divine, and declared His glory in terms still more impressive. How long we gazed I never knew. The glorious vision passed away in a gradual, fading change through a thousand tones of color to pale yellow and white, and then the work of the ice-world went on again in everyday beauty. The green waters of the fiord were filled with sun-spangles; the fleet of icebergs set forth on their voyages with the upspringing breeze; and on the innumerable mirrors and prisms of these bergs, and on those of the shattered crystal walls of the glaciers, common white light and rainbow light began to burn, while the mountains shone in their frosty jewelry, and loomed again in the thin azure in serene terrestrial majesty. We turned and sailed away, joining the outgoing bergs, while "Gloria in excelsis" still seemed to be sounding over all the white landscape, and our burning hearts were ready for any fate, feeling that, whatever the future might have in store, the treasures we had gained this glorious morning would enrich our lives forever.

(From *Travels in Alaska*, Ch. 10)

Land of the White Bear

In 1881, Muir left his wife and newborn daughter at home in Cali-fornia to make his third Alaska trip, this time to join an expedition going in search of three vessels that had been lost in the Arctic Sea.

The trip brought Muir into territory that had never before felt human footprints.

❧❧❧❧❧

STEAMER CORWIN, WRANGELL LAND, AUGUST 12, 1881

A notable addition was made to the national domain when Captain Calvin L. Hooper landed on Wrangell Land, and took formal possession of it in the name of the United States. We landed near the southeast cape, at the mouth of a river, in latitude 71° 4', longitude 177° 40' 30" W. The extent of the new territory thus acquired is not definitely known, nor is likely to be for many a century, or until some considerable change has taken place in the polar climate, rendering the new land more attractive and more accessible. For at present even its southmost portion is almost constantly beset with ice of a kind that renders it all but inaccessible during both the winter and summer, while to the northward it extends far into the frozen ocean.

Going inland, along the left bank of the river, we found it much larger than it at first appeared to be. There was no snow left on the lowlands or any of the hills or mountains in sight, excepting the remnants of heavy drifts; nevertheless, it was still about seventy-five yards wide, twelve feet deep, and was flowing on with a clear, stately current, at a speed of about three miles an hour. While the snow is melting it must be at least two hundred yards wide and twenty feet deep, and its sources must lie well back in the interior of the island.

Not the slightest trace, however, could we find along the river, along the shore, or on the bluff to the northeastward, of the Jeannette party, or of any human inhabitant. A land more severely solitary could hardly be found anywhere on the face of the globe.

The beach was well tracked by polar bears, but none of the party could discover any sign of reindeer or musk oxen, though the country seems to abound in the kind of food they require. A single fox track was observed, and some burrows of a species of spermophile; also a number of birds, and about twenty species of plants, most of them in bloom. The rock is clay slate, which weathers smoothly, and is covered with a sparse growth of mosses, lichens, and flowering plants, not unlike that of the adjacent coasts of Siberia and Alaska.

Some small fragments of knowledge concerning this mysterious country have been in existence for nearly a century, mostly, however, of so vague and foggy a character as to be scarce at all available as geography, while up to the time of Captain Hooper's visit no explorer so far as known had set foot on it. In the year 1820 Lieutenant Wrangell was ordered by Alexander, Emperor of Russia, to proceed from the mouth of the Kolyma as far as Cape Schelagskoj, and from thence in a northerly direction over the ice with sledges drawn by dogs, to ascertain whether an inhabited country existed in that quarter, as asserted by the Chukchis and others.

But the land in question was far from being generally known even by tradition among the Chukchis inhabiting the Siberian coast nearest to it. Wrangell seems to have found only one person during his long search for this land that had heard or could tell him anything concerning it. This man, an intelligent chief or head of a family, drew with charcoal a correct sketch of Cape Schelagskoj, Aratuan Island, and another to the east of the Cape, and then assured Wrangell in the most positive manner that there was no other island along the coast. When asked whether there was any other land to the north beyond the visible horizon, he seemed to reflect a little, and then said that, between Cape Schelagskoj and Cape North, there was a part of the coast where, from some cliffs near the mouth of a river, one might on a clear summer day descry snow-covered mountains at a great distance to the north, but that in winter it was impossible to see so far. He said also that formerly herds of reindeer sometimes came across the ice, probably from thence, but that they had been frightened back by hunters and wolves. He claimed to have himself once seen a herd returning to the north in this way in April, and followed them in a sledge drawn by two deer for a whole day until the roughness of the ice forced him to turn back. His opinion was that these distant mountains he had seen were not on an island, but on an extensive land similar to his own country.

He had been told by his father that a Chukchi elder had once gone there with a few followers in large boats, but what they found there, or whether they ever returned, he did not know. Still he maintained that the distant land was inhabited, and adduced as proof of it that some years ago a dead whale was found at Aratuan Island pierced by spears pointed with slate; and as his people did not use such weapons he supposed that the whale must have been killed by the people of the northland.

After spending three winters Baron Wrangell wrote concerning this country: "Our return to Nishne Kolymsk closed the series of attempts made by us to discover a northern land, which though not seen by us, may never-theless exist, and be attainable under a combination of very favorable circumstances, the principal of which would be a long, cold, and stormless winter, and a late spring. If another attempt should be made, it would be advisable to leave the coast about Cape Yakán, which all the native accounts concur in representing as the nearest point to the supposed northern region."

The Corwin made a very short stay at Wrangell Land, partly because of the condition of the ice, which threatened to shut us in; and partly because it seemed improbable that a prolonged search in the region about our landing-point could in any way advance the main objects of the expedition. A considerable stretch of the bluff coast where we landed was scanned closely as we approached. Captain Hooper, Mr. Nelson, and myself examined a mile or two of the left bank of the river, a gently sloping hillside back from the river, and a stretch of smooth beach at its mouth. Meanwhile a party of officers, after erecting a cairn, depositing records in it, and setting the flag on the edge of the bluff fronting the ocean, went northeastward along the brow of the shore-bluff to a prominent headland a distance of three or four miles, searching carefully for traces of the Jeannette explorers, and of any native inhabitants that might chance to be in the country; then all were hurriedly recalled, and we forced our way back through ten miles of heavy drifting ice to open water.

On the shore we found the skeleton of a large bowhead whale, an oak barrel stave, a piece of a boat mast about seven feet long and four inches in diameter, a double kayak paddle with both blades broken, and a small quantity of driftwood. Every bit of flotsam was much scoured and abraded, showing that the articles had long been exposed to the action of waves and ice.

Back on the hills and along the river-bank the tracks of geese, marmots, foxes, and bears were seen, but no trace whatever of human beings, though the mouth of a river would above all others be the place to find them if the country were inhabited or had been visited by Europeans within a decade or two. Not a stick of the driftwood seemed to have been turned over or stirred in any way, though, from the steepness of the slate bluffs for miles along the coast, and the heavy snowbanks drifted over them, this low, open portion of the shore is about the only place in the neighborhood where driftwood could come to rest on a beach and be easily accessible to natives or others while traveling along the coast either on the ice or on land, and where they would also find a good camp-ground and water.

A few yards back from high-water mark there is a low pile of broken slate, with level ground about it, where any traveler passing this way would naturally choose to camp. But the surface of the slate is covered with gray, brown, and yellow rock-lichens of slow growth, showing that not one of these stones had been moved for many a year. Again, neither the low nor the high ground in this vicinity is at all mantled with spongy tundra mosses and lichens like most of the Arctic shores over which a man might walk without leaving a footprint. On the contrary, it is mostly bare, presenting a soft clay soil, derived from the disintegration of slates, the scanty dwarf vegetation—saxifrages, drabas, potentillas, carices, etc.—occurring in small tufts at intervals of a yard or so, with bare ground between them, smooth and mellow and plastic, with gentle drainage, admirably adapted for the reception and preservation of footprints. Had any person walked on this ground any time in summer when the snow was gone, and where the drainage slopes are not too steep, his track would remain legible to the dullest observer for years.

We concluded, therefore, that this part of the country was not inhabited. Nor should the absence of inhabitants be wondered at, notwithstanding they might be derived from the Siberian coast at long intervals in accordance with the traditions bearing on the question among the Chukchis, or even from the coast of Alaska about Point Barrow or Cape Lisburne. For, though small parties of Eskimos or Chukchis might reach the land on floes detached from the pack while they chanced to be out hunting seals, or in boats driven by storm-winds or otherwise, such parties would probably seek to get back to their old homes again, or would die of famine. The seal and walrus, the two animals on which the natives of the Arctic shores chiefly depend for subsistence, are not to any great extent available, inasmuch as the ice seldom or never leaves the south Wrangell shores, and journeys twenty or thirty miles long would have to be made over rough ice to reach them.

Reindeer and musk oxen may exist in some other portions of the country, but if they occur in such numbers as would be required for the support of any considerable population the tracks of at least some few stragglers should have been seen hereabouts. Migratory water birds are no doubt abundant during the breeding and moulting season, producing sufficient food to last through a few of the summer months, and there are plenty of white bears, huge animals weighing from ten to twenty hundred pounds. Most of them, however, roam far out from land on the rugged edge of the ice-pack among the seals and walruses, and even under the most advantageous circumstances polar bears are poor cattle to depend on for a living. They certainly do not seem to have been fed upon lately to any marked extent, for we found them everywhere in abundance along the edge of the ice, and they appeared to be very fat and prosperous, and very much at home, as if the country had belonged to them always. They are the unrivaled master-existences of this ice-bound solitude, and Wrangell Land may well be called the Land of the White Bear.

(From *The Cruise of the Corwin*, Ch. 15)

Author, Environmental Advocate

The Yellowstone Park

In the heart of the Rocky Mountains, on the broad rugged summit of the Continent, amid snow and ice, and dark shaggy forests, where the great rivers take their rise, there is a region full of wonders, surpassing in wakeful, exciting interest any other region yet discovered on the face of the globe.

The greater portion of this new wonderland is comprehended in what is beginning to be known as the Yellowstone National Park. It measures sixty-five miles in length from north to south, and fifty-five miles in width. And, fortunately, while it was as yet almost wholly unknown to the world in general, it was dedicated and set apart in all its strange wild beauty for the benefit and enjoyment of the people—a most noticeable piece of legislation, for which everybody should give thanks. The withdrawal of this large tract from the public domain has caused no appreciable loss to any one, for its height—6,000 to 12,000 feet above the sea—and its rugged mantle of volcanic rocks, would prevent its ever becoming available to any great extent for agricultural or mining purposes, while its climate, geographical position and marvelous scenery combine to make it a grand gathering-place for travelers from every land seeking new health and life for body and soul.

The National Park as a Camping-place

It is a capital camping-ground: wood, water and grass in abundance; lakes with beautiful shores, garden-like parks and meadows in the evergreen woods, cool, dashing streams with flowery banks, waterfalls and cascades of every form, some of them ranking with those of Yosemite in grandeur, rough volcanic mountains and cañons of bewildering variety of form and color, affording fine work for the climber; while a thousand hot springs and geysers, reeking and spouting in their coral-like fountains, display an exuberance of strange motion and energy admirably calculated to shake up, and surprise, and frighten the dullest observer out of soul-wasting apathy, and make him begin to grow and live again. A wilderness full of striking marvels is delightfully refreshing to the weary toilers of civilization, whether in town or country, and too often becomes a necessity to anything like mental and bodily health, so dark and invisible become the most splendid phenomena if only they be common. The daily show of the sun might well keep one awake and alert, but seen always is not seen at all, and a geyser spouting at length becomes far more effective.

In this strange wonderland one is brought awe-stricken to a standstill before phenomena wholly new. In the heart of the cool, snowy mountains a thousand crystal fountains are plashing, and laving, and boiling, as if a fierce furnace fire were burning beneath every one of them; and a hundred massive torrents of boiling water are rushing into the sky with wild boom and roar like inverted waterfalls, falling up instead of down. Ponderous shafts of water large as sequoias with a diameter of from three to thirty feet or more and two hundred feet high, are sustained at that height with tremendous energy for a few minutes, or hours even, standing erect rigid as trees, their sides delicately roughened and fluted, and dissolving at the top in feathery side branches and sprays; the white, misty vapor about them, blown aside by the wind, revealing the massive boles and branches shining in the sun against a background of dark, pine woods on the hills. Others are fan-shaped, issuing from irregular slits in the silex pavement with radiate structure, the sunbeams sifting through them in rainbow colors with ravishing beauty; all rising and falling night or day in fairy rhythmic dance; growing up into the air and light, tossing their pearly branches in the wind, and sinking again far underground into their dark, hot caves. And thus over and over again at varying periods of minutes, hours, or days, like some strange sort of water-plants of which Nature raises a thousand crops a year, with no apparent exhaustion of the fiery soil.

The so-called "Geyser Basins" in which this rare kind of vegetation is growing are not, strictly speaking, basins at all, but valleys on the slopes of the mountains through which the ancient glaciers ground their way long after the greater volcanic fires had here ceased to burn.

Overlooking the Geyser Valleys

Approaching any of the larger of these Geyser valleys from the heights about them, and looking over the encircling forests, one sees a multitude of tall, white columns of misty vapor ascending from the bottom of the valley, along the banks of the river and up on the sides among the rocks and trees, suggesting the fires of some busy manufacturing town, or the camp-fires of an army. These columns indicate the position of each hot spring and geyser, or "gusher," as the Icelandic word means, and so numerous they are, and so crowded together, and so varied, they seem to have been collected as specimens of every form and color from every country under the sun. They are old geological kitchens, in which one may see Nature at work as a cook amid a thousand boiling, simmering pots and jets, cunningly compounding an infinite variety of mineral messes. Quartz boulders boiled to a smooth, fine paste, with various colors worked in— yellow and brown, red and pink, and pure creamy white, like paint—boiled probably thousands of years and boiling yet with a great show of eager concern, as if not yet half-cooked. Pots of sulphurous mush, pots of broth black as pitch, tossed and stirred with never-ceasing care, and thin, transparent essences, pure and blue as the sky, simmering gently in beautiful coral basins that are growing ever more beautiful the more they are used. Some, though still warm, not boiling at all, but perfectly calm, like bright mirror pools and fringed with grasses and flowers that lean over their edges, as if these dishes were finished and laid aside on a shelf to settle and cool. Others boiling over as if running to waste, tons of the precious liquids tossed into the air and falling in scalding showers on the clean coral floor, keeping onlookers at a distance; every pot, cup and fountain having something special in it, no two being exactly alike in color, temperature or composition.

One needs a big faith to feel at ease in a shop like this. The ground itself, usually so substantial, sounds hollow under foot, and the awful bellowing and roaring shakes one's mind as the ground is shaken, especially at night beneath the moon and stars, or when the sky is overcast with clouds. The Geysers then look like monster dancing ghosts, and the sounds they make seem doubly terrible, as if Divine Government were at an end and the world given over to utter chaos and ruin.

But up comes the sun pouring his steady, hopeful beams over the mountains and the hills, and woods, lighting the ghostly geysers from top to bottom, and shining into the eyes of the reeking springs, covering all with rainbow dust and dissolving the chaos of night into varied forms of eternal love. Harmony again becomes visible, and the work of the world goes on as before. The birds feed their young in the trees, the squirrels gather the pine-cones around the sides of the valleys, and down on the banks of the cool, gliding rivers the blessed ouzels are singing and dipping confidingly in the shallows, as if saying to every one of these grand manifestations of power round about them, "You also are one of us, each in your place, doing the work appointed you to do ere time began."

What the Geysers Are Doing

The coral-like formations with which these valleys are paved may well excite admiring attention, as well as the strange movements of the waters from which they have been made. They grow up in silence, like coral in the sea, forming beautiful cones about the Geysers and springs; and from these, as centers, slope gradually away over all the valley in thin, overlapping layers and bosses. Or, as in the case of the Mammoth Springs, at the north end of the Park, where the building waters issue from the heights above the valley, they form terraced hills of marble or silex, pearly white, tinged here and there with delicate pink; appearing at a distance like cascades pouring over shelving rocks, frozen and fixed in all their glory of snowy foam, with no hint of the deliberation required in the building invisible particles of silex and lime, the stones of this Divine masonry, mined in darkness in quarries no eye has seen, marching to their appointed places through all the dash and roar of the restless waters, and producing these marvelous buildings as the sure result; the glaciers building downward, volcanoes building upward, grinding and laving and making beauty only.

The Great Canyon

The Yellowstone Cañon makes another grand show. It is about thirty miles long and from one thousand to two thousand feet deep, a weird uncanny-looking gorge of most fantastic architecture. The river leaps into it at the head in a fall of 350 feet, making a fine display as it sets out on its long journey of 5,000 miles to the sea. But it is not the depth of the cañon, nor the falls, nor the clear glancing river roaring its brave song as it goes on its way that most impresses the observer. It is the color of the rocks in which the cañon is cut. Heretofore wherever we have gone, however much the vegetation and general views may have changed, from the palms and vines of the tropics to the dwarf willows and saxifrages of the north, the ground seemed ever familiar and the same. But here the ground also has changed as if we had arrived in another world. The walls of the cañon, from top to bottom, throughout its whole extent flame like a sunset in wild vivid colors—vermillion, yellow, blue, green and white variously blended—fairly dazzling in brightness when the sun is shining. The rocks seem to be completely saturated with color put on and rubbed in with wild audacity without any fear, or caution, or moderation. Mountain masses of paint, millions of tons of it, ever being washed away yet more and more of it coming into sight; the whole effect being so entirely strange and exciting that even a river might be afraid to enter such a place. Nevertheless, here also harmony rules supreme. Linnaea hangs her twin bells over the rugged edges of the cliffs, forests and gardens are spread in lavish beauty round about, the nuts and berries ripen well, making good pastures for the birds and bees, and the bears also, and elk, and deer, and buffalo— God's cattle—all find food and are at home in the strange wilderness and make part and parcel of the whole.

Sources of Great Rivers

A more interesting river center than this park region I have never seen, or water more varied in color and form. In the mountains to the northward are the sources of the Yellowstone, on the west those of three forks of the Missouri flowing to the Atlantic, to the southwest the sources of the Snake river flowing to the Columbia and on to the Pacific, and the upper tributaries of Green river flowing into the Colorado and reaching the sea by the Gulf of California. To everybody over all the world water is beautiful forever, whether falling upward into the sky in snowy geysers, or downward into deep resounding cañons, or gliding and resting in calm rivers and lakes. Through frost or fire, tranquil or in storm, massed in seas or in drops of dew, or drifting in clouds on the mountains; through all its forms forever and forever water is beautiful.

(*San Francisco Daily Evening Bulletin*, October 27, 1885)

A Wind-Storm in the Forests

John Muir co-founded the Sierra Club in 1892 and served as its president for the rest of his life. His first book, **The Mountains of California,** *a compilation of previously printed articles and new material, was published in 1894.*

The mountain winds, like the dew and rain, sunshine and snow, are measured and bestowed with love on the forests to develop their strength and beauty. However restricted the scope of other forest influences, that of the winds is universal. The snow bends and trims the upper forests every winter, the lightning strikes a single tree here and there, while avalanches mow down thousands at a swoop as a gardener trims out a bed of flowers. But the winds go to every tree, fingering every leaf and branch and furrowed bole; not one is forgotten; the Mountain Pine towering with outstretched arms on the rugged buttresses of the icy peaks, the lowliest and most retiring tenant of the dells; they seek and find them all, caressing them tenderly, bending them in lusty exercise, stimulating their growth, plucking off a leaf or limb as required, or removing an entire tree or grove, now whispering and cooing through the branches like a sleepy child, now roaring like the ocean; the winds blessing the forests, the forests the winds, with ineffable beauty and harmony as the sure result.

After one has seen pines six feet in diameter bending like grasses before a mountain gale, and ever and anon some giant falling with a crash that shakes the hills, it seems astonishing that any, save the lowest thickset trees, could ever have found a period sufficiently stormless to establish themselves; or, once established, that they should not, sooner or later, have been blown down. But when the storm is over, and we behold the same forests tranquil again, towering fresh and unscathed in erect majesty, and consider what centuries of storms have fallen upon them since they were first planted,—hail, to break the tender seedlings; lightning, to scorch and shatter; snow, winds, and avalanches, to crush and overwhelm,—while the manifest result of all this wild storm-culture is the glorious perfection we behold; then faith in Nature's forestry is established, and we cease to deplore the violence of her most destructive gales, or of any other storm-implement whatsoever....

... One of the most beautiful and exhilarating storms I ever enjoyed in the Sierra occurred in December, 1874, when I happened to be exploring one of the tributary valleys of the Yuba River. The sky and the ground and the trees had been thoroughly rain-washed and were dry again. The day was intensely pure, one of those incomparable bits of California winter, warm and balmy and full of white sparkling sunshine, redolent of all the purest influences of the spring, and at the same time enlivened with one of the most bracing wind-storms conceivable. Instead of camping out, as I usually do, I then chanced to be stopping at the house of a friend. But when the storm began to sound, I lost no time in pushing out into the woods to enjoy it. For on such occasions Nature has always something rare to show us, and the danger to life and limb is hardly greater than one would experience crouching deprecatingly beneath a roof.

It was still early morning when I found myself fairly adrift. Delicious sunshine came pouring over the hills, lighting the tops of the pines, and setting free a steam of summery fragrance that contrasted strangely with the wild tones of the storm. The air was mottled with pine-tassels and bright green plumes, that went flashing past in the sunlight like birds pursued. But there was not the slightest dustiness, nothing less pure than leaves, and ripe pollen, and flecks of withered bracken and moss. I heard trees falling for hours at the rate of one every two or three minutes; some uprooted, partly on account of the loose, water-soaked condition of the ground; others broken straight across, where some weakness caused by fire had determined the spot. The gestures of the various trees made a delightful study. Young Sugar Pines, light and feathery as squirrel-tails, were bowing almost to the ground; while the grand old patriarchs, whose massive boles had been tried in a hundred storms, waved solemnly above them, their long, arching branches streaming fluently on the gale, and every needle thrilling and ringing and shedding off keen lances of light like a diamond. The Douglas Spruces, with long sprays drawn out in level tresses, and needles massed in a gray, shimmering glow, presented a most striking appearance as they stood in bold relief along the hilltops. The madroños in the dells, with their red bark and large glossy leaves tilted every way, reflected the sunshine in throbbing spangles like those one so often sees on the rippled surface of a glacier lake. But the Silver Pines were now the most impressively beautiful of all. Colossal spires 200 feet in height waved like supple goldenrods chanting and bowing low as if in worship, while the whole mass of their long, tremulous foliage was kindled into one continuous blaze of white sun-fire. The force of the gale was such that the most steadfast monarch of them all rocked down to its roots with a motion plainly perceptible when one leaned against it. Nature was holding high festival, and every fiber of the most rigid giants thrilled with glad excitement.

I drifted on through the midst of this passionate music and motion, across many a glen, from ridge to ridge; often halting in the lee of a rock for shelter, or to gaze and listen. Even when the grand anthem had swelled to its highest pitch, I could distinctly hear the varying tones of individual trees,—Spruce, and Fir, and Pine, and leafless Oak,—and even the infinitely gentle rustle of the withered grasses at my feet. Each was expressing itself in its own way,—singing its own song, and making its own peculiar gestures,—manifesting a richness of variety to be found in no other forest I have yet seen. The coniferous woods of Canada, and the Carolinas, and Florida, are made up of trees that resemble one another about as nearly as blades of grass, and grow close together in much the same way. Coniferous trees, in general, seldom possess individual character, such as is manifest among Oaks and Elms. But the California forests are made up of a greater number of distinct species than any other in the world. And in them we find, not only a marked differentiation into special groups, but also a marked individuality in almost every tree, giving rise to storm effects indescribably glorious.

Toward midday, after a long, tingling scramble through copses of hazel and ceanothus, I gained the summit of the highest ridge in the neighborhood; and then it occurred to me that it would be a fine thing to climb one of the trees to obtain a wider outlook and get my ear close to the Æolian music of its topmost needles. But under the circumstances the choice of a tree was a serious matter. One whose instep was not very strong seemed in danger of being blown down, or of being struck by others in case they should fall; another was branchless to a considerable height above the ground, and at the same time too large to be grasped with arms and legs in climbing; while others were not favorably situated for clear views. After cautiously casting about, I made choice of the tallest of a group of Douglas Spruces that were growing close together like a tuft of grass, no one of which seemed likely to fall unless all the rest fell with it. Though comparatively young, they were about 100 feet high, and their lithe, brushy tops were rocking and swirling in wild ecstasy. Being accustomed to climb trees in making botanical studies, I experienced no difficulty in reaching the top of this one, and never before did I enjoy so noble an exhilaration of motion. The slender tops fairly flapped and swished in the passionate torrent, bending and swirling backward and forward, round and round, tracing indescribable combinations of vertical and horizontal curves, while I clung with muscles firm braced, like a bobo-link on a reed.

In its widest sweeps my tree-top described an arc of from twenty to thirty degrees, but I felt sure of its elastic temper, having seen others of the same species still more severely tried—bent almost to the ground indeed, in heavy snows—without breaking a fiber. I was therefore safe, and free to take the wind into my pulses and enjoy the excited forest from my superb outlook. The view from here must be extremely beautiful in any weather. Now my eye roved over the piny hills and dales as over fields of waving grain, and felt the light running in ripples and broad swelling undulations across the valleys from ridge to ridge, as the shining foliage was stirred by corresponding waves of air. Oftentimes these waves of reflected light would break up suddenly into a kind of beaten foam, and again, after chasing one another in regular order, they would seem to bend forward in concentric curves, and disappear on some hillside, like sea-waves on a shelving shore. The quantity of light reflected from the bent needles was so great as to make whole groves appear as if covered with snow, while the black shadows beneath the trees greatly enhanced the effect of the silvery splendor.

Excepting only the shadows there was nothing somber in all this wild sea of pines. On the contrary, notwithstanding this was the winter season, the colors were remarkably beautiful. The shafts of the pine and libocedrus were brown and purple, and most of the foliage was well tinged with yellow; the laurel groves, with the pale undersides of their leaves turned upward, made masses of gray; and then there was many a dash of chocolate color from clumps of manzanita, and jet of vivid crimson from the bark of the madroños, while the ground on the hillsides, appearing here and there through openings between the groves, displayed masses of pale purple and brown.

The sounds of the storm corresponded gloriously with this wild exuberance of light and motion. The profound bass of the naked branches and boles booming like waterfalls; the quick, tense vibrations of the pine-needles, now rising to a shrill, whistling hiss, now falling to a silky murmur; the rustling of laurel groves in the dells, and the keen metallic click of leaf on leaf—all this was heard in easy analysis when the attention was calmly bent.

The varied gestures of the multitude were seen to fine advantage, so that one could recognize the different species at a distance of several miles by this means alone, as well as by their forms and colors, and the way they reflected the light. All seemed strong and comfortable, as if really enjoying the storm, while responding to its most enthusiastic greetings. We hear much nowadays concerning the universal struggle for existence, but no struggle in the common meaning of the word was manifest here; no recognition of danger by any tree; no deprecation; but rather an invincible gladness as remote from exultation as from fear.

I kept my lofty perch for hours, frequently closing my eyes to enjoy the music by itself, or to feast quietly on the delicious fragrance that was streaming past. The fragrance of the woods was less marked than that produced during warm rain, when so many balsamic buds and leaves are steeped like tea; but, from the chafing of resiny branches against each other, and the incessant attrition of myriads of needles, the gale was spiced to a very tonic degree. And besides the fragrance from these local sources there were traces of scents brought from afar. For this wind came first from the sea, rubbing against its fresh, briny waves, then distilled through the redwoods, threading rich ferny gulches, and spreading itself in broad undulating currents over many a flower-enameled ridge of the coast mountains, then across the golden plains, up the purple foot-hills, and into these piny woods with the varied incense gathered by the way.

Winds are advertisements of all they touch, however much or little we may be able to read them; telling their wanderings even by their scents alone. Mariners detect the flowery perfume of land-winds far at sea, and sea-winds carry the fragrance of dulse and tangle far inland, where it is quickly recognized, though mingled with the scents of a thousand land-flowers. As an illustration of this, I may tell here that I breathed sea-air on the Firth of Forth, in Scotland, while a boy; then was taken to Wisconsin, where I remained nineteen years; then, without in all this time having breathed one breath of the sea, I walked quietly, alone, from the middle of the Mississippi Valley to the Gulf of Mexico, on a botanical excursion, and while in Florida, far from the coast, my attention wholly bent on the splendid tropical vegetation about me, I suddenly recognized a sea-breeze, as it came sifting through the palmettos and blooming vine-tangles, which at once awakened and set free a thousand dormant associations, and made me a boy again in Scotland, as if all the intervening years had been annihilated.

Most people like to look at mountain rivers, and bear them in mind; but few care to look at the winds, though far more beautiful and sublime, and though they become at times about as visible as flowing water. When the north winds in winter are making upward sweeps over the curving summits of the High Sierra, the fact is sometimes published with flying snow-banners a mile long. Those portions of the winds thus embodied can scarce be wholly invisible, even to the darkest imagination. And when we look around over an agitated forest, we may see something of the wind that stirs it, by its effects upon the trees. Yonder it descends in a rush of water-like ripples, and sweeps over the bending pines from hill to hill. Nearer, we see detached plumes and leaves, now speeding by on level currents, now whirling in eddies, or, escaping over the edges of the whirls, soaring aloft on grand, upswelling domes of air, or tossing on flame-like crests. Smooth, deep currents, cascades, falls, and swirling eddies, sing around every tree and leaf, and over all the varied topography of the region with telling changes of form, like mountain rivers conforming to the features of their channels.

After tracing the Sierra streams from their fountains to the plains, marking where they bloom white in falls, glide in crystal plumes, surge gray and foam-filled in boulder-choked gorges, and slip through the woods in long, tranquil reaches—after thus learning their language and forms in detail, we may at length hear them chanting all together in one grand anthem, and comprehend them all in clear inner vision, covering the range like lace. But even this spectacle is far less sublime and not a whit more substantial than what we may behold of these storm-streams of air in the mountain woods.

We all travel the milky way together, trees and men; but it never occurred to me until this storm-day, while swinging in the wind, that trees are travelers, in the ordinary sense. They make many journeys, not extensive ones, it is true; but our own little journeys, away and back again, are only little more than tree-wavings—many of them not so much.

When the storm began to abate, I dismounted and sauntered down through the calming woods. The storm-tones died away, and, turning toward the east, I beheld the countless hosts of the forests hushed and tranquil, towering above one another on the slopes of the hills like a devout audience. The setting sun filled them with amber light, and seemed to say, while they listened, "My peace I give unto you."

As I gazed on the impressive scene, all the so-called ruin of the storm was forgotten, and never before did these noble woods appear so fresh, so joyous, so immortal.

(From *The Mountains of California*, Ch. 10)

Avalanche Ride

Few Yosemite visitors ever see snow avalanches and fewer still know the exhilaration of riding on them. In all my mountaineering I have enjoyed only one avalanche ride, and the start was so sudden and the end came so soon I had but little time to think of the danger that attends this sort of travel, though at such times one thinks fast.

One fine Yosemite morning after a heavy snowfall, being eager to see as many avalanches as possible and wide views of the forest and summit peaks in their new white robes before the sunshine had time to change them, I set out early to climb by a side cañon to the top of a commanding ridge a little over three thousand feet above the Valley. On account of the looseness of the snow that blocked the cañon I knew the climb would require a long time, some three or four hours as I estimated; but it proved far more difficult than I had anticipated. Most of the way I sank waist deep, almost out of sight in some places. After spending the whole day to within half an hour or so of sundown, I was still several hundred feet below the summit. Then my hopes were reduced to getting up in time to see the sunset. But I was not to get summit views of any sort that day, for deep trampling near the cañon head, where the snow was strained, started an avalanche, and I was swished down to the foot of the cañon as if by enchantment. The wallowing ascent had taken nearly all day, the descent only about a minute.

When the avalanche started I threw myself on my back and spread my arms to try to keep from sinking. Fortunately, though the grade of the cañon is very steep, it is not interrupted by precipices large enough to cause outbounding or free plunging. On no part of the rush was I buried. I was only moderately imbedded on the surface or at times a little below it, and covered with a veil of back-streaming dust particles; and as the whole mass beneath and about me joined in the flight there was no friction, though I was tossed here and there and lurched from side to side. When the avalanche swedged and came to rest I found myself on top of the crumpled pile without bruise or scar.

This was a fine experience. Hawthorne says somewhere that steam has spiritualized travel; though unspiritual smells, smoke, etc., still attend steam travel. This flight in what might be called a milky way of snow-stars was the most spiritual and exhilarating of all the modes of motion I have ever experienced. Elijah's flight in a chariot of fire could hardly have been more gloriously exciting.

(From *The Yosemite*, Ch. 3)

Deer

The Sierra deer—the blacktail—spend the winters in the brushy and exceedingly rough region just below the main timber-belt, and are less accessible to hunters there than when they are passing through the comparatively open forests to and from their summer pastures near the summits of the range. They go up the mountains early in the spring as the snow melts, not waiting for it all to disappear; reaching the high Sierra about the first of June, and the coolest recesses at the base of the peaks a month or so later. I have tracked them for miles over compacted snow from three to ten feet deep.

Deer are capital mountaineers, making their way into the heart of the roughest mountains; seeking not only pasturage, but a cool climate, and safe hidden places in which to bring forth their young. They are not supreme as rock-climbing animals; they take second rank, yielding the first to the mountain sheep, which dwell above them on the highest crags and peaks. Still, the two meet frequently; for the deer climbs all the peaks save the lofty summits above the glaciers, crossing piles of angular boulders, roaring swollen streams, and sheer-walled cañons by fords and passes that would try the nerves of the hardiest mountaineers,—climbing with graceful ease and reserve of strength that cannot fail to arouse admiration. Everywhere some species of deer seems to be at home,—on rough or smooth ground, lowlands or highlands, in swamps and barrens and the densest woods, in varying climates, hot or cold, over all the continent; maintaining glorious health, never making an awkward step. Standing, lying down, walking, feeding, running even for life, it is always invincibly graceful, and adds beauty and animation to every landscape,—a charming animal, and a great credit to nature.

I never see one of the common blacktail deer, the only species in the Park, without fresh admiration; and since I never carry a gun I see them well: lying beneath a juniper or dwarf pine, among the brown needles on the brink of some cliff or the end of a ridge commanding a wide outlook; feeding in sunny openings among chaparral, daintily selecting aromatic leaves and twigs; leading their fawns out of my way, or making them lie down and hide; bounding past through the forest, or curiously advancing and retreating again and again.

One morning when I was eating breakfast in a little garden spot on the Kaweah, hedged around with chaparral, I noticed a deer's head thrust through the bushes, the big beautiful eyes gazing at me. I kept still, and the deer ventured forward a step, then snorted and withdrew. In a few minutes she returned, and came into the open garden, stepping with infinite grace, followed by two others. After showing themselves for a moment, they bounded over the hedge with sharp, timid snorts and vanished. But curiosity brought them back with still another, and all four came into my garden, and, satisfied that I meant them no ill, began to feed, actually eating breakfast with me, like tame, gentle sheep around a shepherd,—rare company, and the most graceful in movements and attitudes. I eagerly watched them while they fed on ceanothus and wild cherry, daintily culling single leaves here and there from the side of the hedge, turning now and then to snip a few leaves of mint from the midst of the garden flowers. Grass they did not eat at all. No wonder the contents of the deer's stomach are eaten by the Indians.

While exploring the upper cañon of the north fork of the San Joaquin, one evening, the sky threatening rain, I searched for a dry bed, and made choice of a big juniper that had been pushed down by a snow avalanche, but was resting stubbornly on its knees high enough to let me lie under its broad trunk. Just below my shelter there was another juniper on the very brink of a precipice, and, examining it, I found a deer-bed beneath it, completely protected and concealed by drooping branches,—a fine refuge and lookout as well as resting-place. About an hour before dark I heard the clear, sharp snorting of a deer, and looking down on the brushy, rocky cañon bottom, discovered an anxious doe that no doubt had her fawns concealed near by. She bounded over the chaparral and up the farther slope of the wall, often stopping to look back and listen,—a fine picture of vivid, eager alertness. I sat perfectly still, and as my shirt was colored like the juniper bark I was not easily seen. After a little she came cautiously toward me, sniffing the air and grazing, and her movements, as she descended the cañon side over boulder piles and brush and fallen timber, were admirably strong and beautiful; she never strained or made apparent efforts, although jumping high here and there. As she drew nigh she sniffed anxiously, trying the air in different directions until she caught my scent; then bounded off, and vanished behind a small grove of firs. Soon she came back with the same caution and insatiable curiosity,—coming and going five or six times. While I sat admiring her, a Douglas squirrel, evidently excited by her noisy alarms, climbed a boulder beneath me, and witnessed her performances as attentively as I did, while a frisky chipmunk, too restless or hungry for such shows, busied himself about his supper in a thicket of shadbushes, the fruit of which was then ripe, glancing about on the slender twigs lightly as a sparrow.

(From *Our National Parks*, Ch. 6)

Squirrels

The two squirrels of the Park, the Douglas and the California gray, keep all the woods lively. The former is far more abundant and more widely distributed, being found all the way up from the foothills to the dwarf pines on the Summit peaks. He is the most influential of the Sierra animals, though small, and the brightest of all the squirrels I know,—a squirrel of squirrels, quick mountain vigor and valor condensed, purely wild, and as free from disease as a sunbeam. One cannot think of such an animal ever being weary or sick. He claims all the woods, and is inclined to drive away even men as intruders. How he scolds, and what faces he makes! If not so comically small he would be a dreadful fellow.

The gray, *Sciurus fossor*, is the handsomest, I think, of all the large American squirrels. He is something like the Eastern gray, but is brighter and clearer in color, and more lithe and slender. He dwells in the oak and pine woods up to a height of about five thousand feet above the sea, is rather common in Yosemite Valley, Hetch-Hetchy, Kings River Cañon, and indeed in all the main cañons and Yosemites, but does not like the high fir-covered ridges. Compared with the Douglas, the gray is more than twice as large; nevertheless, he manages to make his way through the trees with less stir than his small, peppery neighbor, and is much less influential in every way. In the spring, before the pine-nuts and hazel-nuts are ripe, he examines last year's cones for the few seeds that may be left in them between the half-open scales, and gleans fallen nuts and seeds on the ground among the leaves, after making sure that no enemy is nigh. His fine tail floats, now behind, now above him, level or gracefully curled, light and radiant as dry thistledown. His body seems hardly more substantial than his tail.

The Douglas is a firm, emphatic bolt of life, fiery, pungent, full of brag and show and fight, and his movements have none of the elegant deliberation of the gray. They are so quick and keen they almost sting the onlooker, and the acrobatic harlequin gyrating show he makes of himself turns one giddy to see. The gray is shy and often-times stealthy, as if half expecting to find an enemy in every tree and bush and behind every log; he seems to wish to be let alone, and manifests no desire to be seen, or admired, or feared. He is hunted by the Indians, and this of itself is cause enough for caution. The Douglas is less attractive for game, and probably increasing in numbers in spite of every enemy. He goes his ways bold as a lion, up and down and across, round and round, the happiest, merriest of all the hairy tribe, and at the same time tremendously earnest and solemn, sunshine incarnate, making every tree tingle with his electric toes. If you prick him, you cannot think he will bleed. He seems above the chance and change that beset common mortals, though in busily gathering burs and nuts he shows that he has to work for a living, like the rest of us. I never found a dead Douglas. He gets into the world and out of it without being noticed; only in prime is he seen, like some little plants that are visible only when in bloom.

(From *Our National Parks*, Ch. 6)

The Sierra Bear

The Sierra bear, brown or gray, the sequoia of the animals, tramps over all the park, though few travelers have the pleasure of seeing him. On he fares through the majestic forests and cañons, facing all sorts of weather, rejoicing in his strength, everywhere at home, harmonizing with the trees and rocks and shaggy chaparral. Happy fellow! his lines have fallen in pleasant places,—lily gardens in silver-fir forests, miles of bushes in endless variety and exuberance of bloom over hill-waves and valleys and along the banks of streams, cañons full of music and waterfalls, parks fair as Eden,—places in which one might expect to meet angels rather than bears.

In this happy land no famine comes nigh him. All the year round his bread is sure, for some of the thousand kinds that he likes are always in season and accessible, ranged on the shelves of the mountains like stores in a pantry. From one to another, from climate to climate, up and down he climbs, feasting on each in turn,—enjoying as great variety as if he traveled to far-off countries north and south. To him almost every thing is food except granite. Every tree helps to feed him, every bush and herb, with fruits and flowers, leaves and bark; and all the animals he can catch,— badgers, gophers, ground squirrels, lizards, snakes, etc., and ants, bees, wasps, old and young, together with their eggs and larvae and nests. Craunched and hashed, down all go to his marvelous stomach, and vanish as if cast into a fire. What digestion! A sheep or a wounded deer or a pig he eats warm, about as quickly as a boy eats a buttered muffin; or should the meat be a month old, it still is welcomed with tremendous relish. After so gross a meal as this, perhaps the next will be strawberries and clover, or raspberries with mushrooms and nuts, or puckery acorns and choke-cherries. And as if fearing that anything eatable in all his dominions should escape being eaten, he breaks into cabins to look after sugar, dried apples, bacon, etc. Occasionally he eats the mountaineer's bed; but when he has had a full meal of more tempting dainties he usually leaves it undisturbed, though he has been known to drag it up through a hole in the roof, carry it to the foot of a tree, and lie down on it to enjoy a siesta. Eating everything, never is he himself eaten except by man, and only man is an enemy to be feared. "B'ar meat," said a hunter from whom I was seeking information, "b'ar meat is the best meat in the mountains; their skins make the best beds, and their grease the best butter. Biscuit shortened with b'ar grease goes as far as beans; a man will walk all day on a couple of them biscuit."

In my first interview with a Sierra bear we were frightened and embarrassed, both of us, but the bear's behavior was better than mine. When I discovered him, he was standing in a narrow strip of meadow, and I was concealed behind a tree on the side of it. After studying this appearance as he stood at rest, I rushed toward him to frighten him, that I might study his gait in running. But, contrary to all I had heard about the shyness of bears, he did not run at all; and when I stopped short within a few steps of him, as he held his ground in a fighting attitude, my mistake was monstrously plain. I was then put on my good behavior, and never afterward forgot the right manners of the wilderness.

This happened on my first Sierra excursion in the forest to the north of Yosemite Valley. I was eager to meet the animals, and many of them came to me as if willing to show themselves and make my acquaintance; but the bears kept out of my way.

An old mountaineer, in reply to my questions, told me that bears were very shy, all save grim old grizzlies, and that I might travel the mountains for years without seeing one, unless I gave my mind to them and practiced the stealthy ways of hunters. Nevertheless, it was only a few weeks after I had received this information that I met the one mentioned above, and obtained instruction at first-hand.

I was encamped in the woods about a mile back of the rim of Yosemite, beside a stream that falls into the valley by the way of Indian Cañon. Nearly every day for weeks

I went to the top of the North Dome to sketch; for it commands a general view of the valley, and I was anxious to draw every tree and rock and waterfall. Carlo, a St. Bernard dog, was my companion,—a fine, intelligent fellow that belonged to a hunter who was compelled to remain all summer on the hot plains, and who loaned him to me for the season for the sake of having him in the mountains, where he would be so much better off. Carlo knew bears through long experience, and he it was who led me to my first interview, though he seemed as much surprised as the bear at my unhunter-like behavior. One morning in June, just as the sunbeams began to stream through the trees, I set out for a day's sketching on the dome; and before we had gone half a mile from camp Carlo snuffed the air and looked cautiously ahead, lowered his bushy tail, drooped his ears, and began to step softly like a cat, turning every few yards and looking me in the face with a telling expression, saying plainly enough, "There is a bear a little way ahead." I walked carefully in the indicated direction, until I approached a small flowery meadow that I was familiar with, then crawled to the foot of a tree on its margin, bearing in mind what I had been told about the shyness of bears. Looking out cautiously over the instep of the tree, I saw a big, burly cinnamon bear about thirty yards off, half erect, his paws resting on the trunk of a fir that had fallen into the meadow, his hips almost buried in grass and flowers. He was listening attentively and trying to catch the scent, showing that in some way he was aware of our approach. I watched his gestures, and tried to make the most of my opportunity to learn what I could about him, fearing he would not stay long. He made a fine picture, standing alert in the sunny garden walled in by the most beautiful firs in the world.

After examining him at leisure, noting the sharp muzzle

thrust inquiringly forward, the long shaggy hair on his broad chest, the stiff ears nearly buried in hair, and the slow, heavy way in which he moved his head, I foolishly made a rush on him, throwing up my arms and shouting to frighten him, to see him run. He did not mind the demonstration much; only pushed his head farther forward, and looked at me sharply as if asking," What now? If you want to fight, I'm ready." Then I began to fear that on me would fall the work of running. But I was afraid to run, lest he should be encouraged to pursue me; therefore I held my ground, staring him in the face within a dozen yards or so, putting on as bold a look as I could, and hoping the influence of the human eye would be as great as it is said to be. Under these strained relations the interview seemed to last a long time. Finally, the bear, seeing how still I was, calmly withdrew his huge paws from the log, gave me a piercing look, as if warning me not to follow him, turned, and walked slowly up the middle of the meadow into the forest; stopping every few steps and looking back to make sure that I was not trying to take him at a disadvantage in a rear attack. I was glad to part with him, and greatly enjoyed the vanishing view as he waded through the lilies and columbines.

Thenceforth I always tried to give bears respectful notice of my approach, and they usually kept well out of my way. Though they often came around my camp in the night, only once afterward, as far as I know, was I very near one of them in daylight. This time it was a grizzly I met; and as luck would have it, I was even nearer to him than I had been to the big cinnamon. Though not a large specimen, he seemed formidable enough at a distance of less than a dozen yards. His shaggy coat was well grizzled, his head almost white. When I first caught sight of him he was eating acorns under a Kellogg oak, at a distance of perhaps seventy-five yards, and I tried to slip past without disturbing him. But he had either heard my steps on the gravel or caught my scent, for he came straight toward me, stopping every rod or so to look and listen: and as I was afraid to be seen running, I crawled on my hands and knees a little way to one side and hid behind a libocedrus, hoping he would pass me unnoticed. He soon came up opposite me, and stood looking ahead, while I looked at him, peering past the bulging trunk of the tree. At last, turning his head, he caught sight of mine, stared sharply a minute or two, and then, with fine dignity, disappeared in a manzanita-covered earthquake talus.

(From *Our National Parks*, Ch. 6)

The National Parks and Forest Reservations

In the summer of 1896, Muir accompanied members of the newly appointed National Forestry Commission on a tour aimed at making policy recommendations for the management of western forests. The experience prompted a series of articles aimed at influencing public opinion on the importance of wilderness preservation.

⚜⚜⚜⚜⚜

One fine calm day last summer, when Professor Sargent, General Abbot, and myself were going through the California redwoods, admiring their wondrous beauty and grandeur and silence, we came suddenly upon a scene of disorder. At the foot of a shallow dell, where a little stream crosses the way, we discovered three Indians, a white man, and a horse, all in wild motion—especially the horse. He was a good-looking animal, well bred apparently, but laboring under furious excitement—snorting, groaning, springing up on his hind legs and beating the air, then dropping on his knees as if trying to stand on his head, plunging back and forth in blind fury, butting his master like a goat, butting the bank on one side of the road and the gnarled base of one of the giant trees on the other, as if trying to break his neck, his eyes staring wildly, while he steamed and quivered and threw off splashes of froth from his widely distended nostrils. The Indians scrambled into the bushes out of danger, and the bewildered white man, holding on to the halter and dodging about to avoid being crushed, was swearing aloud in despair. We all knew something about horses, but could give no assistance. Everybody was puzzled. What could be the matter with the animal? He seemed to be torn and tossed by devils. At length, when we were at our wits' end, a yellow-jacket was found in his ear. Then the excitement seemed excessively reasonable, and of course, after the maddening insect was got rid of, the storm subsided as quickly as it rose.

And last February, when the wild storm of protest came out of the West against the grand new forest reservations proclaimed by President Cleveland, I thought of that poor horse, and said, "These men must have yellow-jackets in their ears." Gold stings worse than the wasps of the woods, and gives rise to far more unreasonable and unexplainable behavior. "All our precious mountains," they screamed, "with their stores of timber and grass, silver and gold, fertile valleys and streams—all the natural resources of our great growing States are set aside from use, smothered up in mere pleasure-grounds for wild beasts and a set of sick, rich, dawdling sentimentalists. For this purpose business is blocked and every current of industry dammed. Will our people stand this? No-o-o!" Which in plain English means, "Let us steal and destroy in peace."

Judging by the number and violence of these protests, one would be led to believe that 'most everybody was against the reservation system, none heartily for it. But in truth it is far otherwise. Probably more than ninety per cent of the people in the States in which the new reservations lie are in favor of them, or at least of some form of government protection and control. On our travels last summer we talked with all sorts of settlers—miners, prospectors, merchants, etc.—and I cannot recall a single instance in which objection was made to a rational government forest policy by anyone not interested in plunder. Now, unfortunately, many of the best men in the country have been drawn over to the opposition through cunningly devised fables.

Much is said on questions of this kind about "the greatest good for the greatest number," but the greatest number is too often found to be number one. It is never the greatest number in the common meaning of the term that make the greatest noise and stir on questions mixed with money. One man with a thousand-dollar yellow-jacket in his ear will make more bewildering noise and do more effective kicking and fighting on certain public measures than a million working-men minding their own business, and whose cash interests are not visibly involved. But as soon as light comes, the awakened million creates a public opinion that overcomes wrong, however cunningly veiled. When the opposition first appeared in the newspapers many friends said, "The reservation system is doomed: the government commission has made the mistake of recommending too many large reserves at once, and this has united the Western Senators and Representatives against them." But I said: "No. Much must be said on both sides of the question, and the sooner it is stirred up and debated before the people the better, for thus the light will be let into it. Now that so much of what is left of the forests has been reserved from sale and entry, Congress will be compelled to take care of them, and enact laws under which a permanent supply of timber for every right use may be obtained, instead of letting the reserves lie idle at the mercy of thieves and fire.

To invent and to set in motion a common-sense management seems easy; but so many varied conditions come forward for consideration, and, under long neglect, so many bad practices have sprung up and become deeply rooted, that a good deal of fighting will have to be done before even the most obviously required reforms can be established. Nothing good is got without fighting. This forest battle is part and parcel of the eternal conflict between right and wrong.

No sooner is any reserve made than it is attacked as being too large, infringing on the "vested rights" of settlers, discouraging industry, etc. Thus every one of the parks and reservations in Oregon and California made by President Harrison, and President Cleveland during his first term of office, has been subjected to stormy protests and objections of every conceivable kind, and strenuous efforts have been made to break and to shove back their boundaries. Only last year a determined effort was made to cut off three-fourths of the magnificent Cascade Mountain Forest Reserve in Oregon. And two years ago an attempt was made in Congress to reduce the area of the Yosemite National Park one-half, in the name of seventy-five poor, honest, much-hurt farmers, but really for a few lumbermen and sheep-owners. And so it is always. Complaints are made in the name of poor settlers and miners, while the wealthy corporations are kept carefully hidden in the background. I know this park well, and say, on the contrary, that there is little or nothing in it that can rightly be called a farm, but only a few small garden spots, hay-meadows, and cattle-ranches, whose owners, far from complaining, are rejoicing in the protection afforded them, especially from the devastating hordes of sheep that formerly cleared the ground about them every summer of every green leaf and twig. But the fight goes on nevertheless, and will go on, no matter how great or small the reserves may be. God began the reservation system in Eden, and this first reserve included only one tree. Yet even so moderate a reserve as this was attacked. And if only one tree of each species in our woods were reserved as types and monuments of all that was noble and glorious in vanished American forests, it would doubtless be but a short time ere you would find lawyers and lumbermen at the feet of them arguing that for the good of the nation, for the sake of the dear people, and to clear a path for prosperity and progress, these trees must come down; and we should have to go on defending them against patriotic thieves that are ever ready to break through and steal, as if each tree were a million-acre reserve. It is only in the Better Land that goods need no defence. There are trees in heaven that are safe from politicians and fire, but there is none here.

California has three national parks, of which she is justly proud, the Yosemite, General Grant, and Sequoia, with an area of more than a million acres in all; and six forest reservations, the Sierra, Stanislaus, San Gabriel, San Bernardino, San Jacinto, and Trabuco—comprising with the parks a total area of over eight million acres. The largest and most important is the Sierra Forest Reserve, with an area of over four million acres, and some of the most novel, beautiful, and majestic scenery and noblest coniferous forests in the world.

When the news came last February that two of the thirteen new reservations had fallen to the lot of California there was general rejoicing, the only regret being that they were not larger. Since the first were proclaimed by President Harrison, public opinion has been growing steadily and rapidly in favor of forest protection, until now this State is overwhelmingly in favor of the reservation system, and the administration of forest affairs in general by the Federal government through the War Department. Of the costly and wholly inadequate and ineffective State laws and commissions we have had enough. But in our parks, during the few years they have been under the care of the military, the only unchanging arm of the government, and free from the blight of politics, we have gained a lesson we shall not forget, and we now pray for the extension of this protection over all the forests of the State remaining in the hands of the government, and of all the national forests everywhere. It is almost universally believed here that only a few lumbermen, sheep-owners, and plunderers in general, without visible means of support, are against this policy.

After the Yosemite National Park had been guarded four years by a small troop of cavalry, I made an extended excursion through it to see what the effect of this protection was. Before the military assumed control the forest floor was swept as bare as the driest desert at the end of every summer, and the sky was full of dust and smoke. Now the ground is covered with grass and flowers like a garden, and the bitten, trampled undergrowth of bushes has put forth fresh shoots and leaves, and is blooming again in wild shaggy beauty and fragrance. Only a few washed gullies on steep mountain-sides and the spots held as cattle-ranches continue to look frowsy and raw, while destructive fires have been almost wholly prevented. All this wonderful change from dust and ashes to beauty was effected by a mere handful of soldiers, without friction or noise. A single soldier armed with the authority of the United States and a gun would suffice to protect a hundred thousand acres of the Sierra forests, however difficult and rough the topography. As more and more orchards and vineyards are planted, and irrigating streams are led ever farther over the fertile lowlands, Californians are beginning to appreciate their forests as by far the most precious and indispensable of natural resources, and also the most destructible, and therefore to be guarded with jealous care. Like nearly all the other forests of the West, they are planted just where they do the most good, and where their removal would be followed by the greatest number of evils, so that their preservation can hardly be regarded as less than a physical necessity. In them, high on the mountains, the rivers that supply water for irrigation draw their sources. The fountain snow falls on to them, and is stored up and prevented from slipping into the bottoms of the cañons in avalanches, from being drifted into irregular heaps by the wind, and from melting with destructive and wasteful rapidity, while loss from evaporation is diminished, and the sod of grasses and bushes nourished in the shade absorbs much of the melting snow, and yields it slowly in oozing fertilizing streams that last all summer. Were the forests of the Western mountains wholly destroyed, the snowfall might not be appreciably diminished, but it would melt much faster. At the beginning of summer there would be a week or two of tremendous floods, all the year's supply would rush down the choked channels at once, carrying away the soil and overspreading the lowlands with raw detritus. Then would come drouth and desert barrenness, to say nothing of the distress that would be caused by want of forest products and the effect on scenery.

The aims of the National Forestry Commission and of the most advanced students of forestry in general are, as far as I know them, briefly as follows:

(1.) To advise the immediate withdrawal from entry and sale of all that is left of the forest-bearing lands still in the possession of the government, as the first necessary step and foundation for a permanent forest policy. This has already, in great part, been accomplished. That it was necessary to reserve these mountain forests few fair-minded Americans will deny. For as soon as the public lands are cut up and sold to private parties nothing in the way of general control and wise far-seeing management for the good of all is possible. These lands now belong to all the people of the East and West alike, and in thus reserving them they are not taken out of the public domain, but kept in it for the benefit and advantage of everybody. Too much of the country has already been denuded. Most of the magnificent woods of the Atlantic slope and the middle West have been destructively cleared for farms. Bread, rather than timber, was needed, and so the trees had to die that men might live. But very little of the forest-covered land still belonging to the United States is fit for agriculture. Nearly all of it is on the mountain ranges of the West, and is too rocky and high for wheat and apples, though of vast importance as fountains for irrigating rivers.

(2.) To recommend that, until other means are provided, Congress enact a law for the protection of the public forest reservations and parks, authorizing the Secretary of War, upon the request of the Secretary of the Interior, to make the necessary details of troops to protect the trees and undergrowth in the national parks and reservations not otherwise protected under existing laws to enforce the rules and regulations prescribed by the Secretary of the Interior, and to prevent, as far as possible, the lighting and spread of forest fires. The main object of this proposed legislation is to stop, or at least greatly diminish, the tremendous ravages of the fires now devouring the woods. And surely no objection can be brought forward against this. Even reckless money-crazed persons with yellow-jackets in their ears must admit that forests are better than ashes. A strip of the grandest woods in the world, fronting the foggy breath of the Pacific Ocean, is, on account of this fog and a copious snow and rain fall, comparatively safe from running fires. But the broad, rough, complicated Rocky Mountain region is swept by most extensive and destructive fires every summer, excepting only the Yellowstone Park, which is protected by a troop of cavalry. *These desolating fires consume probably from five to ten times as much timber as the axe and saw,* even under present grossly wasteful methods of lumbering. Now these fires can only be controlled by the government. What is everybody's business is nobody's. Even in southern California, where the people are most awake to the necessity of saving the tree and brush cover of the mountain streams, on which the prosperity of the region depends, disastrous fires ravaged the San Gabriel Reserve last summer, and of course forest guards are loudly called for. As settlements are multiplied, and hunters, miners, prospectors, and stock-men invade the woods in ever-increasing numbers, of course fires are multiplied. Some of them result from mere carelessness, but it is well known that sheep-owners purposely fire the woods in hundreds of places toward the end of the summer season, when everything is dry, to facilitate the march of their flocks, and perhaps for a time improve the pasturage. Prospectors are also ruthless forest-burners, destroying millions of acres of priceless woods simply to lay the rocky ribs of the mountains bare, to thus increase their chances of discovering a mine. If this timber was only stolen and used, like stolen bread that is eaten, it would be less deplorable; but to burn it is the very climax of forest wickedness. To let this diabolical burning go on is as unrighteous and irrational as if the government should enact laws under which men should be encouraged and protected in the business of burning barns and wheat-fields for a living. No. Let right, commendable industry be fostered; but as to these Goths and Vandals of the wilderness, who are spreading black death in the fairest woods God ever made, let the government up and at 'em.

(3.) After careful study of the varied conditions of the different forest regions and the wants of the people, to invent and recommend a permanent, practical, rational forest management, somewhat like those in force in every other civilized country, by which, while checking needless waste, the forests may be made to yield a perennial supply of timber for every use and to spare by thinning out, cutting only the trees that ought to be cut, without injury to what are left, but rather to their advantage, and thus, without further diminishing the area of the forests, make them grow more beautiful, productive, and useful every year. On this problem, which should devoutly interest every right-minded citizen, the commission are at present engaged. It now remains to be seen how they will be supported....

The commission met in Chicago about the beginning of July, and I joined it there, on the invitation of the chairman. And what rough, broken sleeping we had to endure on our travels, and rough, wicked eating in dismal hotels and huts and musty hay-mows, no comfortable critic will ever know. With rare exceptions, only in the woods, with our own blankets and coffee and crackers, was anything like clean luxury enjoyed. Of course the longest journeys were made by rail, but we travelled at least a thousand miles on back-woods roads in wagons, with the customary quartz-mill jolting, and hundreds of miles on animals of mysterious wearisome gait and motion. I never before saw men who minded hardship less in urging a way through their appointed work.

We first visited the Black Hills in South Dakota, a mass of mountains and hills standing out isolated in the broad dry Western plains.

They are not very high—the highest, Mount Harney, rising only 9700 feet above the sea. But nowhere else in all my wide wanderings have I seen so strangely chopped and chiselled a mass of peaks, pillars, gorges, and glens. Here we spent a week examining the curious growth of feathery-tufted spruces among the rocks, and the sunny yellow-pine parks in the open spaces. Fire and wanton waste here, as everywhere in the West, have already made deplorable headway; and if allowed to go on, timber for the settlements and numerous mines will soon be scarce and dear, and the many small streams used to irrigate the adjacent lowlands will soon fail. For these reasons the commission unanimously recommended the Black Hills Forest Reserve, of about a million acres, in the central part.

Thence we went to the Rocky Mountains, past the Big Horn range and memorable Custer battle-field, to the Yellowstone National Park; and thence through and through the broad Rocky range in every direction, among its widespread and far-reaching bewildering spurs and forests, on which the Teton, Bitter Root, Lewis and Clark, Flathead, and Priest River forest reserves were located. The commonest tree in this vast region is the lodge-pole pine—*Pinus contorta*—a wonderful tree of immense vitality, widely distributed from Alaska along the sea-coast far southward, and over all the main Western chains of mountains, with infinitely varied forms, in accordance with climate and soil. Here it is a small, hardy, slender tree, forming close growths like canebrakes, and as inflammable as grass. At the age of 150 or 200 years it is about six to eight inches in diameter and seventy-five feet high. As timber it is of little account, except for local use, but of the utmost importance as cover for the fountains of the great rivers that head here. On the western slopes the timber is much better, where the yellow pine, mountain-pine, and the giant Western larch grow to a height of nearly two hundred feet in some places, with a diameter of from three to eight feet.

From the Rocky Mountain woods we made our way to the vast unrivalled forests of the Pacific coast in Oregon and Washington, where we passed through hundreds of miles of Douglas spruce 800 feet high, mixed with the grand Western arbor-vitae and Sitka spruce, scarcely inferior to the Douglas. Even these well-watered woods, we found, were wasted in many places by fire, as well as by destructive lumbering, notwithstanding the heavy rain-fall they enjoy. These trees, growing close together like gigantic weeds, are the wonder and admiration of the world. It took nature many a century to make them, but fools can destroy them in a few years. Only the government can save them. Here the wild, picturesque, and most valuable Olympic Forest Reserve was located, and the grand Washington and Mount Rainier reserves.

Thence we turned southward and examined the great Cascade Mountain Forest Reserve, going up through it by Klamath Lake to Crater Lake on the summit of the range, and down by way of the Rogue River Valley, noting its marvellous wealth of lodge-pole pine, yellow pine, sugar-pine, mountain-pine, Sitka spruce, incense-cedar, noble silver fir, and pure forests of the Paton hemlock—the most graceful of evergreens, but, like all the dry woods everywhere, horribly blackened and devastated by devilish fires. Here the commission divided—Professors Brewer and Hague going southward to examine the Mount Shasta region and the Sierra at the head-waters of the American

River; Mr. Pinchot, to make a lonely excursion through the Yosemite National Park, across the High Sierra, and southward along the eastern flank to Fort Independence, and thence westward, recrossing the High Sierra by the Kearsarge Pass, and down through the Sierra Forest Reserve by way of the Grand Cañon of Kings River and the General Grant National Park; while Professor Sargent, General Abbot, and myself crossed to the westward from Grant's Pass, in Oregon, through the wild complicated Siskiyou Mountains to Crescent City, on the coast, and thence made our way southward through the redwood belt, meeting again in San Francisco. From San Francisco we made short trips into the Santa Lucia and other Coast mountains, and then set off for the Sequoia National Park in the Sierra, by way of Visalia and the famous groves of "big trees" on the Kahweah. Thence, continuing southward, we next examined the San Gabriel and San Bernardino reserves and the San Jacinto Mountains, where one of the new California reserves is located. Thence we went by rail to Flagstaff, Arizona, and from there pushed off into the charming and tremendous wilderness of the Grand Cañon Reserve. Here I turned homeward to California, while the commission went to the forest reserves of Colorado.

To describe all the forests we passed through and examined would require a book of many volumes. I have only space enough left here to say that all we saw last summer, added to what we had seen in these woods on excursions made in many other summers, only showed more fully that not only should all the reserves established be maintained, but that every remaining acre of unentered forest-bearing land in all the country, not more valuable for agriculture than for tree-growing, should be reserved, protected, and administered by the Federal government for the public good forever.

(From *Harper's Weekly*, June 5, 1897)

Hermit Among the Big Trees

One of my own best excursions among the Sequoias was made in the autumn of 1875, when I explored the then unknown or little known Sequoia region south of the Mariposa Grove for comprehensive views of the belt, and to learn what I could of the peculiar distribution of the species and its history in general. In particular I was anxious to try to find out whether it had ever been more widely distributed since the glacial period; what conditions favorable or otherwise were affecting it; what were its relations to climate, topography, soil, and the other trees growing with it, etc.; and whether, as was generally supposed, the species was nearing extinction. I was already acquainted in a general way with the northern groves, but excepting some passing glimpses gained on excursions into the high Sierra about the head-waters of Kings and Kern rivers I had seen nothing of the south end of the belt.

Nearly all my mountaineering has been done on foot, carrying as little as possible, depending on camp-fires for warmth, that so I might be light and free to go wherever my studies might lead. On this Sequoia trip, which promised to be long, I was persuaded to take a small wild mule with me to carry provisions and a pair of blankets. The friendly owner of the animal, having noticed that I sometimes looked tired when I came down from the peaks to replenish my bread sack, assured me that his "little Brownie mule" was just what I wanted, tough as a knot, perfectly untirable, low and narrow, just right for squeezing through brush, able to climb like a chipmunk, jump from boulder to boulder like a wild sheep, and go anywhere a man could go. But tough as he was and accomplished as a climber, many a time in the course of our journey when he was jaded and hungry, wedged fast in rocks or struggling in chaparral like a fly in a spiderweb, his troubles were sad to see, and I wished he would leave me and find his way home alone.

We set out from Yosemite about the end of August, and our first camp was made in the well-known Mariposa Grove. Here and in the adjacent pine woods I spent nearly a week, carefully examining the boundaries of the grove for traces of its greater extension without finding any. Then I struck out into the majestic trackless forest to the south-eastward, hoping to find new groves or traces of old ones in the dense silver fir and pine woods about the head of Big Creek, where soil and climate seemed most favorable to their growth, but not a single tree or old monument of any sort came to light until I climbed the high rock called Wamellow by the Indians. Here I obtained telling views of the fertile forest-filled basin of the upper Fresno. Innumerable spires of the noble yellow pine were displayed rising above one another on the braided slopes, and yet nobler sugar pines with superb arms outstretched in the rich autumn light, while away toward the southwest, on the verge of the glowing horizon, I discovered the majestic dome-like crowns of Big Trees towering high over all, singly and in close grove congregations. There is something wonderfully attractive in this king tree, even when beheld from afar, that draws us to it with indescribable enthu-siasm; its superior height and massive smoothly rounded outlines proclaiming its character in any company; and when one of the oldest attains full stature on some commanding ridge it seems the very god of the woods. I ran back to camp, packed Brownie, steered over the divide and down into the heart of the Fresno Grove. Then choosing a camp on the side of a brook where the grass was good, I made a cup of tea, and set off free among the brown giants, glorying in the abundance of new work about me. One of the first special things that caught my attention was an extensive landslip. The ground on the side of a stream had given way to a depth of about fifty feet and with all its trees had been launched into the bottom of the stream ravine. Most of the trees—pines, firs, incense cedar, and Sequoia—were still standing erect and uninjured, as if unconscious that anything out of the common had happened. Tracing the ravine alongside the avalanche, I saw many trees whose roots had been laid bare, and in one instance discovered a Sequoia about fifteen feet in diameter growing above an old prostrate trunk that seemed to belong to a former generation. This slip had occurred seven or eight years ago, and I was glad to find that not only were most of the Big Trees uninjured, but that many companies of hopeful seedlings and saplings were growing confidently on the fresh soil along the broken front of the avalanche. These young trees were already eight or ten feet high, and were shooting up vigorously, as if sure of eternal life, though young pines, firs, and libocedrus were running a race with them for the sunshine with an even start. Farther down the ravine I counted five hundred and thirty-six promising young Sequoias on a bed of rough bouldery soil not exceeding two acres in extent.

The Fresno Big Trees covered an area of about four square miles, and while wandering about surveying the boundaries of the grove, anxious to see every tree, I came suddenly on a handsome log cabin, richly embowered and so fresh and unweathered it was still redolent of gum and balsam like a newly felled tree. Strolling forward, wondering who could have built it, I found an old, weary-eyed, speculative, gray-haired man on a bark stool by the door, reading a book. The discovery of his hermitage by a stranger seemed to surprise him, but when I explained that I was only a tree-lover sauntering along the mountains to study Sequoia, he bade me welcome, made me bring my mule down to a little slanting meadow before his door and camp with him, promising to show me his pet trees and many curious things bearing on my studies.

After supper, as the evening shadows were falling, the good hermit sketched his life in the mines, which in the main was like that of most other pioneer gold-hunters—a succession of intense experiences full of big ups and downs like the mountain topography. Since "49" he had wandered over most of the Sierra, sinking innumerable prospect holes like a sailor making soundings, digging new channels for streams, sifting gold-sprinkled boulder and gravel beds with unquenchable energy, life's noon the meanwhile passing unnoticed into late afternoon shadows. Then, health and gold gone, the game played and lost, like a wounded deer creeping into this forest solitude, he awaits the sundown call. How sad the undertones of many a life here, now the noise of the first big gold battles has died away! How many interesting wrecks lie drifted and stranded in hidden nooks of the gold region! Perhaps no other range contains the remains of so many rare and interesting men. The name of my hermit friend is John A. Nelder, a fine kind man, who in going into the woods has at last gone home; for he loves nature truly, and realizes that these last shadowy days with scarce a glint of gold in them are the best of all. Birds, squirrels, plants get loving, natural recognition, and delightful it was to see how sensitively he responds to the silent influences of the woods. His eyes brightened as he gazed on the trees that stand guard around his little home; squirrels and mountain quail came to his call to be fed, and he tenderly stroked the little snowbent sapling Sequoias, hoping they yet might grow straight to the sky and rule the grove. One of the greatest of his trees stands a little way back of his cabin, and he proudly led me to it, bidding me admire its colossal proportions and measure it to see if in all the forest there could be another so grand. It proved to be only twenty-six feet in diameter, and he seemed distressed to learn that the Mariposa Grizzly Giant was larger. I tried to comfort him by observing that his was the taller, finer formed, and perhaps the more favorably situated. Then he led me to some noble ruins, remnants of gigantic trunks of trees that he supposed must have been larger than any now standing, and though they had lain on the damp ground exposed to fire and the weather for centuries, the wood was perfectly sound. Sequoia timber is not only beautiful in color, rose red when fresh, and as easily worked as pine, but it is almost absolutely unperishable. Build a house of Big Tree logs on granite and that house will last about as long as its foundation. Indeed fire seems to be the only agent that has any appreciable effect on it. From one of these ancient trunk remnants I cut a specimen of the wood, which neither in color, strength, nor soundness could be distinguished from specimens cut from living trees, although it had certainly lain on the damp forest floor for more than three hundred and eighty years, probably more than thrice as long. The time in this instance was determined as follows: When the tree from which the specimen was derived fell it sunk itself into the ground, making a ditch about two hundred feet long and five or six feet deep; and in the middle of this ditch, where a part of the fallen trunk had been burned, a silver fir four feet in diameter and three hundred and eighty years old was growing, showing that the Sequoia trunk had lain on the ground three hundred and eighty years plus the unknown time that it lay before the part whose place had been taken by the fir was burned out of the way, and that which had elapsed ere the seed from which the monumental fir sprang fell into the prepared soil and took root. Now because Sequoia trunks are never wholly consumed in one forest fire and these fires recur only at considerable intervals, and because Sequoia ditches, after being cleared, are often left unplanted for centuries, it becomes evident that the trunk remnant in question may have been on the ground a thousand years or more. Similar vestiges are common, and together with the root-bowls and long straight ditches of the fallen monarchs, throw a sure light back on the post-glacial history of the species, bearing on its distribution. One of the most interesting features of this grove is the apparent ease and strength and comfortable independence in which the trees occupy their place in the general forest. Seedlings, saplings, young and middle-aged trees are grouped promisingly around the old patriarchs, betraying no sign of approach to extinction. On the contrary, all seem to be saying, "Everything is to our mind and we mean to live forever." But, sad to tell, a lumber company was building a large mill and flume near by, assuring widespread destruction.

In the cones and sometimes in the lower portion of the trunk and roots there is a dark gritty substance which dissolves readily in water and yields a magnificent purple color. It is a strong astringent, and is said to be used by the Indians as a big medicine. Mr. Nelder showed me specimens of ink he had made from it, which I tried and found good, flowing freely and holding its color well.

Indeed everything about the tree seems constant. With these interesting trees, forming the largest of the northern groves, I stopped only a week, for I had far to go before the fall of the snow. The hermit seemed to cling to me and tried to make me promise to winter with him after the season's work was done. Brownie had to be got home, however, and other work awaited me, therefore I could only promise to stop a day or two on my way back to Yosemite and give him the forest news.

The next two weeks were spent in the wide basin of the San Joaquin, climbing, innumerable ridges and surveying the far-extending sea of pines and firs. But not a single Sequoia crown appeared among them all, nor any trace of a fallen trunk, until I had crossed the south divide of the basin, opposite Dinky Creek, one of the northmost tributaries of Kings River. On this stream there is a small grove, said to have been discovered a few years before my visit by two hunters in pursuit of a wounded bear. Just as I was fording one of the branches of Dinky Creek I met a shepherd, and when I asked him whether he knew anything about the Big Trees of the neighborhood he replied, "I know all about them, for I visited them only a few days ago and pastured my sheep in the grove." He was fresh from the East, and as this was his first summer in the Sierra I was curious to learn what impression the Sequoias had made on him. When I asked whether it was true that the Big Trees were really so big as people say, he warmly replied, "Oh, yes sir, you bet. They're whales. I never used to believe half I heard about the awful size of California trees, but they're monsters and no mistake. One of them over here, they tell me, is the biggest tree in the whole world, and I guess it is, for it's forty foot through and as many good long paces around." He was very earnest, and in fullness of faith offered to guide me to the grove that I might not miss seeing this biggest tree. A fair measurement four feet from the ground, above the main swell of the roots, showed a diameter of only thirty-two feet, much to the young man's disgust. "Only thirty-two feet," he lamented, "only thirty-two, and I always thought it was forty!" Then with a sigh of relief, "No matter, that's a big tree, anyway; no fool of a tree, sir, that you can cut a plank out of thirty feet broad, straight-edged, no bark, all good wood, sound and solid. It would make the brag white pine planks from old Maine look like laths." A good many other fine specimens are distributed along three small branches of the creek, and I noticed several thrifty moderate-sized Sequoias growing on a granite ledge, apparently as independent of deep soil as the pines and firs, clinging to seams and fissures and sending their roots far abroad in search of moisture.

The creek is very clear and beautiful, gliding through tangles of shrubs and flower beds, gay bee and butterfly pastures, the grove's own stream, pure Sequoia water, flowing all the year, every drop filtered through moss and leaves and the myriad spongy rootlets of the giant trees. One of the most interesting features of the grove is a small waterfall with a flowery, ferny, clear brimming pool at the foot of it. How cheerily it sings the songs of the wilderness, and how sweet its tones! You seem to taste as well as hear them, while only the subdued roar of the river in the deep cañon reaches up into the grove, sounding like the sea and the winds. So charming a fall and pool in the heart of so glorious a forest good pagans would have consecrated to some lovely nymph.

(From *Our National Parks*, Ch. 9)

Fire

In the forest between the Middle and East forks of the Kaweah, I met a great fire, and as fire is the master scourge and controller of the distribution of trees, I stopped to watch it and learn what I could of its works and ways with the giants. It came racing up the steep chaparral-covered slopes of the East Fork cañon with passionate enthusiasm in a broad cataract of flames, now bending down low to feed on the green bushes, devouring acres of them at a breath, now towering high in the air as if looking abroad to choose a way, then stooping to feed again, the lurid flapping surges and the smoke and terrible rushing and roaring hiding all that is gentle and orderly in the work. But as soon as the deep forest was reached the ungovernable flood became calm like a torrent entering a lake, creeping and spreading beneath the trees where the ground was level or sloped gently, slowly nibbling the cake of compressed needles and scales with flames an inch high, rising here and there to a foot or two on dry twigs and clumps of small bushes and brome grass. Only at considerable intervals were fierce bonfires lighted, where heavy branches broken off by snow had accumulated, or around some venerable giant whose head had been stricken off by lightning.

I tethered Brownie on the edge of a little meadow beside a stream a good safe way off, and then cautiously chose a camp for myself in a big stout hollow trunk not likely to be crushed by the fall of burning trees, and made a bed of ferns and boughs in it. The night, however, and the strange wild fireworks were too beautiful and exciting to allow much sleep. There was no danger of being chased and hemmed in, for in the main forest belt of the Sierra, even when swift winds are blowing, fires seldom or never sweep over the trees in broad all-embracing sheets as they do in the dense Rocky Mountain woods and in those of the Cascade Mountains of Oregon and Washington. Here they creep from tree to tree with tranquil deliberation, allowing close observation, though caution is required in venturing around the burning giants to avoid falling limbs and knots and fragments from dead shattered tops. Though the day was best for study, I sauntered about night after night, learning what I could and admiring the wonderful show vividly displayed in the lonely darkness, the ground-fire advancing in long crooked lines gently grazing and smoking on the close-pressed leaves, springing up in thousands of little jets of pure flame on dry tassels and twigs, and tall spires and flat sheets with jagged flapping edges dancing here and there on grass tufts and bushes, big bonfires blazing in perfect storms of energy where heavy branches mixed with small ones lay smashed together in hundred cord piles, big red arches between spreading root-swells and trees growing close together, huge-fire-mantled trunks on the hill slopes glowing like bars of hot iron, violet-colored fire running up the tall trees, tracing the furrows of the bark in quick quivering rills, and lighting magnificent torches on dry shattered tops, and ever and anon, with a tremendous roar and burst of light, young trees clad in low-descending feathery branches vanishing in one flame two or three hundred feet high.

One of the most impressive and beautiful sights was made by the great fallen trunks lying on the hillsides all red and glowing like colossal iron bars fresh from a furnace, two hundred feet long some of them, and ten to twenty feet thick. After repeated burnings have consumed the bark and sapwood, the sound charred surface, being full of cracks and sprinkled with leaves, is quickly overspread with a pure, rich, furred, ruby glow almost flameless and smokeless, producing a marvelous effect in the night. Another grand and interesting sight are the fires on the tops of the largest living trees flaming above the green branches at a height of perhaps two hundred feet, entirely cut off from the ground-fires, and looking like signal beacons on watch towers. From one standpoint I sometimes saw a dozen or more, those in the distance looking like great stars above the forest roof. At first I could not imagine how these Sequoia lamps were lighted, but the very first night, strolling about waiting and watching, I saw the thing done again and again. The thick, fibrous bark of old trees is divided by deep, nearly continuous furrows, the sides of which are bearded with the bristling ends of fibres broken by the growth swelling of the trunk, and when the fire comes creeping around the feet of the trees, it runs up these bristly furrows in lovely pale blue quivering, bickering rills of flame with a low, earnest whispering sound to the lightning-shattered top of the trunk, which, in the dry Indian summer, with perhaps leaves and twigs and squirrel-gnawed cone-scales and seed-wings lodged in it, is readily ignited. These lamp-lighting rills, the most beautiful fire streams I ever saw, last only a minute or two, but the big lamps burn with varying brightness for days and weeks, throwing off sparks like the spray of a fountain, while ever and anon a shower of red coals comes sifting down through the branches, followed at times with startling effect by a big burned-off chunk weighing perhaps half a ton.

The immense bonfires where fifty or a hundred cords of peeled, split, smashed wood has been piled around some old giant by a single stroke of lightning is another grand sight in the night. The light is so great I found I could read common print three hundred yards from them, and the illumination of the circle of onlooking trees is indescribably impressive. Other big fires, roaring and booming like waterfalls, were blazing on the upper sides of trees on hillslopes, against which limbs broken off by heavy snow had rolled, while branches high overhead, tossed and shaken by the ascending air current, seemed to be writhing in pain. Perhaps the most startling phenomenon of all was the quick death of childlike Sequoias only a century or two of age. In the midst of the other comparatively slow and steady fire work one of these tall, beautiful saplings, leafy and branchy, would be seen blazing up suddenly, all in one heaving, booming, passionate flame reaching from the ground to the top of the tree and fifty to a hundred feet or more above it, with a smoke column bending forward and streaming away on the upper, free-flowing wind. To burn these green trees a strong fire of dry wood beneath them is required, to send up a current of air hot enough to distill inflammable gases from the leaves and sprays; then instead of the lower limbs gradually catching fire and igniting the next and next in succession, the whole tree seems to explode almost simultaneously, and with awful roaring and throbbing a round, tapering flame shoots up two or three hundred feet, and in a second or two is quenched, leaving the green spire a black, dead mast, bristled and roughened with down-curling boughs. Nearly all the trees that have been burned down are lying with their heads uphill, because they are burned far more deeply on the upper side, on account of broken limbs rolling down against them to make hot fires, while only leaves and twigs accumulate on the lower side and are quickly consumed without injury to the tree. But green, resinless Sequoia wood burns very slowly, and many successive fires are required to burn down a large tree. Fires can run only at intervals of several years, and when the ordinary amount of firewood that has rolled against the gigantic trunk is consumed, only a shallow scar is made, which is slowly deepened by recurring fires until far beyond the centre of gravity, and when at last the tree falls, it of course falls uphill. The healing folds of wood layers on some of the deeply burned trees show that centuries have elapsed since the last wounds were made.

When a great Sequoia falls, its head is smashed into fragments about as small as those made by lightning, which are mostly devoured by the first running, hunting fire that finds them, while the trunk is slowly wasted away by centuries of fire and weather. One of the most interesting fire actions on the trunk is the boring of those great tunnel-like hollows through which horsemen may gallop. All of these famous hollows are burned out of the solid wood, for no Sequoia is ever hollowed by decay. When the tree falls the brash trunk is often broken straight across into sections as if sawed; into these joints the fire creeps, and, on account of the great size of the broken ends, burns for weeks or even months without being much influenced by the weather. After the great glowing ends fronting each other have burned so far apart that their rims cease to burn, the fire continues to work on in the centres, and the ends become deeply concave. Then heat being radiated from side to side, the burning goes on in each section of the trunk independent of the other, until the diameter of the bore is so great that the heat radiated across from side to side is not sufficient to keep them burning. It appears, therefore, that only very large trees can receive the fire-auger and have any shell rim left.

Fire attacks the large trees only at the ground, consuming the fallen leaves and humus at their feet, doing them but little harm unless considerable quantities of fallen limbs happen to be piled about them, their thick mail of spongy, unpitchy, almost unburnable bark affording strong protection. Therefore the oldest and most perfect unscarred trees are found on ground that is nearly level, while those growing on hillsides, against which falling branches roll, are always deeply scarred on the upper side, and as we have seen are sometimes burned down. The saddest thing of all was to see the hopeful seedlings, many of them crinkled and bent with the pressure of winter snow, yet bravely aspiring at the top, helplessly perishing, and young trees, perfect spires of verdure and naturally immortal, suddenly changed to dead masts. Yet the sun looked cheerily down the openings in the forest roof, turning the black smoke to a beautiful brown, as if all was for the best.

(From *Our National Parks*, Ch. 9)

The Birds

The songs of the Yosemite winds and waterfalls are delightfully enriched with bird song, especially in the nesting time of spring and early summer. The most familiar and best known of all is the common robin, who may be seen every day, hopping about briskly on the meadows and uttering his cheery, enlivening call. The black-headed grosbeak, too, is here, with the Bullock oriole, and western tanager, brown song-sparrow, hermit thrush, the purple finch,—a fine singer, with head and throat of a rosy-red hue,—several species of warblers and vireos, kinglets, flycatchers, etc.

But the most wonderful singer of all the birds is the water-ouzel that dives into foaming rapids and feeds at the bottom, holding on in a wonderful way, living a charmed life.

Several species of humming-birds are always to be seen, darting and buzzing among the showy flowers. The little red-bellied nuthatches, the chickadees, and little brown creepers, threading the furrows of the bark of the pines, searching for food in the crevices. The large Steller's jay makes merry in the pine-tops; flocks of beautiful green swallows skim over the streams, and the noisy Clarke's crow may oftentimes be seen on the highest points around the Valley; and in the deep woods beyond the walls you may frequently hear and see the dusky grouse and the pile-ated woodpecker, or woodcock almost as large as a pigeon. The junco or snow-bird builds its nest on the floor of the Valley among the ferns; several species of sparrow are common and the beautiful lazuli bunting, a common bird in the underbrush, flitting about among the azalea and ceanothus bushes and enlivening the groves with his brilliant color; and on gravelly bars the spotted sandpiper is sometimes seen. Many woodpeckers dwell in the Valley; the familiar flicker, the Harris woodpecker and the species which so busily stores up acorns in the thick bark of the yellow pines.

The short, cold days of winter are also sweetened with the music and hopeful chatter of a considerable number of birds. No cheerier choir ever sang in snow. First and best of all is the water-ouzel, a dainty, dusky little bird about the size of a robin, that sings in sweet fluty song all winter and all summer, in storms and calms, sunshine and shadow, haunting the rapids and waterfalls with marvelous constancy, building his nest in the cleft of a rock bathed in spray. He is not web-footed, yet he dives fearlessly into foaming rapids, seeming to take the greater delight the more boisterous the stream, always as cheerful and calm as any linnet in a grove. All his gestures as he flits about amid the loud uproar of the falls bespeak the utmost simplicity and confidence—bird and stream one and inseparable. What a pair! yet they are well related. A finer bloom than the foam bell in an eddying pool is this little bird. We may miss the meaning of the loud-resounding torrent, but the flute-like voice of the bird—only love is in it.

A few robins, belated on their way down from the upper Meadows, linger in the Valley and make out to spend the winter in comparative comfort, feeding on the mistletoe berries that grow on the oaks. In the depths of the great forests, on the high meadows, in the severest altitudes, they seem as much at home as in the fields and orchards about the busy habitations of man, ascending the Sierra as the snow melts, following the green footsteps of Spring, until in July or August the highest glacier meadows are reached on the summit of the Range. Then, after the short summer is over, and their work in cheering and sweetening these lofty wilds is done, they gradually make their way down again in accord with the weather, keeping below the snow-storms, lingering here and there to feed on huckleberries and frost-nipped wild cherries growing on the upper slopes. Thence down to the vineyards and orchards of the lowlands to spend the winter; entering the gardens of the great towns as well as parks and fields, where the blessed wanderers are too often slaughtered for food—surely a bad use to put so fine a musician to; better make stove wood of pianos to feed the kitchen fire.

The kingfisher winters in the Valley, and the flicker and, of course, the carpenter woodpecker, that lays up large stores of acorns in the bark of trees; wrens also, with a few brown and gray linnets, and flocks of the arctic bluebird, making lively pictures among the snow-laden mistletoe bushes. Flocks of pigeons are often seen, and about six species of ducks, as the river is never wholly frozen over. Among these are the mallard and the beautiful wood-duck, now less common on account of being so often shot at. Flocks of wandering geese used to visit the Valley in March and April, and perhaps do so still, driven down by hunger or stress of weather while on their way across the Range. When pursued by the hunters I have frequently seen them try to fly over the walls of Lee Valley until tired out and compelled to re-alight. Yosemite magnitudes seem to be as deceptive to geese as to men, for after circling to a considerable height and forming regular harrow-shaped ranks they would suddenly find themselves in danger of being dashed against the face of the cliff, much nearer the bottom than the top. Then turning in confusion with loud screams they would try again and again until exhausted and compelled to descend. I have occasionally observed large flocks on their travels crossing the summits of the Range at a height of 12,000 to 13,000 feet above the level of the sea, and even in so rare an atmosphere as this they seemed to be sustaining themselves without extra effort. Strong, however, as they are of wind and wing, they cannot fly over Yosemite walls, starting from the bottom.

A pair of golden eagles have lived in the Valley ever since I first visited it, hunting all winter along the northern cliffs and down the river cañon. Their nest is on a ledge of the cliff over which pours the Nevada Fall. Perched on the top of a dead spar, they were always interested observers of the geese when they were being shot at. I once noticed one of the geese compelled to leave the flock on account of being sorely wounded, although it still seemed to fly pretty well. Immediately the eagles pursued it and no doubt struck it down, although I did not see the result of the hunt. Anyhow, it flew past me up the Valley, closely pursued.

One wild, stormy winter morning after five feet of snow had fallen on the floor of the Valley and the flying flakes driven by a strong wind still thickened the air, making darkness like the approach of night, I sallied forth to see what I might learn and enjoy. It was impossible to go very far without the aid of snow-shoes, but I found no great difficulty in making my way to a part of the river where one of my ouzels lived. I found him at home busy about his breakfast, apparently unaware of anything uncomfortable in the weather. Presently he flew out to a stone against which the icy current was beating, and turning his back to the wind, sang as delightfully as a lark in springtime.

After spending an hour or two with my favorite, I made my way across the Valley, boring and wallowing through the loose snow, to learn as much as possible about the way the other birds were spending their time. In winter one can always find them because they are then restricted to the north side of the Valley, especially the Indian Cañon groves, which from their peculiar exposure are the warmest.

I found most of the robins cowering on the lee side of the larger branches of the trees, where the snow could not fall on them, while two or three of the more venturesome were making desperate efforts to get at the mistletoe berries by clinging to the underside of the snow-crowned masses, back downward, something like woodpeckers. Every now and then some of the loose snow was dislodged and sifted down on the hungry birds, sending them screaming back to their companions in the grove, shivering and muttering like cold, hungry children.

Some of the sparrows were busy scratching and pecking at the feet of the larger trees where the snow had been shed off, gleaning seeds and benumbed insects, joined now and then by a robin weary of his unsuccessful efforts to get at the snow-covered mistletoe berries. The brave woodpeckers were clinging to the snowless sides of the larger boles and overarching branches of the camp trees, making short flights from side to side of the grove, pecking now and then at the acorns they had stored in the bark, and chattering aimlessly as if unable to keep still, evidently putting in the time in a very dull way. The hardy nuthatches were threading the open furrows of the barks in their usual industrious manner and uttering their quaint notes, giving no evidence of distress. The Steller's jays were, of course, making more noise and stir than all the other birds combined; ever coming and going with loud bluster, screaming as if each had a lump of melting sludge in his throat, and taking good care to improve every opportunity afforded by the darkness and confusion of the storm to steal from the acorn stores of the woodpeckers. One of the golden eagles made an impressive picture as he stood bolt upright on the top of a tall pine-stump, braving the storm, with his back to the wind and a tuft of snow piled on his broad shoulders, a monument of passive endurance. Thus every storm-bound bird seemed more or less uncomfortable, if not in distress. The storm was reflected in every gesture, and not one cheerful note, not to say song, came from a single bill. Their cowering, joyless endurance offered striking contrasts to the spontaneous, irrepressible gladness of the ouzel, who could no more help giving out sweet song than a rose sweet fragrance. He must sing, though the heavens fall.

(*The Yosemite*, Ch. 9)

The American Forests

The forests of America, however slighted by man, must have been a great delight to God; for they were the best he ever planted. The whole continent was a garden, and from the beginning it seemed to be favored above all the other wild parks and gardens of the globe. To prepare the ground, it was rolled and sifted in seas with infinite loving deliberation and fore-thought, lifted into the light, submerged and warmed over and over again, pressed and crumpled into folds and ridges, mountains, and hills, subsoiled with heaving volcanic fires, ploughed and ground and sculptured into scenery and soil with glaciers and rivers,—every feature growing and changing from beauty to beauty, higher and higher. And in the fullness of time it was planted in groves, and belts, and broad, exuberant, mantling forests, with the largest, most varied, most fruitful, and most beautiful trees in the world. Bright seas made its border, with wave embroidery and icebergs; gray deserts were outspread in the middle of it, mossy tundras on the north, savannas on the south, and blooming prairies and plains; while lakes and rivers shone through all the vast forests and openings, and happy birds and beasts gave delightful animation. Everywhere, everywhere over all the blessed continent, there were beauty and melody and kindly, wholesome, foodful abundance.

These forests were composed of about five hundred species of trees, all of them in some way useful to man, ranging in size from twenty-five feet in height and less than one foot in diameter at the ground to four hundred feet in height and more than twenty feet in diameter,—lordly monarchs proclaiming the gospel of beauty like apostles. For many a century after the ice-ploughs were melted, nature fed them and dressed them every day,—working like a man, a loving, devoted, painstaking gardener; fingering every leaf and flower and mossy furrowed bole; bending, trimming, modeling, balancing; painting them with the loveliest colors; bringing over them now clouds with cooling shadows and showers, now sunshine; fanning them with gentle winds and rustling their leaves; exercising them in every fibre with storms, and pruning them; loading them with flowers and fruit, loading them with snow, and ever making them more beautiful as the years rolled by. Wide-branching oak and elm in endless variety, walnut and maple, chestnut and beech, ilex and locust, touching limb to limb, spread a leafy translucent canopy along the coast of the Atlantic over the wrinkled folds and ridges of the Alleghanies,—a green billowy sea in summer, golden and purple in autumn, pearly gray like a steadfast frozen mist of interlacing branches and sprays in leafless, restful winter.

To the southward stretched dark, level-topped cypresses in knobby, tangled swamps, grassy savannas in the midst of them like lakes of light, groves of gay, sparkling spice-trees, magnolias and palms, glossy-leaved and blooming and shining continually. To the northward, over Maine and Ottawa, rose hosts of spiry, rosiny evergreens,—white pine and spruce, hemlock and cedar, shoulder to shoulder, laden with purple cones, their myriad needles sparkling and shimmering, covering hills and swamps, rocky headlands and domes, ever bravely aspiring and seeking the sky; the ground in their shade now snow-clad and frozen, now mossy and flowery; beaver meadows here and there, full of lilies and grass; lakes gleaming like eyes, and a silvery embroidery of rivers and creeks watering and brightening all the vast glad wilderness.

Thence westward were oak and elm, hickory and tupelo, gum and liriodendron, sassafras and ash, linden and laurel, spreading on ever wider in glorious exuberance over the great fertile basin of the Mississippi, over damp level bottoms, low dimpling hollows, and round dotting hills, embosoming sunny prairies and cheery park openings, half sunshine, half shade; while a dark wilderness of pines covered the region around the Great Lakes. Thence still westward swept the forests to right and left around grassy plains and deserts a thousand miles wide: irrepressible hosts of spruce and pinoberte, aspen and willow, nut-pine and juniper, cactus and yucca, caring nothing for drought, extending undaunted from mountain to mountain, over mesa and desert, to join the darkening multitudes of pines that covered the high Rocky ranges and the glorious forests along the coast of the moist and balmy Pacific, where new species of pine, giant cedars and spruces, silver firs and Sequoias, kings of their race, growing close together like grass in a meadow, poised their brave domes and spires in the sky, three hundred feet above the ferns and the lilies that enameled the ground; towering serene through the long centuries, preaching God's forestry fresh from heaven.

Here the forests reached their highest development. Hence they went wavering northward over icy Alaska, brave spruce and fir, poplar and birch, by the coasts and the rivers, to within sight of the Arctic Ocean. American forests! the glory of the world! Surveyed thus from the east to the west, from the north to the south, they are rich beyond thought, immortal, immeasurable, enough and to spare for every feeding, sheltering beast and bird, insect and son of Adam; and nobody need have cared had there been no pines in Norway, no cedars and deodars on Lebanon and the Himalayas, no vine-clad selvas in the basin of the Amazon. With such variety, harmony, and triumphant exuberance, even nature, it would seem, might have rested content with the forests of North America, and planted no more.

So they appeared a few centuries ago when they were rejoicing in wildness. The Indians with stone axes could do them no more harm than could gnawing beavers and browsing moose. Even the fires of the Indians and the fierce shattering lightning seemed to work together only for good in clearing spots here and there for smooth garden prairies, and openings for sunflowers seeking the light. But when the steel axe of the white man rang out on the startled air their doom was sealed. Every tree heard the bodeful sound, and pillars of smoke gave the sign in the sky.

I suppose we need not go mourning the buffaloes. In the nature of things they had to give place to better cattle, though the change might have been made without barbarous wickedness. Likewise many of nature's five hundred kinds of wild trees had to make way for orchards and cornfields. In the settlement and civilization of the country, bread more than timber or beauty was wanted; and in the blindness of hunger, the early settlers, claiming Heaven as their guide, regarded God's trees as only a larger kind of pernicious weeds, extremely hard to get rid of. Accordingly, with no eye to the future, these pious destroyers waged interminable forest wars; chips flew thick and fast; trees in their beauty fell crashing by millions, smashed to confusion, and the smoke of their burning has been rising to heaven more than two hundred years. After the Atlantic coast from Maine to Georgia had been mostly cleared and scorched into melancholy ruins, the over-flowing multitude of bread and money seekers poured over the Alleghanies into the fertile middle West, spreading ruthless devastation ever wider and farther over the rich valley of the Mississippi and the vast shadowy pine region about the Great Lakes. Thence still westward, the invading horde of destroyers called settlers made its fiery way over the broad Rocky Mountains, felling and burning more fiercely than ever, until at last it has reached the wild side of the continent, and entered the last of the great aboriginal forests on the shores of the Pacific.

Surely, then, it should not be wondered at that lovers of their country, bewailing its baldness, are now crying aloud, "Save what is left of the forests!" Clearing has surely now gone far enough; soon timber will be scarce, and not a grove will be left to rest in or pray in. The remnant protected will yield plenty of timber, a perennial harvest for every right use, without further diminution of its area, and will continue to cover the springs of the rivers that rise in the mountains and give irrigating waters to the dry valleys at their feet, prevent wasting floods and be a blessing to everybody forever.

Every other civilized nation in the world has been compelled to care for its forests, and so must we if waste and destruction are not to go on to the bitter end, leaving America as barren as Palestine or Spain. In its calmer moments, in the midst of bewildering hunger and war and restless over-industry, Prussia has learned that the forest plays an important part in human progress, and that the advance in civilization only makes it more indispensable. It has, therefore, as shown by Mr. Pinchot, refused to deliver its forests to more or less speedy destruction by permitting them to pass into private ownership. But the state woodlands are not allowed to lie idle. On the contrary, they are made to produce as much timber as is possible without spoiling them. In the administration of its forests, the state righteously considers itself bound to treat them as a trust for the nation as a whole, and to keep in view the common good of the people for all time.

In France no government forests have been sold since 1870. On the other hand, about one half of the fifty million francs spent on forestry has been given to engineering works, to make the replanting of denuded areas possible. The disappearance of the forests in the first place, it is claimed, may be traced in most cases directly to mountain pasturage. The provisions of the Code concerning private woodlands are substantially these: no private owner may clear his woodlands without giving notice to the government at least four months in advance, and the forest service may forbid the clearing on the following grounds,—to maintain the soil on mountains, to defend the soil against erosion and flooding by rivers or torrents, to insure the existence of springs or watercourses, to protect the dunes and seashore, etc. A proprietor who has cleared his forest without permission is subject to heavy fine, and in addition may be made to replant the cleared area.

In Switzerland, after many laws like our own had been found wanting, the Swiss forest school was established in 1865, and soon after the federal forest law was enacted, which is binding over nearly two thirds of the country. Under its provisions, the cantons must appoint and pay the number of suitably educated foresters required for the fulfillment of the forest law; and in the organization of a normally stocked forest, the object of first importance must be the cutting each year of an amount of timber equal to the total annual increase, and no more.

The Russian government passed a law in 1888, declaring that clearing is forbidden in protected forests, and is allowed in others "only when its effects will not be to disturb the suitable relations which should exist between forest and agricultural lands."

Even Japan is ahead of us in the management of her forests. They cover an area of about twenty-nine million acres. The feudal lords valued the woodlands, and enacted vigorous protective laws; and when, in the latest civil war, the Mikado government destroyed the feudal system, it declared the forests that had belonged to the feudal lords to be the property of the state, promulgated a forest law binding on the whole kingdom, and founded a school of forestry in Tokyo. The forest service does not rest satisfied with the present proportion of woodland, but looks to planting the best forest trees it can find in any country, if likely to be useful and to thrive in Japan.

In India systematic forest management was begun about forty years ago, under difficulties—presented by the character of the country, the prevalence of running fires, opposition from lumbermen, settlers, etc.—not unlike those which confront us now. Of the total area of government forests, perhaps seventy million acres, fifty-five million acres have been brought under the control of the forestry department,—a larger area than that of all our national parks and reservations. The chief aims of the administration are effective protection of the forests from fire, an efficient system of regeneration, and cheap transportation of the forest products; the results so far have been most beneficial and encouraging.

It seems, therefore, that almost every civilized nation can give us a lesson on the management and care of forests. So far our government has done nothing effective with its forests, though the best in the world, but is like a rich and foolish spendthrift who has inherited a magnificent estate in perfect order, and then has left his fields and meadows, forests and parks, to be sold and plundered and wasted at will, depending on their inexhaustible abundance. Now it is plain that the forests are not inexhaustible, and that quick measures must be taken if ruin is to be avoided. Year by year the remnant is growing smaller before the axe and fire, while the laws in existence provide neither for the protection of the timber from destruction nor for its use where it is most needed....

... Under the timber and stone act of 1878, which might well have been called the "dust and ashes act," any citizen of the United States could take up one hundred and sixty acres of timber land, and by paying two dollars and a half an acre for it obtain title. There was some virtuous effort made with a view to limit the operations of the act by requiring that the purchaser should make affidavit that he was entering the land exclusively for his own use, and by not allowing any association to enter more than one hundred and sixty acres. Nevertheless, under this act wealthy corporations have fraudulently obtained title to from ten thousand to twenty thousand acres or more. The plan was usually as follows: A mill company, desirous of getting title to a large body of redwood or sugar-pine land, first blurred the eyes and ears of the land agents, and then hired men to enter the land they wanted, and immediately deed it to the company after a nominal compliance with the law; false swearing in the wilderness against the government being held of no account. In one case which came under the observation of Mr. Bowers, it was the practice of a lumber company to hire the entire crew of every vessel which might happen to touch at any port in the redwood belt, to enter one hundred and sixty acres each and immediately deed the land to the company, in consideration of the company's paying all expenses and giving the jolly sailors fifty dollars apiece for their trouble.

By such methods have our magnificent redwoods and much of the sugar-pine forests of the Sierra Nevada been absorbed by foreign and resident capitalists. Uncle Sam is not often called a fool in business matters, yet he has sold millions of acres of timber land at two dollars and a half an acre on which a single tree was worth more than a hundred dollars. But this priceless land has been patented, and nothing can be done now about the crazy bargain. According to the everlasting law of righteousness, even the fraudulent buyers at less than one per cent of its value are making little or nothing, on account of fierce competition. The trees are felled, and about half of each giant is left on the ground to be converted into smoke and ashes; the better half is sawed into choice lumber and sold to citizens of the United States or to foreigners: thus robbing the country of its glory and impoverishing it without right benefit to anybody,—a bad, black business from beginning to end....

...Notwithstanding all the waste and use which have been going on unchecked like a storm for more than two centuries, it is not yet too late—though it is high time for the government to begin a rational administration of its forests. About seventy million acres it still owns,—enough for all the country, if wisely used. These residual forests are generally on mountain slopes, just where they are doing the most good, and where their removal would be followed by the greatest number of evils; the lands they cover are too rocky and high for agriculture, and can never be made as valuable for any other crop as for the present crop of trees. It has been shown over and over again that if these mountains were to be stripped of their trees and underbrush, and kept bare and sodless by hordes of sheep and the innumerable fires the shepherds set, besides those of the millmen, prospectors, shake-makers, and all sorts of adventurers, both lowlands and mountains would speedily become little better than desert, compared with their present beneficent fertility. During heavy rainfalls and while the winter accumulations of snow were melting, the large streams would swell into destructive torrents, cutting deep, rugged-edged gullies, carrying away the fertile humus and soil as well as sand and rocks, filling up and overflowing their lower channels, and covering the lowland fields with raw detritus. Drought and barrenness would follow.

In their natural condition, or under wise management, keeping out destructive sheep, preventing fires, selecting the trees that should be cut for lumber, and preserving the young ones and the shrubs and sod of herbaceous vegetation, these forests would be a never failing fountain of wealth and beauty. The cool shades of the forest give rise to moist beds and currents of air, and the sod of grasses and the various flowering plants and shrubs thus fostered, together with the network and sponge of tree roots, absorb and hold back the rain and the waters from melting snow, compelling them to ooze and percolate and flow gently through the soil in streams that never dry. All the pine needles and rootlets and blades of grass, and the fallen, decaying trunks of trees, are dams, storing the bounty of the clouds and dispensing it in perennial life-giving streams, instead of allowing it to gather suddenly and rush headlong in short-lived devastating floods. Everybody on the dry side of the continent is beginning to find this out, and, in view of the waste going on, is growing more and more anxious for government protection. The outcries we hear against forest reservations come mostly from thieves who are wealthy and steal timber by wholesale. They have so long been allowed to steal and destroy in peace that any impediment to forest robbery is denounced as a cruel and irreligious interference with "vested rights," likely to endanger the repose of all ungodly welfare.

Gold, gold, gold! How strong a voice that metal has!

"O wae for the siller, it is sae preva'lin'!"

Even in Congress a sizable chunk of gold, carefully concealed, will outtalk and outfight all the nation on a subject like forestry, well smothered in ignorance, and in which the money interests of only a few are conspicuously involved. Under these circumstances, the bawling, blethering oratorical stuff drowns the voice of God himself. Yet the dawn of a new day in forestry is breaking. Honest citizens see that only the rights of the government are being trampled, not those of the settlers. Only what belongs to all alike is reserved, and every acre that is left should be held together under the federal government as a basis for a general policy of administration for the public good. The people will not always be deceived by selfish opposition, whether from lumber and mining corporations or from sheepmen and prospectors, however cunningly brought forward underneath fables and gold.

Emerson says that things refuse to be mismanaged long. An exception would seem to be found in the case of our forests, which have been mismanaged rather long, and now come desperately near being like smashed eggs and spilt milk. Still, in the long run the world does not move backward. The wonderful advance made in the last few years, in creating four national parks in the West, and thirty forest reservations, embracing nearly forty million acres; and in the planting of the borders of streets and highways and spacious parks in all the great cities, to satisfy the natural taste and hunger for landscape beauty and righteousness that God has put, in some measure, into every human being and animal, shows the trend of awakening public opinion. The making of the far-famed New York Central Park was opposed by even good men, with misguided pluck, perseverance, and ingenuity; but straight right won its way, and now that park is appreciated. So we confidently believe it will be with our great national parks and forest reservations. There will be a period of indifference on the part of the rich, sleepy with wealth, and of the toiling millions, sleepy with poverty, most of whom never saw a forest; a period of screaming protest and objection from the plunderers, who are as unconscionable and enterprising as Satan. But light is surely coming, and the friends of destruction will preach and bewail in vain.

The United States government has always been proud of the welcome it has extended to good men of every nation, seeking freedom and homes and bread. Let them be welcomed still as nature welcomes them, to the woods as well as to the prairies and plains. No place is too good for good men, and still there is room. They are invited to heaven, and may well be allowed in America. Every place is made better by them. Let them be as free to pick gold and gems from the hills, to cut and hew, dig and plant, for homes and bread, as the birds are to pick berries from the wild bushes, and moss and leaves for nests. The ground will be glad to feed them, and the pines will come down from the mountains for their homes as willingly as the cedars came from Lebanon for Solomon's temple. Nor will the woods be the worse for this use, or their benign influences be diminished any more than the sun is diminished by shining. Mere destroyers, however, tree-killers, wool and mutton men, spreading death and confusion in the fairest groves and gardens ever planted,—let the government hasten to cast them out and make an end of them. For it must be told again and again, and be burningly borne in mind, that just now, while protective measures are being deliberated languidly, destruction and use are speeding on faster and farther every day. The axe and saw are insanely busy, chips are flying thick as snowflakes, and every summer thousands of acres of priceless forests, with their underbrush, soil, springs, climate, scenery, and religion, are vanishing away in clouds of smoke, while, except in the national parks, not one forest guard is employed.

All sorts of local laws and regulations have been tried and found wanting, and the costly lessons of our own experience, as well as that of every civilized nation, show conclusively that the fate of the remnant of our forests is in the hands of the federal government, and that if the remnant is to be saved at all, it must be saved quickly.

Any fool can destroy trees. They cannot run away; and if they could, they would still be destroyed,—chased and hunted down as long as fun or a dollar could be got out of their bark hides, branching horns, or magnificent bole backbones. Few that fell trees plant them; nor would planting avail much towards getting back anything like the noble primeval forests. During a man's life only saplings can be grown, in the place of the old trees—tens of centuries old—that have been destroyed. It took more than three thousand years to make some of the trees in these Western woods,—trees that are still standing in perfect strength and beauty, waving and singing in the mighty forests of the Sierra. Through all the wonderful, eventful centuries since Christ's time—and long before that—God has cared for these trees, saved them from drought, disease, avalanches, and a thousand straining, leveling tempests and floods; but he cannot save them from fools,—only Uncle Sam can do that.

(From *Our National Parks,* Ch. 10)

The Grand Canyon of the Colorado

Happy nowadays is the tourist, with earth's wonders, new and old, spread invitingly open before him, and a host of able workers as his slaves making everything easy, padding plush about him, grading roads for him, boring tunnels, moving hills out of his way, eager, like the Devil, to show him all the kingdoms of the world and their glory and foolishness, spiritualizing travel for him with lightning and steam, abolishing space and time and almost everything else. Little children and tender, pulpy people, as well as storm-seasoned explorers, may now go almost everywhere in smooth comfort, cross oceans and deserts scarce accessible to fishes and birds, and, dragged by steel horses, go up high mountains, riding gloriously beneath starry showers of sparks, ascending like Elijah in a whirlwind and chariot of fire.

First of the wonders of the great West to be brought within reach of the tourist were the Yosemite and the Big Trees, on the completion of the first transcontinental railway; next came the Yellowstone and icy Alaska, by the northern roads; and last the Grand Canyon of the Colorado, which, naturally the hardest to reach, has now become, by a branch of the Santa Fe, the most accessible of all.

Of course, with this wonderful extension of steel ways through our wildness there is loss as well as gain. Nearly all railroads are bordered by belts of desolation. The finest wilderness perishes as if stricken with pestilence. Bird and beast people, if not the dryads, are frightened from the groves. Too often the groves also vanish, leaving nothing but ashes. Fortunately, nature has a few big places beyond man's power to spoil — the ocean, the two icy ends of the globe, and the Grand Canyon.

When I first heard of the Santa Fe trains running to the edge of the Grand Canyon of Arizona, I was troubled with thoughts of the disenchantment likely to follow. But last winter, when I saw those trains crawling along through the pines of the Coconino Forest and close up to the brink of the chasm at Bright Angel, I was glad to discover that in the presence of such stupendous scenery they are nothing. The locomotives and trains are mere beetles and caterpillars, and the noise they make is as little disturbing as the hooting of an owl in the lonely woods.

In a dry, hot, monotonous forested plateau, seemingly boundless, you come suddenly and without warning upon the abrupt edge of a gigantic sunken landscape of the wildest, most multitudinous features, and those features, sharp and angular, are made out of flat beds of limestone and sandstone forming a spiry, jagged, gloriously colored mountain range countersunk in a level gray plain. It is a hard job to sketch it even in scrawniest outline; and, try as I may, not in the least sparing myself, I cannot tell the hundredth part of the wonders of its features — the side canyons, gorges, alcoves, cloisters, and amphitheaters of vast sweep and depth, carved in its magnificent walls; the throng of great architectural rocks it contains resembling castles, cathedrals, temples, and palaces, towered and spired and painted, some of them nearly a mile high, yet beneath one's feet. All this, however, is less difficult than to give any idea of the impression of wild, primeval beauty and power one receives in merely gazing from its brink. The view down the gulf of color and over the rim of its wonderful wall, more than any other view I know, leads us to think of our earth as a star with stars swimming in light, every radiant spire pointing the way to the heavens....

... Every feature of Nature's big face is beautiful, — height and hollow, wrinkle, furrow, and line, — and this is the main master-furrow of its kind on our continent, incomparably greater and more impressive than any other yet discovered, or likely to be discovered, now that all the great rivers have been traced to their heads.

The Colorado River rises in the heart of the continent on the dividing ranges and ridges between the two oceans, drains thousands of snowy mountains through narrow or spacious valleys, and thence through canyons of every color, sheer-walled and deep, all of which seem to be represented in this one grand canyon of canyons.

It is very hard to give anything like an adequate conception of its size; much more of its color, its vast wall-sculpture, the wealth of ornate architectural buildings that fill it, or, most of all, the tremendous impression it makes. According to Major Powell, it is about two hundred and seventeen miles long, from five to fifteen miles wide from rim to rim, and from about five thousand to six thousand feet deep. So tremendous a chasm would be one of the world's greatest wonders even if, like ordinary canyons cut in sedimentary rocks, it were empty and its walls were simple. But instead of being plain, the walls are so deeply and elaborately carved into all sorts of recesses — alcoves, cirques, amphitheaters, and side canyons — that, were you to trace the rim closely around on both sides, your journey would be nearly a thousand miles long. Into all these recesses the level, continuous beds of rock in ledges and benches, with their various colors, run like broad ribbons, marvelously beautiful and effective even at a distance of ten or twelve miles. And the vast space these glorious walls inclose, instead of being empty, is crowded with gigantic architectural rock forms gorgeously colored and adorned with towers and spires like works of art.

Looking down from this level plateau, we are more impressed with a feeling of being on the top of everything than when looking from the summit of a mountain. From side to side of the vast gulf, temples, palaces, towers, and spires come soaring up in thick array half a mile or nearly a mile above their sunken, hidden bases, some to a level with our standpoint, but none higher. And in the inspiring morning light all are so fresh and rosy-looking that they seem new-born; as if, like the quick-growing crimson snowplants of the California woods, they had just sprung up, hatched by the warm, brooding, motherly weather.

In trying to describe the great pines and sequoias of the Sierra, I have often thought that if one of these trees could be set by itself in some city park, its grandeur might there be impressively realized; while in its home forests, where all magnitudes are great, the weary, satiated traveler sees none of them truly. It is so with these majestic rock structures.

Though mere residual masses of the plateau, they are dowered with the grandeur and repose of mountains, together with the finely chiseled carving and modeling of man's temples and palaces, and often, to a considerable extent, with their symmetry. Some, closely observed, look like ruins; but even these stand plumb and true, and show architectural forms loaded with lines strictly regular and decorative, and all are arrayed in colors that storms and time seem only to brighten. They are not placed in regular rows in line with the river, but "a' through ither," as the Scotch say, in lavish, exuberant crowds, as if nature in wildest extravagance held her bravest structures as common as gravel-piles. Yonder stands a spiry cathedral nearly five thousand feet in height, nobly symmetrical, with sheer buttressed walls and arched doors and windows, as richly finished and decorated with sculptures as the great rock temples of India or Egypt. Beside it rises a huge castle with arched gateway, turrets, watch-towers, ramparts, etc., and to right and left palaces, obelisks, and pyramids fairly fill the gulf, all colossal and all lavishly painted and carved. Here and there a flat-topped structure may be seen, or one imperfectly domed; but the prevailing style is ornate Gothic, with many hints of Egyptian and Indian.

Throughout this vast extent of wild architecture — nature's own capital city — there seem to be no ordinary dwellings. All look like grand and important public structures, except perhaps some of the lower pyramids, broad-based and sharp-pointed, covered with down-flowing talus like loosely set tents with hollow, sagging sides. The roofs often have disintegrated rocks heaped and draggled over them, but in the main the masonry is firm and laid in regular courses, as if done by square and rule.

Nevertheless they are ever changing; their tops are now a dome, now a flat table or a spire, as harder or softer strata are reached in their slow degradation, while the sides, with all their fine moldings, are being steadily undermined and eaten away. But no essential change in style or color is thus effected. From century to century they stand the same. What seems confusion among the rough earth-quake-shaken crags nearest one comes to order as soon as the main plan of the various structures appears. Every building, however complicated and laden with ornamental lines, is at one with itself and every one of its neighbors, for the same characteristic controlling belts of color and solid strata extend with wonderful constancy for very great distances, and pass through and give style to thousands of separate structures, however their smaller characters may vary.

Of all the various kinds of ornamental work displayed — carving, tracery on cliff faces, moldings, arches, pinnacles — none is more admirably effective or charms more than the webs of rain-channeled taluses. Marvelously extensive, without the slightest appearance of waste or excess, they cover roofs and dome tops and the base of every cliff, belt each spire and pyramid and massy, towering temple, and in beautiful continuous lines go sweeping along the great walls in and out around all the intricate system of side canyons, amphitheaters, cirques, and scallops into which they are sculptured. From one point hundreds of miles of the fairy embroidery may be traced. It is all so fine and orderly that it would seem that not only had the clouds and streams been kept harmoniously busy in the making of it, but that every raindrop sent like a bullet to a mark had been the subject of a separate thought, so sure is the outcome of beauty through the stormy centuries. Surely nowhere else are there illustrations so striking of the natural beauty of desolation and death, so many of nature's own mountain buildings wasting in glory of high desert air — going to dust. See how steadfast in beauty they all are in their going. Look again and again how the rough, dusty boulders and sand of disintegration from the upper ledges wreathe in beauty for ashes — as in the flowers of a prairie after fires — but here the very dust and ashes are beautiful.

Gazing across the mighty chasm, we at last discover that it is not its great depth nor length, nor yet these wonderful buildings, that most impresses us. It is its immense width, sharply defined by precipitous walls plunging suddenly down from a flat plain, declaring in terms instantly apprehended that the vast gulf is a gash in the once unbroken plateau, made by slow, orderly erosion and removal of huge beds of rocks. Other valleys of erosion are as great — in all their dimensions some are greater — but none of these produces an effect on the imagination at once so quick and profound, coming without study, given at a glance. Therefore by far the greatest and most influential feature of this view from Bright Angel or any other of the canyon views is the opposite wall. Of the one beneath our feet we see only fragmentary sections in cirques and amphitheaters and on the sides of the out-jutting promontories between them, while the other, though far distant, is beheld in all its glory of color and noble proportions — the one supreme beauty and wonder to which the eye is ever turning. For while charming with its beauty it tells the story of the stupendous erosion of the canyon — the foundation of the unspeakable impression made on everybody. It seems a gigantic statement for even nature to make, all in one mighty stone word, apprehended at once like a burst of light, celestial color its natural vesture, coming in glory to mind and heart as to a home prepared for it from the very beginning. Wildness so godful, cosmic, primeval, bestows a new sense of earth's beauty and size. Not even from high mountains does the world seem so wide, so like a star in glory of light on its way through the heavens....

(From *Century* Magazine, Nov. 1, 1902)

Sage

Around the World

Martinez, California, July 20, 1904

I have been away more than a year on a long, crooked trip around the world and have seen a little of many countries—the parks and gardens and art galleries of Europe; broad, fertile Russia, the Crimea, and grand forests and glaciers and snowy peaks of the Caucasus; the wide, billowy, densely forested Ural mountains; the vast, fertile levels, plains and woods of Siberia; beautiful Manchuria with its charming hills and dales and low, richly wooded mountains, endless wheat and millet fields, great rivers and plains; picturesque Japan; the mountainous island-dotted coast of China; the loftiest ice-laden summits of the Himalaya and their deodar forests and rivers, and the swarming cities at their feet, temples, etc.; old Egypt, its one green valley stretching between hot, tawny deserts, and its stupendous monuments of auld lang syne; balmy, palmy Ceylon, wonderful and beautiful; Australia and New Zealand where people, animals, plants and rocks all are strange and novel to me; the gloriously beautiful Malay archipelago; the Philippines, etc. How I wish you had been with me! This sketch, however slight, will, I hope, help you to recall some of your own wide, round-the-world wanderings.

(Excerpt from letter to Prof. J.D. Butler)

A Tribute to Robert Burns

In this speech read aloud to a group of prominent local Scots at a 1907 banquet in Southern California, Muir described how he charmed the animals he met on his long wanderings by singing and whistling Burns's poems.

It is surely a fine thing to stop now and then in the throng of our common everyday work to contemplate the works and ways of God's great men, sent down from time to time to guide and bless mankind. And it is glorious to know that the greatest of all that have appeared in the last century was a Scotsman, Robert Burns. And therefore we Scotsmen tonight are celebrating the birthday of not only the greatest of Scotsmen but one of the greatest of all the world's great men. His lessons of divine love and sympathy to humanity—the morals and religion, God's unchangeable foundational truth and righteousness, which he preached in his poems and sent forth white hot from his heart, have gone ringing and singing around the globe, stirring the heart of every nation and race. And so universally and gladly have these lessons been learned and adopted, nowadays almost everybody worth mentioning claims to be Scottish or half Scottish, with the right to help to celebrate this blessed day of his birth. No wonder then Robert Burns is our joy and pride, and that we love and almost worship him, now that we have come to know him, and all the world knows him and loves him.

And yet what a hard, sad life he had in his own Scotland, among his ain folk. "The largest soul of all the British lands," says Carlyle, "and perhaps no man had so false a reception from his fellow men." Wae's me that Scotsmen let our best Scotsman starve. And though he now has love and honor beyond bounds, and noble monuments to his worth are rising in every land on the globe, the idea of Burns forlorn, starving in Scotland blinds us with tears. He died a hundred and ten years ago in a storm of trouble and pain, full of despairing care about his wife and bairns, deserted by his canny fault-counting friends. But in the midst of it all he knew something of the worth of his short life's work. "The sterling of his honest worth," he said, "no poverty could debase," and his independent British mind oppression might bend but could not subdue. And when lying forsaken in the shadow of death he said to his despairing wife, "Never mind, I'll be more respected a hundred years after I am dead than I am now." How gloriously this prophecy has been fulfilled! His fame began to grow from the day of his death, and year by year it has grown higher and brighter, cheering and enriching all mankind. In the halls of fame there is none like his. "The birthday of no other human being is so universally celebrated," and as Lord Rosebery well says, "He reigns over a greater dominion than any empire the world has yet seen, and his name excites a more enthusiastic worship than that of any saint in the calendar." And this marvelous evergrowing admiring devotion is perfectly natural. Could Burns have seen it how glad he would have been. What is the secret of it all? It is his glorious inspiring genius derived from heaven, with glowing all-embracing sympathy. The man of science, the naturalist, too often loses sight of the essential oneness of all living beings in seeking to classify them in kingdoms, orders, families, genera, species, etc., taking note of the kind and arrangement of limbs, teeth, toes, scales, hair, feathers, etc., measured and set forth in meters, centimeters, and millimeters, while the eye of the poet, the seer, never closes on the kinship of all God's creatures, and his heart ever beats in sympathy with great and small alike as "earth-born companions and fellow mortals" equally dependent on heaven's eternal love. As far as I know none in all the world so clearly recognized the loving fatherhood of God as our ain Robert Burns, and none in whose heart there flowed so quick and kind and universal a sympathy. Call to mind his field mouse, "Wee sleekit cowrin' tim'rous beastie," turned out of house and home, its store of food scattered, and cold winter coming on; the tender pity for the silly sheep and cattle, and ilk hopping bird "wee help-less thing" shelterless in a winter snowstorm; the wounded hare crying like a child—the unfortunate daisy, "wee modest crimson-tippet flower" crushed amang the stoure. He extended pity and sympathy even to the deil, entering into his feelings and hoping he might perhaps be able to repent and escape from his gloomy den:

> "Hear me auld hangie for a wee,
> An' let poor damned bodies be;
> I'm sure sma' pleasure it can gie,
> E'n to a deil
> To skelp an' scaud poor dogs like me
> An' hear us squeel!
> But fare you weel auld Nickie-ben,
> O wad ye tak a thought an' men!
> Ye aiblins mught—I dinna ken,
> Still hae a stake
> I'm wae to think upo' yon den
> Even for your sake."

Nothing could abate one jot his passionate love for Scotland. In his early days in the midst of poortith cauld and the weary endless battle for bread he thus tells his patriotic ambition:

"A wish that to my latest hour
Will strongly heave my breast,
That I for poor auld Scotland's sake
Some useful plan or book might make
Or sing a song at least."

And he sang: "Scots Wha Hae With Wallace Bled,"
"A Man's a Man For A' That," "The Banks and Braes O'
Bonnie Doon," "Mary in Heaven," "Auld Lang Syne,"
"The Cotter's Saturday Night," charming and electrifying
the great and lowly alike, and showing that "From scenes
like these old Scotia's grandeur springs, that makes her
loved at home, revered abroad."

These and many others he sang in the few troubled
years alloted him and made all the world his debtor. But
Scotland's debt is in several ways peculiar. He brought her
forward into bright light and made her great and glorious
among the nations, and he saved the grand Scottish
language when it was in danger of sinking in English.
Though unfit for science it is wonderfully rich in love-
words for telling "A' the pleasure o' the heart, the lover
and the friend." And since Burns' poems are enshrined in
gude braid Scots the world will never allow it to perish.

None in this land of plenty can realize the hardships
under which Burns' immortal work was accomplished.
Of what we call education he had almost nothing. He was
brought up on the Bible in his father's auld clay biggin.
This was his school and college, his poor neighbors and
the fields and the sky his university. He sang untrained
like a stream or a bird, while under the crushing weight of
doure unchangeable poverty—a kind of poverty unknown
in America where doors open everywhere to affluence
and ease. When he was in the fullness of strength of early
manhood, standing five feet ten, his great eyes flashing,

such eyes as Walter Scott said he had never seen in any other countenance; as bold and brave and bonnie a chiel as ever trod yird, he toiled from daybreak till dark digging, plowing, reaping, thrashing for three dollars a month!

On my lonely walks I often thought how fine it would be to have the company of Burns. And indeed he was always with me, for I had him by heart. On my first long walk from Indiana to the Gulf of Mexico I carried a copy of Burns' poems and sang them all the way. The whole country and the people, beasts and birds, seemed to like them. In the Sierra I sang and whistled them to the squirrels and birds and they were charmed out of fear and gathered close about me. So real was his companionship he oftentimes seemed to be with me in the flesh however wild and strange the places where I wandered—the Arctic tundras so like the heathery muirlands of Scotland, the leafy Alleghanies, icy Alps and Himalaya, Manchuria, Siberia, Australia, New Zealand—everywhere Burns seemed at home and his poems fitted everybody.

Wherever a Scotsman goes there goes Burns. His grand whole Catholic soul squares with the good of it all, therefore we find him in everything everywhere. Throughout these last hundred and ten years thousands of good men have been telling God's love; but the man who has done most to warm human hearts and bring to light the kinship of the world is Burns, Robert Burns, the Scotsman.

(From *The Pasadena Evening Star*, Jan. 26, 1907)

Nature and God

In 1909, Muir was a widower living alone in the Martinez family homestead, lobbying on environmental issues and trying to organize his articles and journals accumulated over the years into new book projects. In a talk given to the California Federation of Women's Clubs in San Francisco that spring, he remarked, "I'm glad that I got to California soon enough to see the State in all its original untrammelled beauty. I have walked five hundred miles through the San Joaquin and Sacramento Valleys when they were an unbroken mass of golden bloom. I made my bed among the wildflowers where the march of commerce has obliterated God's handiwork. There is not much left to us of beauty because commerce seizes upon all it can reach that is dollarable." He shared the following reflections with a journalist who spent three days with him in the Alhambra Valley.

There are no accidents in Nature. Every motion of the constantly shifting bodies in the world is timed to the occasion for some definite, fore-ordered end. The flowers blossom in obedience to the same law that marks the course of constellations, and the song of a bird is the echo of a universal symphony. Nature is one, and to me the greatest delight of observation and study is to discover new unities in this all-embracing and eternal harmony.

Little men, with only a book knowledge of science, have seized upon evolution as an escape from the idea of a God. 'Evolution!'— a wonderful, mouth-filling word, isn't it? It covers a world of ignorance. Just say 'evolution' and you have explained every phenomenon of Nature and explained away God. It sounds big and wise. Evolution, they say, brought the earth through its glacial periods, caused the snow blanket to recede, and the flower carpet to follow it, raised the forests of the world, developed animal life from the jelly-fish to the thinking man.

But what caused evolution? There they stick. To my mind, it is inconceivable that a plan that has worked out, through unthinkable millions of years, without one hitch or one mistake, the development of beauty that has made every microscopic particle of matter perform its function in harmony with every other in the universe — that such a plan is the blind product of an unthinking abstraction. No; somewhere, before evolution was, was an Intelligence that laid out the plan, and evolution is the process, not the origin, of the harmony. You may call that Intelligence what you please: I cannot see why so many people object to call it God....

... People talk about creation as a remote fact of history, as if it were something that was attended to a long time ago, and finished at the time. But creation was not an act; it is a process; and it is going on today as much as it ever was. But Nature is not in a hurry. With God 'a thousand years is as a day.' Suppose you could have been a spirit in one of the past periods of the creation of the world, and that the Archangel Gabriel had taken you to a place where you could see the earth as it was then covered miles deep with snow and ice, the air still full of swirling snowflakes that seemed to be burying the world forever. Suppose he showed you this silent, frozen, characterless waste (as it would seem to you), and told you that God was creating here a world of beauty, of seas and mountains, of flowers and forests, of song-birds and men. Suppose you flew away and were gone for a thousand years, and then looked again. You could not see that the scene had altered a particle. Another thousand years. Still no change that you could see.

'Creation?' you cry out, 'I see nothing being done here.'

'Patience,' is the angel's answer. 'Down beneath these miles of snow the ice is shifting, grinding, slicing, leveling, building, making a sierra here, a broad valley there, scooping out a Yosemite, leveling off a plain, polishing boulders, marking rock ledges with the handwriting of God, making ready warm glades for grass and flowers, mountain slopes for majestic forests, homes for birds — breaking ground for beauty.'

At the end of a few million years your visits are rewarded. The ice-cap has receded from parts of the earth. Seas are exposed, land has come into view, flowers have followed the retreating ice, trees nestle in the cañons and climb the mountain shoulders, birds are caroling, fish dart along the singing streams, man is abroad to enjoy the beauties of the earth.

This is creation. All this is going on today, only men are blind to see it. They think only of food. They are not content to provide three meals a day; they must have enough for a thousand meals. And so they build ships to carry the food that they call commerce, and they build houses to store food in, and other houses to buy and sell it in, and houses to eat it in, and load themselves down with the care of it so that they cannot get away. They cannot pause long enough to go out into the wilderness where God has provided every sparrow enough to eat and to spare, and contemplate for even an hour the wonderful world that they live in. You say that what I write may bring this beauty to the hearts of those that do not get out to see it. They have no right to it. The good Lord put those things here as a free gift that he who chooses may take with joy, and he who will not walk out of the smoke of the cities to see them has no right to them....

...See how painstaking Nature is in her minutest creations. I picked up this piece of petrified wood in Arizona. It is millions of years old. Millions of years ago the tree that it is from was covered about two miles deep in alluvial mud. Then Nature set about making it imperishably beautiful. All living organisms are composed of microscopic cells that are linked together to make the organism. These cells are so minute that millions of them would have to be laid side by side to extend the length of an inch. But each cell is perfectly formed and individual.

When the process of decay began in this bit of wood, these cells began to break down and lost their shape. But, as they did this, Nature repaired each tiny break with a bit of mineral from the water of the ooze in which this lay, so that when a cell disappeared it was replaced by a piece of enduring masonry that is an exact reproduction of the living cell. It is as if you had a brick building and wanted to change it into a stone replica without tearing it down all at once, and so you took out a brick at a time and substituted a block of marble so carefully carved that it reproduced every microscopic peculiarity of the brick in structure and surface. In time your brick house would be all of marble, but identical in appearance and structure. So with this bit of wood, except that the replacing of cells was done on a scale of millionths of an inch. The result is that piece of wood translated into stone, in exact replica, except that Nature has added, with the mineral, a rainbow of coloring that rivals the finest gems. Think of it: millions of years of silent labor under miles of dirt, all that at some day there might come to light a new beauty to adorn the earth....

(From "Three Days With John Muir" by French Strother, *The World's Work*, March, 1, 1909)

Hetch Hetchy Valley (1912)

By the 1890s, the growing city of San Francisco was eyeing Hetch Hetchy Valley as a possible location for a dam that would create a relatively inexpensive, high quality municipal water supply. John Muir and the Sierra Club sprang into action to oppose the idea, but the San Francisco earthquake and fire of 1906 turned the tide of public opinion. Muir kept up the good fight until the bitter end.

<center>~~~~~~~~~~~~~~~~~</center>

Yosemite is so wonderful that we are apt to regard it as an exceptional creation, the only valley of its kind in the world; but Nature is not so poor as to have only one of anything. Several other Yosemites have been discovered in the Sierra that occupy the same relative positions on the Range and were formed by the same forces in the same kind of granite. One of these, the Hetch Hetchy Valley, is in the Yosemite National Park about twenty miles from Yosemite and is easily accessible to all sorts of travelers by a road and trail that leaves the Big Oak Flat road at Bronson Meadows a few miles below Crane Flat, and to mountaineers by way of Yosemite Creek basin and the head of the middle fork of the Tuolumne.

It is said to have been discovered by Joseph Screech, a hunter, in 1850, a year before the discovery of the great Yosemite. After my first visit to it in the autumn of 1871, I have always called it the "Tuolumne Yosemite," for it is a wonderfully exact counterpart of the Merced Yosemite, not only in its sublime rocks and waterfalls but in the gardens, groves and meadows of its flowery park-like floor. The floor of Yosemite is about 4000 feet above the sea; the Hetch Hetchy floor about 3700 feet. And as the Merced River flows through Yosemite, so does the Tuolumne through Hetch Hetchy. The walls of both are of gray granite, rise abruptly from the floor, are sculptured in the same style and in both every rock is a glacier monument.

Standing boldly out from the south wall is a strikingly picturesque rock called by the Indians, Kolana, the outermost of a group 2300 feet high, corresponding with the Cathedral Rocks of Yosemite both in relative position and form. On the opposite side of the Valley, facing Kolana, there is a counterpart of the El Capitan that rises sheer and plain to a height of 1800 feet, and over its massive brow flows a stream which makes the most graceful fall I have ever seen. From the edge of the cliff to the top of an earthquake tálus it is perfectly free in the air for a thousand feet before it is broken into cascades among talus boulders. It is in all its glory in June, when the snow is melting fast, but fades and vanishes toward the end of summer. The only fall I know with which it may fairly be compared is the Yosemite Bridal Veil; but it excels even that favorite fall both in height and airy-fairy beauty and behavior. Lowlanders are apt to suppose that mountain streams in their wild career over cliffs lose control of themselves and tumble in a noisy chaos of mist and spray. On the contrary, on no part of their travels are they more harmonious and self-controlled. Imagine yourself in Hetch Hetchy on a sunny day in June, standing waist-deep in grass and flowers (as I have often stood), while the great pines sway dreamily with scarcely perceptible motion. Looking northward across the Valley you see a plain, gray granite cliff rising abruptly out of the gardens and groves to a height of 1800 feet, and in front of it Tueeulala's silvery scarf burning with irised sun-fire. In the first white outburst at the head there is abundance of visible energy, but it is speedily hushed and concealed in divine repose, and its tranquil progress to the base of the cliff is like that of a downy feather in a still room. Now observe the fineness and marvelous distinctness of the various sun-illumined fabrics into which the water is woven; they sift and float from form to form down the face of that grand gray rock in so leisurely and unconfused a manner that you can examine their texture, and patterns and tones of color as you would a piece of embroidery held in the hand. Toward the top of the fall you see groups of booming, comet-like masses, their solid, white heads separate, their tails like combed silk interlacing among delicate gray and purple shadows, ever forming and dissolving, worn out by friction in their rush through the air. Most of these vanish a few hundred feet below the summit, changing to varied forms of cloud-like drapery. Near the bottom the width of the fall has increased from about twenty-five feet to a hundred feet. Here it is composed of yet finer tissues, and is still without a trace of disorder—air, water and sunlight woven into stuff that spirits might wear.

So fine a fall might well seem sufficient to glorify any valley; but here, as in Yosemite, Nature seems in nowise moderate, for a short distance to the eastward of Tueeulala booms and thunders the great Hetch Hetchy Fall, Wapama, so near that you have both of them in full view from the same standpoint. It is the counterpart of the Yosemite Fall, but has a much greater volume of water, is about 1700 feet in height, and appears to be nearly vertical, though considerably inclined, and is dashed into huge outbounding bosses of foam on projecting shelves and knobs. No two falls could be more unlike—Tueeulala out in the open sunshine descending like thistledown; Wapama in a jagged, shadowy gorge roaring and thundering, pounding its way like an earthquake avalanche.

Besides this glorious pair there is a broad, massive fall on the main river a short distance above the head of the Valley. Its position is something like that of the Vernal in Yosemite, and its roar as it plunges into a surging trout-pool may be heard a long way, though it is only about twenty feet high. On Rancheria Creek, a large stream, corresponding in position with the Yosemite Tenaya

Creek, there is a chain of cascades joined here and there with swift flashing plumes like the one between the Vernal and Nevada Falls, making magnificent shows as they go their glacier-sculptured way, sliding, leaping, hurrahing, covered with crisp clashing spray made glorious with sifting sunshine. And besides all these a few small streams come over the walls at wide intervals, leaping from ledge to ledge with birdlike song and watering many a hidden cliff-garden and fernery, but they are too unshowy to be noticed in so grand a place.

The correspondence between the Hetch Hetchy walls in their trends, sculpture, physical structure, and general arrangement of the main rock-masses and those of the Yosemite Valley has excited the wondering admiration of every observer. We have seen that the El Capitan and Cathedral rocks occupy the same relative positions in both valleys; so also do their Yosemite points and North Domes. Again, that part of the Yosemite north wall immediately to the east of the Yosemite Fall has two horizontal benches, about 500 and 1500 feet above the floor, timbered with golden-cup oak. Two benches similarly situated and timbered occur on the same relative portion of the Hetch Hetchy north wall, to the east of Wapama Fall, and on no other. The Yosemite is bounded at the head by the great Half Dome. Hetch Hetchy is bounded in the same way though its head rock is incomparably less wonderful and sublime in form.

The floor of the Valley is about three and a half miles long, and from a fourth to half a mile wide. The lower portion is mostly a level meadow about a mile long, with the trees restricted to the sides and the river banks, and partially separated from the main, upper, forested portion by a low bar of glacier-polished granite across which the river breaks in rapids.

The principal trees are the yellow and sugar pines, digger pine, incense cedar, Douglas spruce, silver fir, the California and golden-cup oaks, balsam cottonwood, Nuttall's flowering dogwood, alder, maple, laurel, tumion, etc. The most abundant and influential are the great yellow or silver pines like those of Yosemite, the tallest over two hundred feet in height, and the oaks assembled in magnificent groves with massive rugged trunks four to six feet in diameter, and broad, shady, wide-spreading heads. The shrubs forming conspicuous flowery clumps and tangles are manzanita, azalea, spiræa, brier-rose, several species of ceanothus, calycanthus, philadelphus, wild cherry, etc.; with abundance of showy and fragrant herbaceous plants growing about them or out in the open in beds by themselves—lilies, Mariposa tulips, brodi-aeas, orchids, iris, spraguea, draperia, collomia, collinsia, castilleja, nemophila, larkspur, columbine, goldenrods, sunflowers, mints of many species, honeysuckle, etc. Many fine ferns dwell here also, especially the beautiful and interesting rock-ferns—pellaea, and cheilanthes of several species—fringing and rosetting dry rock-piles and ledges; woodwardia and asplenium on damp spots with fronds six or seven feet high; the delicate maiden-hair in mossy nooks by the falls, and the sturdy, broad-shouldered pteris covering nearly all the dry ground beneath the oaks and pines.

It appears, therefore, that Hetch Hetchy Valley, far from being a plain, common, rock-bound meadow, as many who have not seen it seem to suppose, is a grand landscape garden, one of Nature's rarest and most precious mountain temples. As in Yosemite, the sublime rocks of its walls seem to glow with life, whether leaning back in repose or standing erect in thoughtful attitudes, giving welcome to storms and calms alike, their brows in the sky, their feet set in the groves and gay flowery meadows, while birds, bees, and butterflies help the river and waterfalls to stir all the air into music—things frail and fleeting and types of permanence meeting here and blending, just as they do in Yosemite, to draw her lovers into close and confiding communion with her.

Sad to say, this most precious and sublime feature of the Yosemite National Park, one of the greatest of all our natural resources for the uplifting joy and peace and health of the people, is in danger of being dammed and made into a reservoir to help supply San Francisco with water and light, thus flooding it from wall to wall and burying its gardens and groves one or two hundred feet deep. This grossly destructive commercial scheme has long been planned and urged (though water as pure and abundant can be got from outside of the people's park, in a dozen different places), because of the comparative cheapness of the dam and of the territory which it is sought to divert from the great uses to which it was dedicated in the Act of 1890 establishing the Yosemite National Park.

The making of gardens and parks goes on with civilization all over the world, and they increase both in size and number as their value is recognized. Everybody needs beauty as well as bread, places to play in and pray in, where Nature may heal and cheer and give strength to body and soul alike. This natural beauty-hunger is made manifest in the little window-sill gardens of the poor, though perhaps only a geranium slip in a broken cup, as well as in the carefully tended rose and lily gardens of the rich, the thousands of spacious city parks and botanical gardens, and in our magnificent National parks—the Yellowstone, Yosemite, Sequoia, etc.—Nature's sublime wonderlands, the admiration and joy of the world. Nevertheless, like anything else worth while, from the very beginning, however well guarded, they have always been subject to attack by despoiling gainseekers and mischief-makers of every degree from Satan to Senators, eagerly trying to make everything immediately and selfishly commercial, with schemes disguised in smug-smiling philanthropy, industriously, shampiously crying, "Conservation, conservation, panutilization," that man and beast may be fed and the dear Nation made great. Thus long ago a few enterprising merchants utilized the Jerusalem temple as a place of business instead of a place of prayer, changing money, buying and selling cattle and sheep and doves; and earlier still, the first forest reservation, including only one tree, was likewise despoiled. Ever since the establishment of the Yosemite National Park, strife has been going on around its borders and I suppose this will go on as part of the universal battle between right and wrong, however much its boundaries may be shorn, or its wild beauty destroyed.

The first application to the Government by the San Francisco Supervisors for the commercial use of Lake Eleanor and the Hetch Hetchy Valley was made in 1903, and on December 22nd of that year it was denied by the Secretary of the Interior, Mr. Hitchcock, who truthfully said:

"Presumably the Yosemite National Park was created such by law because of the natural objects of varying degrees of scenic importance located within its boundaries, inclusive alike of its beautiful small lakes, like Eleanor, and its majestic wonders, like Hetch Hetchy and Yosemite Valley. It is the aggregation of such natural scenic features that makes the Yosemite Park a wonderland which the Congress of the United States sought by law to reserve for all coming time as nearly as practicable in the condition fashioned by the hand of the Creator—a worthy object of national pride and a source of healthful pleasure and rest for the thousands of people who may annually sojourn there during the heated months."

In 1907 when Mr. Garfield became Secretary of the Interior the application was renewed and granted; but under his successor, Mr. Fisher, the matter has been referred to a Commission, which as this volume goes to press still has it under consideration.

The most delightful and wonderful camp grounds in the Park are its three great valleys—Yosemite, Hetch Hetchy, and Upper Tuolumne; and they are also the most important places with reference to their positions relative to the other great features—the Merced and Tuolumne Cañons, and the High Sierra peaks and glaciers, etc., at the head of the rivers. The main part of the Tuolumne Valley is a spacious flowery lawn four or five miles long, surrounded by magnificent snowy mountains, slightly separated from other beautiful meadows, which together make a series about twelve miles in length, the highest reaching to the feet of Mount Dana, Mount Gibbs, Mount Lyell and Mount McClure. It is about 8500 feet above the sea, and forms the grand central High Sierra camp ground from which excursions are made to the noble mountains, domes, glaciers, etc.; across the Range to the Mono Lake and volcanoes and down the Tuolumne Cañon to Hetch Hetchy. Should Hetch Hetchy be submerged for a reservoir, as proposed, not only would it be utterly destroyed, but the sublime cañon way to the heart of the High Sierra would be hopelessly blocked and the great camping ground, as the watershed of a city drinking system, virtually would be closed to the public. So far as I have learned, few of all the thousands who have seen the park and seek rest and peace in it are in favor of this outrageous scheme.

One of my later visits to the Valley was made in the autumn of 1907 with the late William Keith, the artist. The leaf-colors were then ripe, and the great godlike rocks in repose seemed to glow with life. The artist, under their spell, wandered day after day along the river and through the groves and gardens, studying the wonderful scenery; and, after making about forty sketches, declared with enthusiasm that although its walls were less sublime in height, in picturesque beauty and charm Hetch Hetchy surpassed even Yosemite.

That any one would try to destroy such a place seems incredible; but sad experience shows that there are people good enough and bad enough for anything. The proponents of the dam scheme bring forward a lot of bad arguments to prove that the only righteous thing to do with the people's parks is to destroy them bit by bit as they are able. Their arguments are curiously like those of the devil, devised for the destruction of the first garden—so much of the very best Eden fruit going to waste; so much of the best Tuolumne water and Tuolumne scenery going to waste. Few of their statements are even partly true, and all are misleading.

Thus, Hetch Hetchy, they say, is a "low-lying meadow." On the contrary, it is a high-lying natural landscape garden, as the photographic illustrations show.

"It is a common minor feature, like thousands of others." On the contrary it is a very uncommon feature; after Yosemite, the rarest and in many ways the most important in the National Park.

"Damming and submerging it 175 feet deep would enhance its beauty by forming a crystal-clear lake." Landscape gardens, places of recreation and worship, are never made beautiful by destroying and burying them. The beautiful sham lake, forsooth, would be only an eyesore, a dismal blot on the landscape, like many others to be seen in the Sierra. For, instead of keeping it at the same level all the year, allowing Nature centuries of time to make new shores, it would, of course, be full only a month or two in the spring, when the snow is melting fast; then it would be gradually drained, exposing the slimy sides of the basin and shallower parts of the bottom, with the gathered drift and waste, death and decay of the upper basins, caught here instead of being swept on to decent natural burial along the banks of the river or in the sea. Thus the Hetch Hetchy dam-lake would be only a rough imitation of a natural lake for a few of the spring months, an open sepulcher for the others.

"Hetch Hetchy water is the purest of all to be found in the Sierra, unpolluted, and forever unpollutable." On the contrary, excepting that of the Merced below Yosemite, it is less pure than that of most of the other Sierra streams, because of the sewerage of camp grounds draining into it, especially of the Big Tuolumne Meadows camp ground, occupied by hundreds of tourists and mountaineers, with their animals, for months every summer, soon to be followed by thousands from all the world.

These temple destroyers, devotees of ravaging commercialism, seem to have a perfect contempt for Nature, and, instead of lifting their eyes to the God of the mountains, lift them to the Almighty Dollar.

Dam Hetch Hetchy! As well dam for water-tanks the people's cathedrals and churches, for no holier temple has ever been consecrated by the heart of man.

(*The Yosemite*, Ch. 16)

N.B. As William Faulkner wrote, "The past is never dead. It's not even past." A movement to restore Hetch Hetchy Valley to its original natural state persists to this day.

Boyhood in Scotland

Friends and publishers spent years encouraging Muir to write an auto-biography so his extraordinary life and adventures could be shared with a worldwide audience. **The Story of My Boyhood and Youth** *finally appeared in 1913.*

అడ్డికిందిందిందిం

When I was a boy in Scotland I was fond of everything that was wild, and all my life I've been growing fonder and fonder of wild places and wild creatures. Fortunately around my native town of Dunbar, by the stormy North Sea, there was no lack of wildness, though most of the land lay in smooth cultivation. With red-blooded playmates, wild as myself, I loved to wander in the fields to hear the birds sing, and along the seashore to gaze and wonder at the shells and seaweeds, eels and crabs in the pools among the rocks when the tide was low; and best of all to watch the waves in awful storms thundering on the black headlands and craggy ruins of the old Dunbar Castle when the sea and the sky, the waves and the clouds, were mingled together as one. We never thought of playing truant, but after I was five or six years old I ran away to the seashore or the fields most every Saturday, and every day in the school vacations except Sundays, though solemnly warned that I must play at home in the garden and back yard, lest I should learn to think bad thoughts and say bad words. All in vain. In spite of the sure sore punishments that followed like shadows, the natural inherited wildness in our blood ran true on its glorious course as invincible and unstoppable as stars.

My earliest recollections of the country were gained on short walks with my grandfather when I was perhaps not over three years old. On one of these walks grandfather took me to Lord Lauderdale's gardens, where I saw figs growing against a sunny wall and tasted some of them, and got as many apples to eat as I wished. On another memorable walk in a hayfield, when we sat down to rest on one of the haycocks I heard a sharp, prickly, stinging cry, and, jumping up eagerly, called grandfather's attention to it. He said he heard only the wind, but I insisted on digging into the hay and turning it over until we discovered the source of the strange exciting sound—a mother field mouse with half a dozen naked young hanging to her teats. This to me was a wonderful discovery. No hunter could have been more excited on discovering a bear and her cubs in a wilderness den....

... Father was proud of his garden and seemed always to be trying to make it as much like Eden as possible, and in a corner of it he gave each of us a little bit of ground for our very own, in which we planted what we best liked, wondering how the hard dry seeds could change into soft leaves and flowers and find their way out to the light; and, to see how they were coming on, we used to dig up the larger ones, such as peas and beans, every day. My aunt had a corner assigned to her in our garden, which she filled with lilies, and we all looked with the utmost respect and admiration at that precious lily-bed and wondered whether when we grew up we should ever be rich enough to own one anything like so grand. We imagined that each lily was worth an enormous sum of money and never dared to touch a single leaf or petal of them. We really stood in awe of them. Far, far was I then from the wild lily gardens of California that I was destined to see in their glory.

When I was a little boy at Mungo Siddons's school a flower-show was held in Dunbar, and I saw a number of the exhibitors carrying large handfuls of dahlias, the first I had ever seen. I thought them marvelous in size and beauty and, as in the case of my aunt's lilies, wondered if I should ever be rich enough to own some of them.

Although I never dared to touch my aunt's sacred lilies, I have good cause to remember stealing some common flowers from an apothecary, Peter Lawson, who also answered the purpose of a regular physician to most of the poor people of the town and adjacent country. He had a pony which was considered very wild and dangerous, and when he was called out of town he mounted this wonderful beast, which, after standing long in the stable, was frisky and boisterous, and often to our delight reared and jumped and danced about from side to side of the street before he could be persuaded to go ahead. We boys gazed in awful admiration and wondered how the druggist could be so brave and able as to get on and stay on that wild beast's back. This famous Peter loved flowers and had a fine garden surrounded by an iron fence, through the bars of which, when I thought no one saw me, I oftentimes snatched a flower and took to my heels. One day Peter discovered me in this mischief, dashed out into the street and caught me. I screamed that I wouldna steal any more if he would let me go. He didn't say anything but just dragged me along to the stable where he kept the wild pony, pushed me in right back of its heels, and shut the door. I was screaming, of course, but as soon as I was imprisoned the fear of being kicked quenched all noise. I hardly dared breathe. My only hope was in motionless silence. Imagine the agony I endured! I did not steal any more of his flowers. He was a good hard judge of boy nature....

...One of our best playgrounds was the famous old Dunbar Castle, to which King Edward fled after his defeat at Bannockburn. It was built more than a thousand years ago, and though we knew little of its history, we had heard many mysterious stories of the battles fought about its walls, and firmly believed that every bone we found in the ruins belonged to an ancient warrior. We tried to see who could climb highest on the crumbling peaks and crags, and took chances that no cautious mountaineer would try. That I did not fall and finish my rock-scrambling in those adventurous boyhood days seems now a reasonable wonder....

...Our amusements on Saturday afternoons and vacations depended mostly on getting away from home into the country, especially in the spring when the birds were calling loudest. Father sternly forbade David and me from playing truant in the fields with plundering wanderers like ourselves, fearing we might go on from bad to worse, get hurt in climbing over walls, caught by gamekeepers, or lost by falling over a cliff into the sea. "Play as much as you like in the back yard and garden," he said, "and mind what you'll get when you forget and disobey." Thus he warned us with an awfully stern countenance, looking very hard-hearted, while naturally his heart was far from hard, though he devoutly believed in eternal punishment for bad boys both here and hereafter. Nevertheless, like devout martyrs of wildness, we stole away to the seashore or the green, sunny fields with almost religious regularity, taking advantage of opportunities when father was very busy, to join our companions, oftenest to hear the birds sing and hunt their nests, glorying in the number we had discovered and called our own. A sample of our nest chatter was something like this: Willie Chisholm would proudly exclaim—

"I ken (know) seventeen nests, and you, Johnnie, ken only fifteen."

"But I wouldna gie my fifteen for your seventeen, for five of mine are larks and mavises. You ken only three o' the best singers."

"Yes, Johnnie, but I ken six goldies and you ken only

one. Maist of yours are only sparrows and linties and robin-redbreasts."

Then perhaps Bob Richardson would loudly declare that he "kenned mair nests than onybody, for he kenned twenty-three, with about fifty eggs in them and mair than fifty young birds—maybe a hundred. Some of them naething but raw gorblings but lots of them as big as their mithers and ready to flee. And aboot fifty craw's nests and three fox dens."

"Oh, yes, Bob, but that's no fair, for naebody counts craw's nests and fox holes, and then you live in the country at Belle-haven where ye have the best chance."

"Yes, but I ken a lot of bumbee's nests, baith the red-legged and the yellow-legged kind."

"Oh, wha cares for bumbee's nests!"

"Weel, but here's something! Ma father let me gang to a fox hunt, and man, it was grand to see the hounds and the lang-legged horses lowpin the dykes and burns and hedges!"

The nests, I fear, with the beautiful eggs and young birds, were prized quite as highly as the songs of the glad parents, but no Scotch boy that I know of ever failed to listen with enthusiasm to the songs of the skylarks. Oftentimes on a broad meadow near Dunbar we stood for hours enjoying their marvelous singing and soaring. From the grass where the nest was hidden the male would suddenly rise, as straight as if shot up, to a height of perhaps thirty or forty feet, and, sustaining himself with rapid wing-beats, pour down the most delicious melody, sweet and clear and strong, overflowing all bounds, then suddenly he would soar higher again and again, ever higher and higher, soaring and singing until lost to sight even on perfectly clear days, and oftentimes in cloudy weather "far in the downy cloud," as the poet says.

To test our eyes we often watched a lark until he seemed a faint speck in the sky and finally passed beyond the keenest-sighted of us all. "I see him yet!" we would cry, "I see him yet!" "I see him yet!" "I see him yet!" as he soared. And finally only one of us would be left to claim that he still saw him. At last he, too, would have to admit that the singer had soared beyond his sight, and still the music came pouring down to us in glorious profusion, from a height far above our vision, requiring marvelous power of wing and marvelous power of voice, for that rich, delicious, soft, and yet clear music was distinctly heard long after the bird was out of sight. Then, suddenly ceasing, the glorious singer would appear, falling like a bolt straight down to his nest, where his mate was sitting on the eggs.

It was far too common a practice among us to carry off a young lark just before it could fly, place it in a cage, and fondly, laboriously feed it. Sometimes we succeeded in keeping one alive for a year or two, and when awakened by the spring weather it was pitiful to see the quivering imprisoned soarer of the heavens rapidly beating its wings and singing as though it were flying and hovering in the air like its parents. To keep it in health we were taught that we must supply it with a sod of grass the size of the bottom of the cage, to make the poor bird feel as though it were at home on its native meadow,—a meadow perhaps a foot or at most two feet square. Again and again it would try to hover over that miniature meadow from its miniature sky just underneath the top of the cage. At last, conscience-stricken, we carried the beloved prisoner to the meadow west of Dunbar where it was born, and, blessing its sweet heart, bravely set it free, and our exceeding great reward was to see it fly and sing in the sky.

In the winter, when there was but little doing in the fields, we organized running-matches. A dozen or so of us would start out on races that were simply tests of endurance, running on and on along a public road over the breezy hills like hounds, without stopping or getting tired. The only serious trouble we ever felt in these long races was an occasional stitch in our sides. One of the boys started the story that sucking raw eggs was a sure cure for the stitches. We had hens in our back yard, and on the next Saturday we managed to swallow a couple of eggs apiece, a disgusting job, but we would do almost anything to mend our speed, and as soon as we could get away after taking the cure we set out on a ten or twenty mile run to prove its worth. We thought nothing of running right ahead ten or a dozen miles before turning back; for we knew nothing about taking time by the suns and none of us had a watch in those days. Indeed, we never cared about time until it began to get dark. Then we thought of home and the thrashing that awaited us. Late or early, the thrashing was sure, unless father happened to be away. If he was expected to return soon, mother made haste to get us to bed before his arrival. We escaped the thrashing next morning, for father never felt like thrashing us in cold blood on the calm holy Sabbath. But no punishment, however sure and severe, was of any avail against the attraction of the fields and woods. It had other uses, developing memory, etc., but in keeping us at home it was of no use at all. Wildness was ever sounding in our ears, and Nature saw to it that besides school lessons and church lessons some of her own lessons should be learned, perhaps with a view to the time when we should be called to wander in wildness to our heart's content. Oh, the blessed enchantment of those Saturday runaways in the prime of the spring! How our young wondering eyes reveled in the sunny, breezy glory of the hills and the sky, every particle of us thrilling and tingling with the bees and glad birds and glad streams! Kings may be blessed; we were glorious, we were free,—school cares and scoldings, heart thrashings and flesh thrashings alike, were forgotten in the fullness of Nature's glad wildness. These were my first excursions,—the beginnings of life-long wanderings.

(From *The Story of My Boyhood and Youth*, Ch. 1)

Off to America

Our grammar-school reader, called, I think, "Maccou-lough's Course of Reading," contained a few natural-history sketches that excited me very much and left a deep impression, especially a fine description of the fish hawk and the bald eagle by the Scotch ornithologist Wilson, who had the good fortune to wander for years in the American woods while the country was yet mostly wild. I read his description over and over again, till I got the vivid picture he drew by heart,—the long-winged hawk circling over the heaving waves, every motion watched by the eagle perched on the top of a crag or dead tree; the fish hawk poising for a moment to take aim at a fish and plunging under the water; the eagle with kindling eye spreading his wings ready for instant flight in case the attack should prove successful; the hawk emerging with a struggling fish in his talons, and proud flight; the eagle launching himself in pursuit; the wonderful wing-work in the sky, the fish hawk, though encumbered with his prey, circling higher, higher, striving hard to keep above the robber eagle; the eagle at length soaring above him, compelling him with a cry of despair to drop his hard-won prey; then the eagle steadying himself for a moment to take aim, descending swift as a lightning-bolt, and seizing the falling fish before it reached the sea.

Not less exciting and memorable was Audubon's

wonderful story of the passenger pigeon, a beautiful bird flying in vast flocks that darkened the sky like clouds, countless millions ambling to rest and sleep and rear their young in certain forests, miles in length and breadth, fifty or a hundred nests on a single tree; the overloaded branches bending low and often breaking; the farmers gathering from far and near, beating down countless thousands of the young and old birds from their nests and roosts with long poles at Bight, and in the morning driving their bands of hogs, some of them brought from farms a hundred miles distant, to fatten on the dead and wounded covering the ground.

In another of our reading-lessons some of the American forests were described. The most interesting of the trees to us boys was the sugar maple, and soon after we had learned this sweet story we heard everybody talking about the discovery of gold in the same wonder-filled country.

One night, when David and I were at grandfather's fireside solemnly learning our lessons as usual, my father came in with news, the most wonderful, most glorious, that wild boys ever heard. "Bairns," he said, "you needna learn your lessons the nicht, for we're gan to America the morn!" No more grammar, but boundless woods full of mysterious good things; trees full of sugar, growing in ground full of gold; hawks, eagles, pigeons, filling the sky; millions of birds' nests, and no gamekeepers to stop us in all the wild, happy land. We were utterly, blindly glorious. After father left the room, grandfather gave David and me a gold coin apiece for a keepsake, and looked very serious, for he was about to be deserted in his lonely old age. And when we in fullness of young joy spoke of what we were going to do, of the wonderful birds and their nests that we should find, the sugar and gold, etc., and promised to send him a big box full of that tree sugar packed in gold from the glorious paradise over the sea, poor lonely grandfather, about to be forsaken, looked with downcast eyes on the floor and said in a low, trembling, troubled voice, "Ah, poor laddies, poor laddies, you'll find something else ower the sea forbye gold and sugar, birds' nests and freedom fra lessons and schools. You'll find plenty hard, hard work." And so we did. But nothing he could say could cloud our joy or abate the fire of youthful, hopeful, fearless adventure. Nor could we in the midst of such measureless excitement see or feel the shadows and sorrows of his darkening old age. To my schoolmates, met that night on the street, I shouted the glorious news, "I'm gan to Amaraka the morn!" None could believe it. I said, "Weel, just you see if I am at the skule the morn!"

Next morning we went by rail to Glasgow and thence joyfully sailed away from beloved Scotland, flying to our fortunes on the wings of the winds, care-free as thistle seeds. We could not then know what we were leaving, what we were to encounter in the New World, nor what our gains were likely to be. We were too young and full of hope for fear or regret, but not too young to look forward with eager enthusiasm to the wonderful schoolless bookless American wilderness. Even the natural heart-pain of parting from grandfather and grandmother Gilrye, who loved us so well, and from mother and sisters and brother, was quickly quenched in young joy. Father took with him only my sister Sarah (thirteen years of age), myself (eleven), and brother David (nine), leaving my eldest sister, Margaret, and the three youngest of the family, Daniel, Mary, and Anna, with mother, to join us after a farm had been found in the wilderness and a comfortable house made to receive them.

(From *The Story of My Boyhood and Youth*, Ch. 2)

Auroras

*John Muir died of pneumonia in a Los Angeles hospital on Christmas Eve, 1914. He left pages from the unfinished manuscript for **Travels in Alaska**, which he had worked on ever since losing the fight over Hetch Hetchy, spread around him on the bed. This description of the Northern Lights from his 1890 trip became the book's final chapter.*

❧❧❧❧❧

A few days later I set out with Professor Reid's party to visit some of the other large glaciers that flow into the bay, to observe what changes have taken place in them since October, 1879, when I first visited and sketched them. We found the upper half of the bay closely choked with bergs, through which it was exceedingly difficult to force a way. After slowly struggling a few miles up the east side, we dragged the whale-boat and canoe over rough rocks into a fine garden and comfortably camped for the night.

The next day was spent in cautiously picking a way across to the west side of the bay; and as the strangely scanty stock of provisions was already about done, and the ice-jam to the northward seemed impenetrable, the party decided to return to the main camp by a comparatively open, round-about way to the southward, while with the canoe and a handful of food-scraps I pushed on northward. After a hard, anxious struggle, I reached the mouth of the Hugh Miller fiord about sundown, and tried to find a camp-spot on its steep, boulder-bound shore. But no landing-place where it seemed possible to drag the canoe above high-tide mark was discovered after examining a mile or more of this dreary, forbidding barrier, and as night was closing down, I decided to try to grope my way across the mouth of the fiord in the starlight to an open sandy spot on which I had camped in October, 1879, a distance of about three or four miles.

With the utmost caution I picked my way through the sparkling bergs, and after an hour or two of this nerve-trying work, when I was perhaps less than halfway across and dreading the loss of the frail canoe which would include the loss of myself, I came to a pack of very large bergs which loomed threateningly, offering no visible thoroughfare. Paddling and pushing to right and left, I at last discovered a sheer-walled opening about four feet wide and perhaps two hundred feet long, formed apparently by the splitting of a huge iceberg. I hesitated to enter this passage, fearing that the slightest change in the tide-current might close it, but ventured nevertheless, judging that the dangers ahead might not be greater than those I had already passed. When I had got about a third of the way in, I suddenly discovered that the smooth-walled ice-lane was growing narrower, and with desperate haste backed out. Just as the bow of the canoe cleared the sheer walls they came together with a growling crunch. Terror-stricken, I turned back, and in an anxious hour or two gladly reached the rock-bound shore that had at first repelled me, determined to stay on guard all night in the canoe or find some place where with the strength that comes in a fight for life I could drag it up the boulder wall beyond ice danger. This at last was happily done about midnight, and with no thought of sleep I went to bed rejoicing.

My bed was two boulders, and as I lay wedged and bent on their up-bulging sides, beguiling the hard, cold time in gazing into the starry sky and across the sparkling bay, magnificent upright bars of light in bright prismatic colors suddenly appeared, marching swiftly in close succession along the northern horizon from west to east as if in diligent haste, an auroral display very different from any I had ever before beheld. Once long ago in Wisconsin I saw the heavens draped in rich purple auroral clouds fringed and folded in most magnificent forms; but in this glory of light, so pure, so bright, so enthusiastic in motion, there was nothing in the least cloud-like. The short color-bars, apparently about two degrees in height, though blending, seemed to be as well defined as those of the solar spectrum.

How long these glad, eager soldiers of light held on their way I cannot tell; for sense of time was charmed out of mind and the blessed night circled away in measureless rejoicing enthusiasm.

In the early morning after so inspiring a night I launched my canoe feeling able for anything, crossed the mouth of the Hugh Miller fiord, and forced a way three or four miles along the shore of the bay, hoping to reach the Grand Pacific Glacier in front of Mt. Fairweather. But the farther I went, the ice-pack, instead of showing inviting little open streaks here and there, became so much harder jammed that on some parts of the shore the bergs, drifting south with the tide, were shoving one another out of the water beyond high-tide line. Farther progress to northward was thus rigidly stopped, and now I had to fight for a way back to my cabin, hoping that by good tide luck I might reach it before dark. But at sundown I was less than half-way home, and though very hungry was glad to land on a little rock island with a smooth beach for the canoe and a thicket of alder bushes for fire and bed and a little sleep. But shortly after sundown, while these arrangements were being made, lo and behold another aurora enriching the heavens! and though it proved to be one of the ordinary almost color-less kind, thrusting long, quivering lances toward the zenith from a dark cloud-like base, after last night's wonderful display one's expectations might well be extravagant and I lay wide awake watching.

On the third night I reached my cabin and food. Professor Reid and his party came in to talk over the results of our excursions, and just as the last one of the visitors opened the door after bidding good-night, he shouted, "Muir, come look here. Here's something fine."

I ran out in auroral excitement, and sure enough here was another aurora, as novel and wonderful as the marching rainbow-colored columns—a glowing silver bow spanning the Muir Inlet in a magnificent arch right under the zenith, or a little to the south of it, the ends resting on the top of the mountain-walls. And though colorless and steadfast, its intense, solid, white splendor, noble proportions, and fineness of finish excited boundless admiration. In form and proportion it was like a rainbow, a bridge of one span five miles wide; and so brilliant, so fine and solid and homogeneous in every part, I fancy that if all the stars were raked together into one windrow, fused and welded and run through some celestial rolling-mill, all would be required to make this one glowing white colossal bridge.

After my last visitor went to bed, I lay down on the moraine in front of the cabin and gazed and watched. Hour after hour the wonderful arch stood perfectly motionless, sharply defined and substantial-looking as if it were a permanent addition to the furniture of the sky. At length while it yet spanned the inlet in serene unchanging splendor, a band of fluffy, pale gray, quivering ringlets came suddenly all in a row over the eastern mountain-top, glided in nervous haste up and down the under side of the bow and over the western mountain-wall. They were about one and a half times the apparent diameter of the bow in length, maintained a vertical posture all the way across, and slipped swiftly along as if they were suspended like a curtain on rings. Had these lively auroral fairies marched across the fiord on the top of the bow instead of shuffling along the under side of it, one might have fancied they were a happy band of spirit people on a journey making use of the splendid bow for a bridge. There must have been hundreds of miles of them; for the time required for each to cross from one end of the bridge to the other seemed only a minute or less, while nearly an hour elapsed from their first appearance until the last of the rushing throng vanished behind the western mountain, leaving the bridge as bright and solid and steadfast as before they arrived. But later, half an hour or so, it began to fade. Fissures or cracks crossed it diagonally through which a few stars were seen, and gradually it became thin and nebulous until it looked like the Milky Way, and at last vanished, leaving no visible monument of any sort to mark its place.

I now returned to my cabin, replenished the fire, warmed myself, and prepared to go to bed, though too aurorally rich and happy to go to sleep. But just as I was about to retire, I thought I had better take another look at the sky, to make sure that the glorious show was over; and, contrary to all reasonable expectations, I found that the pale foundation for another bow was being laid right overhead like the first. Then losing all thought of sleep, I ran back to my cabin, carried out blankets and lay down on the moraine to keep watch until daybreak, that none of the sky wonders of the glorious night within reach of my eyes might be lost.

I had seen the first bow when it stood complete in full splendor, and its gradual fading decay. Now I was to see the building of a new one from the beginning. Perhaps in less than half an hour the silvery material was gathered, condensed, and welded into a glowing, evenly proportioned arc like the first and in the same part of the sky. Then in due time over the eastern mountain-wall came another throng of restless electric auroral fairies, the infinitely fine pale-gray garments of each lightly touching those of their neighbors as they swept swiftly along the under side of the bridge and down over the western mountain like the merry band that had gone the same way before them, all keeping quivery step and time to music too fine for mortal ears.

While the gay throng was gliding swiftly along, I watched the bridge for any change they might make upon it, but not the slightest could I detect. They left no visible track, and after all had passed the glowing arc stood firm and apparently immutable, but at last faded slowly away like its glorious predecessor.

Excepting only the vast purple aurora mentioned above, said to have been visible over nearly all the continent, these two silver bows in supreme, serene, supernal beauty surpassed everything auroral I ever beheld.

(*Travels in Alaska*, Ch. 19)

Bibliography

Books

Gisel, Bonnie Johanna, ed. *Kindred & Related Spirits: The Letters of John Muir and Jeanne C. Carr.* Salt Lake City: The University of Utah Press, 2001.

Kimes, William F., ed. *Rambles of a Botanist Among the Plants and Climates of California: John Muir.* Los Angeles: Dawson's Book Shop, 1974.

Muir, John. *A Thousand-Mile Walk to the Gulf.* Boston and New York: Houghton Mifflin Company, 1916.

— *My First Summer in the Sierra.* San Francisco: Sierra Club Books, 1988.

— *Our National Parks.* Boston and New York: Houghton Mifflin Company, 1901.

— *Steep Trails.* San Francisco: Sierra Club Books, 1994.

— *The Cruise of the Corwin.* Boston and New York: Houghton Mifflin Company, 1917.

— *The Mountains of California.* New York: The Century Company, 1913.

— *The Story of My Boyhood and Youth.* Boston and New York: Houghton Mifflin Company, 1913.

— *The Yosemite.* New York: The Century Company, 1912.

— *Travels in Alaska.* Boston and New York: Houghton Mifflin Company, 1915.

Stetson, Lee, ed. *The Wild Muir: Twenty-two of John Muir's Greatest Adventures.* Yosemite National Park: Yosemite Conservancy, 1994.

Teale, Edwin Way, ed. *The Wilderness World of John Muir.* Boston and New York: Houghton Mifflin Company, 1954.

White, Fred D., ed. *Essential Muir: A Selection of John Muir's Best Writings.* Santa Clara and Berkeley: Santa Clara University and Heyday Books, 2006.

Wolfe, Linnie Marsh, ed. *John of the Mountains.* Boston: Houghton Mifflin Company, 1938.

— *Son of the Wilderness: The Life of John Muir.* New York: Alfred A. Knopf, 1945.

Worster, Donald. *A Passion for Nature: The Life of John Muir.* Oxford: Oxford University Press, 2008.

Websites

Kimes, William & Maymie. *John Muir: A Reading Bibliography;* available online at www.go.pacific.edu/archives

John Muir Papers at the University of the Pacific, Holt-Atherton Special Collections. www.go.pacific.edu/archives

The Sierra Club. *The John Muir Exhibit.* San Francisco: Sierra Club. www.vault.sierraclub.org